One Fine Day in Palm Springs...

Liberace always enjoyed window-shopping down Palm Canyon Drive in Palm Springs. He would stroll casually, devoting special attention to the jewelry stores. He was recognized, of course, but the local residents respected his privacy, and the tourists often couldn't believe they were seeing Liberace.

One day as he strolled down Palm Canyon Drive he overheard the conversation of two women behind him.

"It's him!"

"No, it isn't."

"I *know* it is."

"Well, you're wrong."

Liberace turned around and smiled. "It *is* him!" one of the women said.

"But you look much younger than you do on television," the other one remarked.

"You must have an old set," Liberace replied.

Liberace

THE TRUE STORY

Bob Thomas

ST. MARTIN'S PRESS/NEW YORK

Quotations from *The Magic of Believing* by Claude M. Bristol (copyright © 1948, 1976) reprinted by permission of the publisher, Prentice-Hall, Inc., Englewood Cliffs, N.J.

LIBERACE: THE TRUE STORY

Copyright © 1987 by Bob Thomas.

Front cover photo courtesy Wide World Photos, Inc.

Library of Congress Catalog Card Number: 87-27106

ISBN: 0-312-91352-4   Can. ISBN: 0-312-91354-0

Printed in the United States of America

St. Martin's Press hardcover edition published 1987
First St. Martin's Press mass market edition/January 1989

10 9 8 7 6 5 4 3 2 1

For Robert Gottlieb,
agent extraordinaire

CONTENTS

ACKNOWLEDGMENTS

The author is grateful to the following for sharing their memories and observations about the life and times of Liberace:

Don Ameche	Robert Goulet	Debbie Reynolds
Jimmy Anderson	Marty Halpern	Eddie Rio
David Barr	Hildegarde	Sabas Rosas
Rudy Behlmer	Jim Hlaban	Isabel Sanford
Milton Berle	Jim Hobson	Scott Sanders
Macdonald Carey	Sam Honigberg	Stan Seiden
Denise Collier	Bob Hope	Red Skelton
Linda Dano	Jamie James	Anna Sosenko
Phyllis Diller	Del Krause	Steve Swedish
Red Doff	Carl Lorenz	Michael Travis
Gordon Douglas	Sam Lutz	Irving Wallace
Don Fedderson	Rae Lynn	Bill Watters
Mark Felton	Shirley MacLaine	Paul Weston
Bob Finkel	Phyllis McGuire	Betty White
Ken Fosler	Debbie Munch	Tommy Wonder
Peter Foy	Dale Olson	Ken Zagaro
Vince Fronza	William T. Orr	Joe Zungsheim
Duke Goldstone	Dolly Parton	

I also benefited greatly from the expert research of fellow journalists: Jennifer Juergens, New York; Dave DeGrace, Milwaukee; Bob Macy, Las Vegas; Bonnie Ward and Mark Evje, Palm Springs; Lee Siegel and Fred Shuster, Los Angeles. I am also grateful to Joseph C. McBride for additional research in Milwaukee. The printed sources for this book are too many and too diverse to list here, but of special value were the files of the *Milwaukee Journal* and the *Sentinel*.

As in all things, Liberace was an extravagant storyteller. In weighing the many versions he told of his life's events, I have had to exercise fielder's choice.

My gratitude to Toni Lopopolo, with whom the author-editor relationship has once more proved a singular joy.

The scene in the parking lot was one of superficial gaiety. In the lengthening shadows of the California twilight, the guests in their Christmas finery climbed aboard the silvery luxury bus that rumbled mightily as it air-conditioned the interior to a comfortable temperature. They came bearing gifts, the women in stylish dresses, predominantly red, the men in their finest suits. All knew that their host liked his guests to dress in a manner befitting the opulence of his home.

They had one thing in common: all were closely tied to Liberace, two by blood, a few by friendship, most by being in his employ. These were the people Liberace loved and trusted most in the world, the ones he surrounded himself with at his favorite time of the year.

It was December 14, 1986, and they were leaving from the six-story Liberace building on Beverly Boulevard, heading for his Malibu residence, where limited parking made travel by bus more practical. The passengers included Liberace's sister, Angie, and her daughter, Diane; his steadfast companion for the past five years, Cary James; Michael Travis, the costume designer; Jamie James, Liberace's publicist, and Ray Arnett, the stage manager, both thirty-year veterans; Vince Fronza and Ken Fosler, the Palm Springs neighbors; Tido Minor, the former Mrs. Don Federson, who helped discover Liberace for television and remained his friend over the years; Liberace's lawyer, doctor, fan-club secretary, accountants, restaurant manager, backstage valet, prop and costume movers, husbands and wives. Because they were bringing packages for everyone, Seymour Heller, Liberace's longtime manager, and his wife, Billie, would be coming by limousine.

The passengers settled into the cushioned chairs of the chartered bus high above the pavement and were offered drinks and snacks. The bus lumbered out of the parking lot and turned on Beverly Boulevard heading westward toward the waning sun and the ocean.

"I don't care. . . ."

Liberace was crooning his opening theme song on the television screens, which were playing a black-and-white tape cassette of a 1954 "Liberace" television show at Christmas. This was a thirty-five-year-old Liberace with smooth eager face and wavy black hair streaked with gray dye.

"Although I'm spending Christmas in California, I miss the ones back home in Milwaukee, Wisconsin," the young Liberace said, smiling directly into the camera, and he launched into a rendition of "White Christmas."

The concert continued with Liberace in piano solos or accompanied by his brother, George, and two other violinists, hurrying through a wide range of Christmas songs. Finally a Christmas poem and "Ave Maria," with George playing violin beside the white grand piano.

"And now I'd like you to meet my family," said Liberace. They walked onstage carrying gifts: George and his current wife, Jane; Gordon Robinson, the musical director; brother Rudy and his son; sister Angie and her daughter, Diane; the poodle Suzette bearing a package. Most important of all, "the producer of my show—Mom."

All joined in singing "Jingle Bells," and then Liberace ended the show in customary style: "I'll be looking at the moon, but I'll be seeing you. . . ."

The bus passengers applauded the show heartily. Diane, now a grandmother, commented to her seatmate, Michael Travis: "I hope they don't show that tape at the house. Uncle Lee wouldn't like it. Half the people on it are dead."

The journey continued northward on the Pacific Coast Highway as the crimson sun hovered above the winter sea. Most of the passengers chattered happily, anticipating the festive dinner and the bountiful presents that Liberace was certain to bestow. Only one of the guests, a stranger to most of the others, seemed somber and withdrawn. Seated with his attractive wife, he was a mature man with steel-gray hair but a youthful face. The other passengers learned later that he was Liberace's doctor, Ronald Daniels.

Liberace stood beaming before the Malibu house in a red jacket, white lace shirt, and white silk slacks, a diamond medallion hanging from a gold chain. He greeted passengers affectionately as they stepped off the bus, and he led them inside for cocktails before the massive windows that looked out to the darkening sea. Liberace seemed convivial as ever, though somewhat restrained. His guests attributed that to tiredness. After all, he had completed twenty-one shows in fourteen days at Radio City Music Hall the month before, and then embarked on a strenuous book-promotion tour in New York, Chicago, Dallas, and Los Angeles. He deserved to be tired.

Gladys Luckie, Liberace's longtime housekeeper, had come from Las Vegas to prepare the feast, which was highlighted by her extraordinary fried chicken; the recipe was so secret that she wouldn't reveal it to Liberace for his cookbook. He liked to have Italian dishes for his Christmas dinners, and there was pasta, garlic bread, and a veal roast. After dessert came the annual orgy of gift-opening.

"Save the paper!" someone shouted in fond remembrance of Mom's repeated request at earlier Christmases.

Paper and ribbons collected in a huge mass as presents were opened amid cries of astonishment and delight. The other guests had faced the annual challenge of what to give Liberace for Christmas, and he expressed pleasure with all of them, particularly a compact disc player, compact discs of Horowitz piano music, and a clock that showed time around the world.

Liberace's gift to Seymour was much anticipated, and it involved an incident that only a few in the room were aware of. While Liberace was in Dallas for the book promotion, Seymour came to his hotel suite in a state of excitement. A Texas Porsche dealer had proposed that if Liberace would pose for an advertisement with one of the cars, Seymour could have a Porsche free. "Then you won't have to give me a Christmas present," Seymour suggested. Liberace, who never liked to have his gifts taken for granted, suggested, "Why don't *I* get a Porsche, too?" Seymour returned with the news that the dealer had agreed to the two Porsches. "Maybe I should get some money as well," Liberace replied. Seymour abandoned the proposal.

At the Christmas party, the buildup began when Seymour opened a package that contained a parking sign: "Porsches Only." Later Liberace announced, "Now we'll all have to go out to the garage to see Seymour's gift." The guests stood in front of the garage door, which swung open to reveal—a miniature, toy Porsche. Everyone laughed, and Seymour managed a smile. Back in the house he opened his real gift, a handsome leather jacket lined in mink.

Liberace seemed subdued throughout the evening, and several of the guests noted mentally that he appeared thinner. "How are you feeling, Uncle Lee?" Diane asked concernedly. "I'm all right," he replied. "When I get tired, I just lie down for a while." That was unusual for a man whose energy had long seemed limitless. A few of the guests noticed that his hands trembled slightly as he opened the presents.

The fancy invitations to the party had been accompanied by a note explaining that he would not be giving his usual Christmas party in Palm Springs, adding lightly that he might be at Donald Trump's place in Florida or perhaps in Madrid or even in Hawaii with Imelda and Ferdinand Marcos, counting her shoes. The invitation had indicated that the party would end at 10:30, and it did.

Liberace hugged each of his guests before they reentered the bus for the journey back to Los Angeles. He stood in the driveway waving to them as the driver wheeled onto the Pacific Coast Highway.

Tido Minor was worried. She had visited Liberace at Thanksgiving in Palm Springs, and she had been concerned about his appearance. Now she was shocked.

"Seymour, what's wrong with Lee?" she inquired.

"I don't know," the manager replied.

"Do you mean you don't know, or you know and can't tell me?" she asked.

"No, Tido, I honestly don't know."

Virtually no one knew what was wrong, and that was the way Liberace wanted it. Within six weeks he would be dead.

Liberace

Chapter 1

THE SURVIVING TWIN BECOMES A YOUTHFUL
PRODIGY AND AUGMENTS HIS EDUCATION IN THE
ROADHOUSES OF WISCONSIN

"**O**ne of the babies was born under
the veil," said the midwife in a voice shaded with sadness. "But the
other one, my dear . . ." Her voice suddenly joyful. "A *big* baby boy!"

How pitiful the dead infant looked, its tiny body almost a skeleton,
a film of placenta over its shriveled face like a cloth for burial. "Under
the veil"—it was the phrase that struck terror in the hearts of preg-
nant women in the Old World.

But the other baby—what a pulsing, squalling, robust piece of
humanity. A full thirteen pounds he was, and more.

The mother was too weak to grieve for one son or to rejoice for the other. The deliveries of her first-born son and her daughter had been nothing like this. Never had she known such pain. Now, as she lingered numbly in post-natal twilight, she clutched the live baby in her arms. All she could do was gaze in wonderment at the sanguine, brown-eyed baby at her breast.

His mother, who preferred the romance of movie houses to the drabness of her life in an outlying suburb of Milwaukee, gave her second son the middle name Valentino, after the sloe-eyed hero of desert adventures. Since Rudolph Valentino was Italian, her husband did not complain. He grumbled when she insisted on a Polish first name for the baby: Wladziu. But she would not be dissuaded. When it came time for the christening at the parish church, the priest gave the baby the name of Wladziu Valentino Liberace. The birth certificate, however, listed the baby as Walter, the English version of Wladziu.

Like Rudolph Valentino, Salvatore Liberace had left the poverty of an Italian village for the promise of America. Salvatore saw no future amid a large family in Formia, near Naples, where he was born in 1884. At the Municipal School of Music, he had studied clarinet, trumpet, and French horn, and had excelled in the French horn. His brother Ben, an accomplished trombonist, had emigrated to America, settling in Philadelphia. Salvatore followed his brother, arriving at Ellis Island in 1906 with only a sackful of clothing and his one hope for survival in the new land, a French horn.

It was not an instrument that assured ready employment. Dance orchestras did not include French horns. Only symphony orchestras and military bands had them, so job opportunities were scarce. But Salvatore had enough faith in his talent to audition for John Philip Sousa, the March King, who had first achieved fame as leader of the United States Marine Band and since 1892 had toured with his own band throughout the United States. Sousa approved of the young Italian, and Salvatore donned the white, gold-braided uniform of the Sousa band.

The job with Sousa proved temporary, and Salvatore traveled with his French horn wherever he could find work. He was performing with his own band in Menasha, Wisconsin, in 1909 when he met and married the daughter of Polish immigrant farmers, Frances Zuchowski. Salvatore was twenty-five, and Frances was eighteen. She had a sweet, oval face and a strong, peasant body. Her parents had emigrated from a border town near Russia, having wearied of the battles that had repeatedly changed the nationality of their land. The immigrants settled on a small farm between the towns of Menasha and Neenah.

Frances was overwhelmed by the volatile, darkly handsome musician with the amusing accent and a zest for adventure. She agreed to accompany him to Philadelphia, where his brother Ben lived and where a French horn player could find more chances for employment. The first Liberace child, George, was born in Philadelphia in 1911.

The big-city life held no appeal for Frances Liberace. After a lifetime on the farm, she found Philadelphia too clamorous and dirty, and too dangerous for the family she planned to have. She pleaded with her husband to return to Wisconsin, where she could once again be close to her family.

"How am I going to find work in some hick town?" Salvatore demanded.

"If we move near Milwaukee, you'll find something," Frances replied. Their arguments became heated, neither giving any ground. Finally, when Frances threatened to return to Wisconsin alone with the baby, Salvatore acquiesced.

The Liberaces moved to a Milwaukee suburb, West Allis, a workers' town filled with immigrants who had been attracted to jobs in the factories and mills. Salvatore Liberace could ride the streetcar to Milwaukee and hunt for work. He was fortunate to find a steady job with the International Harvester Band, which played at the Schlitz Palm Garden.

In 1914, Frances gave birth to their second child, who was named Angelina. Then on May 16, 1919, in their new house at 635 51st Street (renumbered 1649 60th Street in 1931), the twins were born. One survived, and his mother often told the neighbors that there was something special about little Wladziu. "He took all the strength from his little brother," she said. "That was a sign."

Neighbors often heard fierce arguments emanating from the Liberace house. Frances screamed that the children were going hungry because her husband was such a poor provider. He responded with Italian fury that if she hadn't persuaded him to leave Philadelphia he might be able to find work with his French horn. When he was forced to take out-of-town jobs, she complained that he was neglecting her and the children. She also suspected him of philandering.

By 1923 it had become bitterly apparent that Salvatore Liberace could no longer support his wife and three children by occasional jobs in movie theaters and beer-hall bands. He bought a grocery store in West Milwaukee, which was closer to the city. He and Frances worked in the store during the day, and he took whatever musical work he could find at night. The family occupied an apartment behind the store.

The second son was now called Walter because his playmates couldn't pronounce Wladziu. His earliest memories were of the grocery store, that place of delights and wonders where he played on the linoleum floor while his mother waited on customers. Despite his robustness at birth, Walter proved a fragile child, vulnerable to the harsh Wisconsin winters. Four times in his early years he fell ill with pneumonia; when he was nine, he almost died of it. His mother always nursed him back to health, sitting all night at his bedside with cold towels to soothe the fever. When he recovered, she prepared delectable Polish dishes, hoping to add weight to his skinny frame. Happily, the grocery store assured food on the table for the Liberaces, even though the family finances were lean.

Because his mother was occupied with the store, Walter was relegated to the care of his sister, Angelina, five years older. She introduced him to an exciting world of make-believe, in which they costumed her dolls with fragments of cloth and feathers and created kings and princesses and movie stars. Sister and brother could wander for hours through fantasies of romance and adventure.

Salvatore Liberace dictated that his children should begin learning music by the age of four. George had started piano lessons while the family still lived in Philadelphia. But during the move to Milwaukee, the storage ticket for the family piano was lost. While the piano was being hunted, Salvatore asked George, "Would you like to start learning the violin?" George agreed.

The piano was finally located and shipped to West Allis, and Angelina began taking lessons from a neighbor, Mrs. Martin. One day when George was practicing his violin upstairs, his father heard four-year-old Walter picking out George's tunes on the piano. Walter's lessons began immediately. Ever afterward Angelina had to fight her little brother for practice time at the living room piano.

After learning to read music from Mrs. Martin, Walter became indefatigable, absorbing every piece of sheet music in the piano bench. Angelina, who was not a facile student, was both frustrated and angry at her little brother's ease at the keyboard. When she was thirteen, she was given the assignment of memorizing seventeen pages of Mendelssohn's *Midsummer Night's Dream*. After several weeks, she was still struggling with it. "Here, let me do it," suggested Walter, who was seven. Within a day he could play the number perfectly.

The Paderewski incident became a major part of the Liberace family legend, and its retelling over the years has made it difficult to discern fact from fiction. The most engaging version was related by Frances Liberace in the years after her son became famous.

Ignace Jan Paderewski had been a towering world figure for more than half a century. A fiercely patriotic Pole, he startled the music world in the 1890s with his dynamic piano style, and his unruly hair, stern face, and erect bearing made him the image of the virtuoso in the concert halls of the world. After the outbreak of World War I, he devoted himself to the establishment of an independent Poland and in 1919 became prime minister of the new nation. He abandoned politics two years later and resumed his concert career.

According to Frances Liberace, her own mother had worked for a music studio in Berlin where a young Pole named Paderewski taught piano. The girl translated his instructions from Polish into High German for the well-to-do pupils.

It is 1926, and Paderewski has embarked on another of his triumph-filled United States tours. Frances's mother writes to ask if he remembers the Polish girl who translated for his piano lessons in Berlin. Indeed he remembers her, the maestro answers, and he would be delighted to see her when he appears in Milwaukee.

The meeting is arranged at the Liberace house in West Milwaukee. Paderewski arrives, a majestic figure in a velvet cape, and he greets his old friend affectionately. He obliges with a few short numbers on the piano in the front parlor, then sits on the horse-hair chair and reminisces about Berlin with Mrs. Zuchowski. She has a high, sweet voice, but her husband doesn't like her to sing, so she doesn't. Her grandson Walter is not so shy.

"Mr. Paderewski, may I play the piano for you?" the boy asks. The visitor gives an indulgent smile, and Walter climbs on the stool and delivers a Chopin piece.

"Very good, my boy," says Paderewski. "Perhaps someday when I am gone, you will take my place."

A nice story, and Liberace himself never tired of telling it in endless variations to interviewers and audiences. He recounted a likelier version in his 1973 autobiography. He wrote that his father had acquired tickets for the entire family to attend a Paderewski concert at the Pabst Theater in Milwaukee. The Liberaces were among those who trooped backstage for a meeting with the great man. The boy Walter remarked that he could play some of the classical pieces

Paderewski had offered in his concert. Impressed, Paderewski placed his hand on Walter's head and remarked, "Some day this boy may take my place."

Walter was a solitary boy, not only because of his devotion to the piano. Even those playmates who didn't shun him for being a sissy found him hard to understand. In his youthful enthusiasm he tumbled out his words in an incoherent mass. His teachers chastised him for speaking so rapidly, and they marked him down when he was unable to correct himself.

"What's the matter with the kid?" his father asked. "Is he dim-witted or something?"

His wife was shocked at the suggestion. "Of course not! Do you see how he plays the piano? He's brilliant. It's just a passing thing, the way he talks. He'll grow out of it."

"I don't think so. I think there's something wrong with him."

Salvatore Liberace expressed his concern to Steve Swedish, a big, robust musician who worked with him in movie house pit bands.

"You know, I've heard about kids like Walter," said Swedish. "Sometimes they talk that way because their tongues are too tight."

"What d'ya mean, their tongues are too tight?"

"There's a little piece of flesh under the tongue that prevents them from speaking clearly. A doctor can make a little snip, and it's fixed."

A week later Liberace told Swedish: "I took Walter to the doctor and did what you said. It didn't make no difference."

"Then it isn't something physical," said Swedish. "Walter needs some speech therapy. The best man I know is Father Raphael Hamilton at Marquette University. He's a priest who specializes in speech problems."

Starting at the age of seven, Walter underwent years of therapy with Father Hamilton, who drilled him in concentrating on vowels so his speech developed a smoother flow. When he was fifteen, Walter underwent a summer course in diction to rid himself of his boyhood accent, the result of hearing a father who spoke Italian-shaded English and a mother who retained evidence of her Polish upbringing. Walter had to concentrate on the "th" sound to avoid saying "dese" and "dem." The result was the deliberate, almost cloying Liberace style of speech duplicated by nightclub impressionists.

Years later when attending a Liberace concert in Milwaukee, Father Hamilton would nudge Steve Swedish conspiratorially and mutter: "Hey, Steve—we made Liberace!"

Salvatore Liberace realized that Walter had progressed beyond the simple piano lessons of Mrs. Walker. But how could he find better training for the boy when the family could hardly make ends meet? If only an accomplished teacher would recognize the promise in Walter and offer to instruct him free. Salvatore remembered a superior pianist with whom he had once played in a concert.

Father and son went hand-in-hand to the Wisconsin College of Music and met with Florence Bettray Kelly, an elegant, warm-hearted pianist and teacher who had studied with the virtuoso Moriz Rosenthal.

"He plays very well for a boy his age, very well indeed," said Mrs. Kelly after Walter offered a few selections on the piano. "I would be willing to take him as a student. And I believe that I can get him a scholarship with the conservatory."

Thus began the most important musical influence of Liberace's professional life. Teacher and student remained together in sometimes contentious partnership for seventeen years—the longest scholarship ever granted by the conservatory—and Mrs. Kelly continued coaching Liberace even after he became famous.

The Depression brought hardship to the Liberace family, and not only because of the economic malaise that crippled the entire nation. By the end of 1929, the revolution of sound had swept the film industry, and talkies eliminated the need for symphony orchestras to accompany the action on the screen. Nor was there other work to be found for serious musicians. Salvatore Liberace was unemployable.

He was bewildered and hurt to find himself divorced from the profession he loved. His Italian pride was damaged when he discovered he was no longer the provider of the family. His wife and children were forced to find jobs that would help put food on the table. And now there was another mouth to feed. Another son was born in 1930 and named Rudolph—another remembrance of Frances's favorite star, Valentino.

Mrs. Liberace worked in a cookie factory, bringing home each night an aura of chocolate and a large bag of damaged cookies for the family. George drove a grocery truck and gave piano lessons. Angelina worked as a secretary and as an assistant nurse. Even before he was a teenager, Walter was bringing home money. He played piano for dance classes and washed dishes in restaurants.

For ten years Salvatore Liberace, who Americanized his name to Sam, had no steady work, except for a time in the W.P.A. Orchestra, part of the Roosevelt Administration's attempt to provide work for unemployed artists. Sometimes he would be absent during the day and return home with grease-stained hands. He made no explanation, unable to admit the shame of taking daywork as a factory hand. As his bitterness grew, he became more abusive toward the children, more quarrelsome with his wife. His absences in the evening led to fierce arguments with Frances, who accused him of philandering— quite correctly, as it turned out.

Young Walter was dismayed by his father's rebukes and repelled by the deprivation the family had been forced to live with. At one point Frances Liberace was desperate enough to seek help from county welfare. Walter was faced with the ignominy of picking up groceries in his coaster wagon from the county relief station.

"Except for music, there wasn't much beauty in my childhood," he lamented in later years. "We lived in one of those featureless bungalows in a featureless neighborhood. My only escape was when I visited my grandparents' farm in the summer. I hated shabbiness. I'd walk twenty-seven blocks and pay fifteen cents to sit in a new, clean movie house when I could have walked five blocks and paid five cents to sit in an old, dirty one."

Although his schoolmates still ragged him about practicing so much, he learned to use his music to win them over. They invited him to birthday parties because he was certain to accept the invitation to sit down at the piano and play the latest tunes. He became a familiar figure at dance recitals and fashion shows. He was known at West Milwaukee High School even before he entered. He left grammar school in the afternoon and played ragtime piano for dancers in the high school gymnasium.

Walter blossomed in high school. He found that his fellow students accepted him for what he was: a talented piano player with a lively sense of fun. No matter that he didn't indulge in sports, like the other boys. "Gotta save these hands," he explained.

He used the piano to broaden his skills as an entertainer. Instead of accepting money for playing at dance studios, he took lessons. With his inborn rhythm, he quickly learned to tap dance, and gave a creditable performance in a duet with one of the instructors at a recital.

He loved to dress up, even then. Every semester the students of West Milwaukee High School celebrated Character Day. Everyone was required to wear costumes of famous figures, and those who didn't were forced to swallow a spoonful of castor oil. That never befell Walter Liberace. He almost always won first prize for the most original costume. Once he dressed as Haile Selassie, who was in the news because of Mussolini's invasion of Ethiopia. On other Character

Days he came to school as Yankee Doodle Dandy, then as Greta Garbo, complete with slinky gown, blond wig, and heavy makeup. While other boys customarily wore sweaters to school, Walter always came in a coat with vest. On cold days he wore spats.

Walter excelled in classes that interested him. With his swift fingers, he outperformed the girls in the typing class. When the orchestra teacher offered a position in the orchestra if Walter would also take her German class, Walter enrolled in German and won straight As for four years. He was a member of the German Club, the Latin Club, and took part in the annual Hi-lights talent show and any other theatrical activity he had time for.

Walter helped organize cooking classes for boys, and his meat loaves and corn muffins were prized by his fellow students. So were the corsages fashioned from cloth that Walter made and sold to those with dates to the June Prom and the Silhouette Dance. Walter generally didn't attend, except to play piano in the orchestra. His classmates recall that he had little interest in dating, although he was believed to have had a crush on a ballet dancer whose recitals he played for. She later married and left Milwaukee.

The high point in Walter's week was his lesson with Florence Kelly. Often she taught him between programs at radio station WTMJ, where she was staff pianist. Both teacher and student were strong-willed, and they sometimes clashed over selections she insisted he learn. One of the disputed pieces was Liszt's "Forest Murmurs."

"Have you learned it?" she demanded one day.

"I did two pages and I'm not going to do any more," Walter replied. "It's a stupid piece, and I hate it."

"All right, get out!" she ordered. "If you won't learn this piece, I'm through with you. I don't want to see you again. Do you understand?" While the other radio musicians watched in amazement, she pushed him out of the studio and threw the music sheets after him.

Mrs. Kelly immediately telephoned Mr. Liberace and told him that

Walter's scholarship was in jeopardy unless he followed her instruction. When Walter arrived home, his father was furious. "No more practice on the piano for one week," Sam Liberace decreed. When Walter returned to Mrs. Kelly, he knew "Forest Murmurs" perfectly. Twenty years later, it amused her when he played it on his television program and announced, "This is my favorite piano number."

An artist of great discipline, Florence Kelly was continually frustrated by the work habits of her star pupil. She couldn't understand his lackadaisical attitude before a concert or recital. "You've got to *prepare!*" she insisted. "Yeah, later," he replied.

On the night before a concert he would stay up all night at the piano. His performance would be flawless, and he exulted to Mrs. Kelly, "I didn't let you down, did I?"

"No, but what hell you put me through beforehand!" she replied.

Most of Mrs. Kelly's students were plagued by nervousness and self-doubt before a performance. Not Walter Liberace. When he was twelve, she entered him against a dozen girls in a contest of the National Federation of Music Clubs at the summer camp of Oconomowoc. Walter was unquestionably the winner. That evening he sat on the couch in his teacher's living room and commented, "Why, I wouldn't think of playing the way some of those girls did, Florence! You wouldn't allow me to play that way. They were terrible, just terrible."

A few years later, Mrs. Kelly decided Walter was overly confident and needed to be taught a lesson. She entered him in a contest at the Athenaeum against some of the best young pianists in Wisconsin. At 11 o'clock that evening she received a telephone call from Walter: "Florence, I had to borrow a nickel so I could call and tell you I won."

In his later apotheosis of Mom as the major influence in his life, Liberace sometimes told the story of how she saved his musical career and perhaps his life.

During his midteens, Walter developed a hangnail which became infected and began to swell his arm. His mother took the boy to a specialist who diagnosed the problem as blood poisoning. "Amputation is the only answer," the doctor said. "But my son is a pianist," Frances Liberace protested. "Can't you save his hand?" The doctor replied: "We'll be lucky to save his arm."

Frances wouldn't consider surgery. She led Walter home and told him she was going to try something her mother had brought from the Old World. She filled the clothes boiler with water and placed it on the lighted burner. As the water was heating, she knelt down and prayed for God to save her son's arm.

As soon as the water came to a rolling boil, she plunged Walter's arm into it, right up to the shoulder. The boy howled with pain as his mother plastered his arm with a poultice of milk and white laundry soap. She wrapped the arm in wax paper. Every half hour during the next four days and nights, she repeated the treatment. On the fifth day pus began to discharge from the hand. The crisis was over, but it would be months before Walter could play the piano again.

While studying Liszt and Chopin with Florence Kelly, Walter Liberace was earning money by playing ragtime and popular melodies in honky-tonks and beer halls and at weddings and anniversary parties. Florence could hardly complain, since she played popular tunes at the radio station.

Walter was fourteen when he started appearing with three other musicians, Del Krause, Joe Zingsheim, and Carl Lorenz. The boys were three years older, but Walter was their peer musically. Their first date was in 1933 at Little Nick's on Muskegon and Mitchell Streets, an ice cream parlor that had been converted to a beer hall with the repeal of Prohibition. No matter that Walter was too young to be working in a place serving alcoholic beverages. He looked old for his age, and besides, nobody cared much about such things during Milwaukee's euphoria over the return of legal beer.

Del Krause played drums, and the band rehearsed in his mother's living room because the drums were heavy to carry around. There was a piano for Walter; Joe Zingsheim brought his trumpet and Carl Lorenz his sax and clarinet.

For the young crowd, the band offered the popular tunes of the 1930s, but for older audiences they played songs of the 1920s and before, often inviting a sing-along. The most surefire medley consisted of "The Darktown Strutters' Ball," "Won't You Come Home, Bill Bailey?" "Has Anybody Seen My Gal?" "When the Saints Go Marching In," and "Sweet Georgia Brown." Requests were invited. If Walter wasn't familiar with the song, he asked the guest to sing or hum it. He was able to play the tune immediately, and the others improvised an accompaniment.

"Where are you going, Walter?" his mother would ask when she saw him dressed after dinner in his best suit, a hand-me-down from George.

"Oh, the boys and I are playing tonight," he replied. "I think it's for a church social."

She was reassured when Del Krause arrived to take the streetcar to the engagement with Walter. Del lived a block and a half away, and he seemed like a nice, responsible boy. Mrs. Liberace was appalled to learn from a neighbor that Walter had been seen playing piano in a beer garden. She forbade him from leaving the house at night for a week.

"What are we gonna do?" Walter wailed to Del Krause. "We've got that date at Little Nick's tonight."

"Wally, I've got an idea," Del replied. That evening after the Liberace parents had gone to bed, he brought a ladder to Walter's bedroom window. Walter climbed down, went off to play for the beery customers at Little Nick's, and returned home undetected.

Only Walter's music could prevent him from being the model son and student. One Friday afternoon, the band was engaged for a mixer at West Division High School. To arrive in time, Walter and Del had to cut their classes at West Milwaukee High. "We'll get caught," Walter said. "No, we won't," Del said confidently. Walter was right. Both students faced a reprimand in the principal's office on Monday morning.

The band started with salaries of fifty cents apiece per evening, but soon were earning $1.25. The engagements Walter liked best were at a beer garden, where the management allowed the young players to partake of the meals. On Friday night there was a fish fry and on Saturday night a chicken fry. Walter always went back for extras.

Leroy Schultz was the only boy in the neighborhood who owned a car, a 1923 Model T Ford that he kept in assembly-line condition. The musicians paid him fifty cents a night to drive them to and from engagements, thus simplifying their operations. Since he was the youngest, Walter sat in the front seat, between the driver and Del Krause's bass drum.

Walter Liberace was indefatigable at the piano. When the band took an intermission, he continued playing for the customers, asking for requests.

The band often appeared at a gin mill that Joe Zingsheim's brother operated at Beloit and Cold Spring Streets. One night Joe's brother was in a playful mood, and he poured beer over Walter's fingers as he was playing. Walter didn't miss a note.

"Stop!" exclaimed the alarmed Zingsheim. "It's going to ruin the piano." But Walter continued to the end of the song.

While Walter played ragtime at night, he continued studying classics with Florence Kelly in the daytime. When he was fourteen, she presented his first recital at the Wisconsin College of Music. "You did me proud," Mrs. Kelly admitted in a rare display of praise for her precocious student. His program of études and sonatas was applauded heartily by the audience of teachers, students, and parents.

"Did you hear about the show at the Riverside Theater?" a high school friend asked Walter one day. "They're putting on something called 'Milwaukee on Parade,' using a lot of local talent. I bet you could make it."

Walter hurried downtown to the movie palace and asked to see the manager. The manager was unimpressed by the kid in knickers and sent him away. Walter came back the next day after school, and the next day, until the exasperated manager agreed to an audition. "Not bad," he conceded after the boy delivered a whirlwind rendition of "Twelfth Street Rag."

Florence Kelly was the first to hear the news from the breathless Walter: a week's engagement at the movie palace in the Fanchon and Marco revue! The theater was going to supply him with a suit, since he didn't own one. Walter didn't tell his family about the date because he knew his father would not approve of his son playing popular songs for the movie-theater audience.

Sam Liberace learned the news from Florence Kelly. "Did you know what Wally is doing? He's playing at the Riverside Theater. And he's damned good, too."

As Walter had anticipated, his father disapproved. But Sam Liberace was less upset when Walter presented his week's salary: $75.

Though he couldn't throw a football or catch a fly ball, Walter Liberace became popular with his fellow students, male and female, at West Milwaukee High. Taunts of being a sissy were seldom heard, and even the school athletes admired his sunny personality and his readiness to entertain. As soon as he gulped down the lunch his mother had made for him, he hurried to the girls' gymnasium and played boogie-woogie and the latest popular songs for them. Walter auditioned for every school play and often was chosen for a role.

Joseph Schwei, the faculty member in charge of assembly programs, knew he could always count on Walter to help fill a vacancy.

One arose on the day the home economics class planned a fashion show of designs created by students. The girl who was scheduled to announce the show became ill. "I'll do it!" Walter told Mr. Schwei. He reported for the show in a beret, artist's smock, and flowing tie. With a long pointer and an easel, he explained the fashions and introduced the models with so much humor that he had the audience laughing throughout the performance.

By day at West Milwaukee High School, Walter Liberace was learning English composition, German, Latin, mathematics, and other basic subjects. His education at night was far different.

Playing piano in beer gardens and roadhouses introduced him to a world far removed from the conservative, basically Catholic neighborhood where he had grown up. Customers could be noisy, lewd, and roaring drunk. Walter, who had been allowed a glass of wine at the family table, was introduced to booze when he was barely fifteen.

The Del Krause band was playing at the silver wedding anniversary party of a Polish couple. The evening had been marked by heartfelt toasts and frenetic dancing. The host lurched up to the bandstand with an unlabeled bottle. "Somethin' for you boys," he said grandly.

Joe Zingsheim took a swallow and passed the bottle to Walter. Walter had a swig and with watery eyes and scalded throat handed the bottle to Carl Lorenz. The moonshine made the circuit of the players three times before it was time to begin another set of numbers. Walter sat down at the piano, played the first eight bars of "The Carioca," and fell off the bench. He was wary of alcohol ever afterward.

Walter was also learning about sex. The primary facts had been imparted to him by his brother George, but Walter had no firsthand knowledge—furtive kisses with the few girls he dated, nothing more. He had never seen a naked woman. He listened to the bragging tales of conquests by boys whose brashness he admired but could not emulate. He couldn't imagine himself forcing his manhood on the demure, virginal girls he knew in school.

His piano engagements introduced him to a different kind of woman. So sheltered had he been that he saw a woman smoke for the first time in a beer garden. He was so astonished that he stopped playing.

Walter reported one evening for a smoker at a men's fraternal organization. As he played honky-tonk on the piano, the hall darkened, and a flickering, scratched movie appeared on the screen. Walter watched in disbelief as the shadowy, naked figures coupled and performed bizarre contortions while the male audience shouted lewd comments and roared with laughter.

The lights came on, and a spotlight shone on the stage, where three women, with dyed hair and heavy makeup, appeared from behind the curtain. While Walter played "St. Louis Blues," the women performed an amateur dance, removing all their clothing to a storm of approval. He continued the music while the women brushed past him provocatively and began mingling with the lodge members.

Walter played a noisy accompaniment to the merriment until the doors swung open and Milwaukee police stormed into the hall amid a shrill chorus of whistles. A bust! Sam Liberace claimed his son at the police station and delivered a blistering tirade on the way home. Mrs. Liberace added her own fury and decreed that Walter could henceforward work only at teas, weddings, and other polite gatherings. But of course that proved impractical, since the boy brought home sizable checks from playing in saloons and roadhouses, and Walter was now the principal earner of the Liberace household.

When Walter was sixteen, George found him work at Pick's Club Madrid, a roadhouse that attracted big spenders from Chicago. He accompanied George's wife, a soprano who specialized in operetta songs. He also played for other women singers who strolled among the tables while Walter followed them with a small piano on wheels. The singers split the tips with him.

George, who played violin in the orchestra, always drove his wife and Walter to and from the Club Madrid. One night the blues singer, a lusty redhead whose busty figure and suggestive songs pleased the male customers, told George there were two men who looked promising for big tips. "Can Walter stay and play for me?" she asked. "I'll split the tips with the kid and drive him home."

The two customers tipped handsomely, and both Walter and the blues singer were elated as they divided the money and began the long drive back to Milwaukee. Virtually no other cars were on the road in the early morning, and on a quiet stretch the singer drove to the side and parked. She began fondling Walter and said with a laugh, "My, you're a big boy!" Before he realized what was happening, she had unbuttoned his pants and was mouthing his erect penis. He had never felt such a sensation in his life. Afterward she aroused him again, then climbed on top of him, and they coupled in a few moments of intense passion.

Walter arrived home in a state of bliss. Then he was horrified. There were lipstick stains all over his white pants. "My God, how will I ever explain that to Mom!" he exclaimed to himself. He scrubbed and scrubbed with laundry soap until he finally removed the damning evidence.

When Walter related the previous night's events to his schoolmates—the same ones who had bragged about their sexual conquests—they didn't believe him. "You're full of shit, Liberace," they said.

Walter had a few more encounters with the blues singer at her apartment, and, as he related in later years, she was impressed by his youthful capacity for multiple orgasms. The passionate interlude ended when she found a singing job in Cleveland. Walter's sexual initiation proved far from satisfactory. His partner had been a boy-hungry trollop twice his age, and their love-making had been mechanical and passionless, nothing like what Walter had expected after all the romantic movies he had seen.

In a rare display of harmony, the entire Liberace family—mother and father, George, Angelina, and Rudy, plus Mom's sister Ann, now a Catholic nun named Sister DeSalles—appeared in June 1937 for Walter's graduation from East Milwaukee High School. He played in the school orchestra, of course, and was cited for his scholastic achievement: an 84 average, twenty-first in the graduating class of seventy-six.

His picture in the high school annual shows a healthy young man of eighteen, already an inch or two under six feet tall, the wide-set eyes beaming, the full lips curved in a confident smile. While other boys in the annual looked stiff in their Sunday suits, Walter seemed comfortable in a jacket and double-breasted vest with lapels. On the coat was a stylish boutonniere. Beneath the photograph was the inscription:

> Our Wally has already made his claim
> With Paderewski, Gershwin, and others of fame.

High school graduation brought no prospect of college, even though Walter's grades would have granted him admission to the University of Wisconsin. With Sam Liberace still unemployed and George on his own and touring with orchestras, it was left for Walter to provide the principal support for the family. Besides, he had no concern for further education. His single, all-consuming interest was music, and he could broaden his knowledge through the continuing scholarship studies with Florence Kelly. His real education, he realized, lay in constantly performing before people, honing his skills to please and amuse and impress his audience with his pianistic talent.

Chapter 2

THE ONCE AND FUTURE WALTER BUSTER KEYS
FINDS HIS DESTINY WITH THE HELP OF ANOTHER
MILWAUKEE NATIVE

Leopold Stokowski was coming to Milwaukee with the Philadelphia Symphony Orchestra, and Walter believed it would lift his father's depressed spirits to attend the concert with him. "Hey, Dad, I've got two tickets to see Stokowski," Walter said. "You wanna go with me?"

"Can't go," Sam Liberace answered. "I gotta rehearsal with the American Legion Band."

Walter was disappointed, but he knew someone else who would be thrilled to hear the Philadelphia Symphony—Florence Kelly. Walter and his teacher were both in a state of excitement as they joined the crowd at the Pabst Theater and took seats in the rear of the orchestra section. As the musicians in their tuxedos and stiff shirts threaded their way through the music stands to take their positions, Walter gazed around at the audience. His heart stopped. Seated a few rows in front of him was his father, talking intimately with a woman!

Tears began to form in Walter's eyes. Florence Kelly looked at him and said, "Walter, what's the matter?" He nodded in the direction of his father, and Mrs. Kelly held her hand over her mouth in astonishment.

"You knew?" he asked.

Mrs. Kelly nodded slowly.

"Who is she?"

"Zona Smrz. She teaches cello and plays in the symphony."

"Does Mom know?"

"I don't think so. But in time she will."

For Walter it was a punishing blow. He had intimate knowledge of the antagonism between his mother and father, but he had persisted in thinking that, like all Catholic couples, they would find some way to coexist. Now Walter had seen firsthand the evidence of his father's duplicity. Never again could Walter believe in his father—he would always sympathize with his mother, who had sacrificed to preserve the fabric of the family, only to be betrayed by a thankless husband.

Unwilling to face his father and afraid that he would somehow disclose the secret to his mother, Walter spent more time away from home. There was much to occupy him. Now that he was free of school, he could intensify his lessons with Mrs. Kelly. And there were jobs to be found for a piano player with his versatility.

His first regular job was in the Red Room bar of the Plankinton Arcade. The pay was $35 a week plus all he could eat, and the manager claimed he lost money on the deal. He also hired himself out for late-night parties, leaving the Red Room at the 1 A.M. closing and entertaining revelers sometimes until dawn.

Florence Kelly made no attempt to discourage Walter from playing popular tunes for boozing Milwaukeeans; she understood firsthand the perils of earning a living from musicianship. But she continued schooling the young man in the classics. "You have it in you to become a concert performer, Walter," she insisted. She managed to win him a contract with a Chicago booking agency which placed him in the Community Concert Course. He was sent to high schools, colleges, women's clubs and other organizations devoted to the uplift of Midwestern culture.

Sam Liberace was playing in the W.P.A. Orchestra, and Mrs. Kelly suggested that he try to win Walter a solo appearance with the federally-financed organization. The conductor agreed, and when his father broke the news of the engagement, the exuberant Walter declared, "And I'm going to wear tails!"

"Not at your age," Sam answered sternly. "You can wear George's tuxedo."

"Oh, no," Walter vowed. "I've worn his hand-me-downs all my life."

On the evening of the concert, Walter walked downstairs in an elegant tuxedo with tails, on which he had lavished his savings of $27.50. Mom was adoring, Dad was wrathful. George was practical: "Have you learned to flip the tails before you sit down?" "Of course," replied Walter. "I've been practicing upstairs."

As he reached for the first high notes at the concert, the coat cuffs pulled toward his elbows. He had forgotten to flip his tails! As soon as he came to a musical rest, the tails went flying, and the audience laughed appreciatively. He had learned another lesson in how to engage an audience.

In 1939 Mrs. Kelly presented her prize student with an extraordinary opportunity. Dr. Frederick Stock of the Chicago Symphony was willing to include Walter among young artists he was auditioning for a possible guest appearance. Teacher and student boarded the Milwaukee-Chicago train during a raging snowstorm, and they fretted through the long delays, realizing that Walter's opportunity might be irretrievably lost. But when they finally arrived at Orchestra Hall, Stock was still auditioning another aspirant.

The place was forbidding: a huge, empty concert hall with no one in sight but the leonine maestro standing in the orchestra pit before a quavering young player at the onstage piano.

"No! No! No!" Stock commanded. "You are pianissimo when you should be fortissimo! Can't you do it right? Now start again!"

The youthful pianist began once more, playing the soloist part while Stock hummed the role of the orchestra. But the pianist's assurance had been destroyed, and his missteps caused another explosion from Stock. "Impossible!" the conductor exclaimed, rapping his baton on the edge of the stage. "Start again!"

"Oh my God, Florence!" Walter whispered to Mrs. Kelly. "What can I do?"

"What you can do, Walter," she replied, "is play the best you have ever played in your life. This is your one great chance."

The other pianist was dismissed, and he fled the stage in tears. "Next!" Stock decreed.

Walter walked hesitantly to the piano and announced he would play Liszt's Second Concerto in A Major. Stock regarded him dubiously and nodded for the young man to begin. Walter started to play, anticipating the crack of the maestro's baton on the stage apron as a signal for him to begin again. It didn't come. Stock listened intently, humming softly the orchestral portions. Walter completed the entire concerto without looking at a note of music.

"Well done," Stock conceded at the end of the concerto. "You will be hearing from me."

Soon came word that Walter was invited to play with the Chicago Symphony in a concert at the Pabst Theater in Milwaukee. Walter was overjoyed, but the concert was not for six months, and in the meantime he needed work. He found a job as pianist in a popular dance band, the Jay Mills Orchestra, which was touring Wisconsin, Minnesota, and Michigan. He became good friends with the singer,

Vivian Stapleton, a lovely seventeen-year-old from Newark. She and Walter were the only teenagers in the band, and they didn't fit into the booze parties of the other band members. The pair spent their off-nights at roller-skating rinks and ice cream parlors. When her name appeared too long for the band's advertising cards, it was changed to Vivian Blaine. She later became a star of Twentieth Century-Fox musicals in the 1940s and played Adelaide in the original stage version and the movie of *Guys and Dolls.*

Jay Mills, who excelled as a promoter as well as orchestra leader, arranged an appearance on the popular radio show "The Fitch Bandwagon." Walter was excited about appearing on a coast-to-coast radio show for the first time, but it almost proved the undoing of his big chance to play classical music. The manager of the Chicago Symphony happened to hear the broadcast and he complained to Stock: "That boy you picked to play piano in Milwaukee—he was on the radio with a dance band! He can't play with the symphony." Stock replied: "I don't care if he played on a street corner with the Salvation Army Band. He will play with us."

The symphony management had one request of Walter: would he use another name until after his Milwaukee appearance? He told Jay Mills his plight, and the next night the billing appeared: "At the piano—WALTER BUSTER KEYS."

He remained Walter Buster Keys for only six months, but the name would be forever enshrined in Liberace legend.

Finally the date of the Chicago Symphony appearance arrived—January 14, 1940. Walter's thrill over the performance was tempered when Frederick Stock became ill and was replaced by Hans Lange as conductor. But he played with total confidence and was cheered by the hometown audience.

His family and neighbors and high school friends poured backstage to congratulate Walter. The most valued accolade came from his father. Rarely had Sam Liberace commented on his son's music except to castigate him for playing popular stuff. Never in his life had Walter been embraced by his father. Now he was.

"Son, I was proud of you," said Sam, as tears flowed down his cheeks. "From now on you can play anything you want to. You've proved to me you can do it."

"Young Pianist Proves Worth," proclaimed the *Milwaukee Journal* in Walter Liberace's first important review. The music critic, Richard S. Davis, cited how the young Milwaukee musician had been chosen in a competition and declared that he had played Liszt's Second Concerto in A Major with great credit to himself and his teacher.

> *The young artist was at no time in difficulty, but it was apparent that he was proceeding with infinite care, and the swaggering approach that goes so well with Liszt was somewhat missed.*
>
> *Mr. Liberace did disclose, however, a very considerable gift for brilliant pianism. His technique, while never tested to the full, was fully adequate, his tone was excellent and his musical sense impressive. In sentimental passages his piano sang with warmth, and there was sparkle in the froth. If at intervals the pianist seemed a little diffident, it was undoubtedly because he felt his great responsibility and was constrained to take no chances.*

The review (which may have been the high point in Liberace's relationship with critics) was celebrated by Walter and Florence Kelly. More than ever she was convinced that he could succeed as a concert artist.

But the opportunities for a serious young musician in the Midwest were scant, and since Jay Mills had disbanded his orchestra, Walter had to retreat to bars and grills. Back at the Plankinton Arcade, he graduated from the Red Room saloon to the Green Room restaurant at $90 a week. At the Green Room the customers paid more attention to Walter's music. Walter Ludwig, the owner, was amazed when the patrons applauded after the numbers. No one had ever done that for a pianist in his restaurant before. Ludwig also found that for the first time customers were lining up for tables, and people were calling on the telephone to ask when the piano player would perform.

Walter, who sought any chance to escape the tensions between his mother and father at home, spent much of his nonperforming time with Ludwig and his wife. When the Ludwigs went on vacation to a lake cabin, Walter accompanied them. He always took along a cardboard piano keyboard, and he would practice on it three hours each day. Walter was a favorite with all the employees of the Green Room. One Christmas he baked sixteen individual fruitcakes, wrapped them in cellophane, and presented them to each of his coworkers.

On October 18, 1940, Walter was given a night off from the Green Room to appear in concert at the Athenaeum concert hall for the Sigma Alpha Iota sorority. The hall was only half-filled but the audience applauded the young pianist's renditions of Beethoven's C Minor "Themes and Variations," two Chopin études, the Liszt "Mazeppa," and more modern pieces by Poulenc and Niemann.

Once more the *Journal*'s Richard S. Davis was complimentary, exhibiting prescience of things to come:

> Again the pianist demonstrated that his nature is warmly musical, that he has the skill for handsome technical flourishes, and that he can bear down dramatically when occasion warrants. ... Mr. Liberace is inclined to be sentimental and perhaps a little soft, which is a tendency to be watched. He can, however, make the piano sing appealingly and that is a gift to be cherished. His work is clean for the most part and uniformly intelligent.

The Milwaukee concert led to others in outlying towns. One of them, Liberace later maintained, was to prove historic.

It was at a small concert hall in LaCrosse, Wisconsin. Walter played his usual smattering of the classics to polite but appreciative applause. When he finished the major works, he turned to the audience and said, "Well, instead of my usual encores, I'd like to play what you'd like to hear. What will it be?"

After an embarrassed silence, a voice in the balcony called out: "Three Little Fishes." The audience laughed. It was the country's most popular song of the moment, a nonsense tune made popular by Kay Kyser's Orchestra, with a chorus that went: " 'Fim, little fishies, fim if you can,' and they fam and the fam all over the dam."

After the laughter subsided, Walter began playing an introduction in the florid style of Chopin, then mingled it with the unmistakable strains of "Three Little Fishes." The audience applauded with delight. Walter continued with the song as it might have been interpreted by Mozart, Beethoven, and John Philip Sousa. The applause was thunderous when he concluded.

A reporter from the LaCrosse newspaper was in the audience, and he telephoned the Associated Press bureau in Milwaukee with an item. The story was carried on the AP's national wire, and newspapers printed it with headlines such as: "Three Little Fishes Swim in a Sea of Classics."

For Walter Liberace the lesson was twofold. He realized he could achieve a greater audience response with a combination of classics and popular music. He also understood for the first time the overwhelming power of publicity.

Inevitably, Frances Liberace learned of her husband's mistress, the cello teacher Zona Smrz. She erupted with Polish fury, throwing Sam and his clothing out of the house. Over the disapproval of the parish priest, she consulted a lawyer about a divorce. She poured out her grievances, not only his adulterous behavior but his failure to provide for his family as well as other misdemeanors. At one point the lawyer interrupted her: "Mrs. Liberace, doesn't your husband have another name besides 'that old bastard'?"

The divorce was granted in 1941. Two years later Sam married Zona Smrz, and they moved to Middleton so she could be close to the University of Wisconsin at Madison. She had become proficient in art with plastics, and the university had made developments in that field. She continued her art career and Sam played with the Madison Symphony. They remained married until her death many years later.

Frances Liberace was married in 1943 to another Italian, Alexander Casadonte. He had come from Sam's village in Italy and had roomed with the Liberaces after his arrival. There was some talk among neighbors that a romance between Frances and the boarder had developed even before she threw Sam out. Casadonte died in 1945, and Frances never married again.

After the divorce of his parents, it would be more than a dozen years before Walter would see his father again.

By 1941 America was mobilizing for war, and George Liberace enlisted in the navy. Walter was called in the draft, but a childhood back injury exempted him from military service.

Walter was becoming more and more confused about his double career, and he poured out his feelings to Florence Kelly. "I don't know who I am," he complained.

"I know what you're going through," she said sympathetically. "You don't know whether to be a concert pianist or a nightclub entertainer. Why don't you combine the two? Play some classics, then give them something popular. Make them think they're getting some uplift, then slide into something melodic and familiar. It'll work, Walter, I know it will."

"But how? I can't play Liszt at the Green Room."

"I think it's time for you to move on. You've gone as far as you can go in Wisconsin. You've got to reach a more sophisticated audience. I think you should go to New York."

Walter had thought about it, of course. He had listened to the radio concerts conducted by Walter Damrosch and Arturo Toscanini, and he had imagined himself playing with them in Carnegie Hall. He had also heard popular pianists like Vincent Lopez and Eddy Duchin appearing in places like the Rainbow Room and the Central Park Casino. Walter had never been east of Chicago, and New York seemed a distant and unattainable dream. Or was it?

Jay Mills provided the opportunity. He broken up his band to accept a position as master of ceremonies and entertainment director at Pal's Cabin, a nightclub in West Orange, New Jersey. Mills wrote his former pianist: "I remember you talked about playing in New York some day. Well, West Orange ain't exactly New York, but it's close. If you want to come here, I'll put you to work. Think about it, kid."

Walter had a tearful farewell with Mom, who offered repeated warnings about the perils of the big city, said good-bye to his former bandmates in The Mixers, and boarded the train for the East.

Pal's Cabin proved to be more impressive than it had sounded. Beginning as a hot dog stand, it proved so popular that the owners kept building on until they had a complete entertainment complex. The New Jersey audiences were friendly and receptive, and Mills assured Walter of steady employment. New York was still Walter's goal, and he went there often to savor its wonders.

New York on first sight was impressive to any midwesterner. New York on the brink of war dazzled the senses. Walter Liberace wandered Times Square with more than the customary awe of a first-time visitor. He stared at the animated signs far overhead, the movie palace marquees heralding Frank Sinatra, Benny Goodman, Danny Kaye, and Betty Hutton in person. He shouldered through the crowd of sailors and soldiers and their brightly painted girls. He listened to the jazz from outside the doorways of the joints on Fifty-second Street; his limited resources wouldn't allow him to enter.

He found other, unexpected pleasures. Attractive young men struck up conversations and invited him to theaters and parties. After years of repression, Walter was suddenly free to admit his homosexual desires and express his affection for other men. He had always been forced to hide those feelings from his schoolmates, his family, his friends. Now in New York there was no one to watch him, no one to whisper. He was liberated at last.

Press clippings and letters of recommendation meant little to Broadway booking agents. Walter's rounds of the agencies brought no prospects for his ambitions to appear in concerts or to play in stylish nightclubs. Finally he won an audition at the Music Corporation of America, and one of the agents, Mae Johnston, agreed to represent him.

One morning Mae Johnston asked him, "How would you like to play the Persian Room at the Plaza?"

"The Persian Room!" Walter replied. "Are you kidding?"

"No, this is the McCoy. I don't mean you're going to be the headliner. They need an intermission piano player over there."

"Oh." Walter had done the job before. It was the most thankless task a pianist could have, playing background music while the patrons gobbled their dinners and swilled their drinks between dance sets by the orchestra and the floor show. "Maybe the job will be different at the Plaza," Walter told himself.

It wasn't. If anything, the Persian Room guests were noisier and more inattentive than any he had faced in other nightclub intermissions. The patrons, many of them army and navy officers paying stiff prices for an evening's entertainment, seemed intent on enjoying it to the utmost. Walter played his Gershwin medley and the Grieg Concerto in A Minor to not a hint of applause.

One part of the Persian Room date thrilled him: the star attraction was Hildegarde.

After Spencer Tracy and Pat O'Brien, she was Milwaukee's most famous show business figure. Walter had listened to her every week on radio and had admired her bubbly sophistication and her supple piano work. She was often written up in the *Milwaukee Journal* and the *Sentinel*. Walter knocked on her dressing room door and introduced himself, and she seemed genuinely pleased that a fellow Milwaukeean was working on the same bill.

Every night Walter stood offstage and scrutinized Hildegarde's performance. He noticed that the orchestra was augmented with additional strings and a harp. The lights in the Persian Room were lowered to darkness and held there until the noise at the tables subsided. The orchestra played a rousing fanfare, and spotlights shone on the stage. Six chorus girls emerged in maids' uniforms, carrying dusters. They danced around a grand piano that had materialized in the middle of the dance floor. As they dusted the piano, they sang of the coming of their mistress, the inimitable, the glamorous Hildegarde!

She swept into the room in a cloud of chiffon, her blond hair piled high on her head. Thunderous applause greeted her, and she sat down at the piano to play and sing "There'll Be Bluebirds Over the White Cliffs of Dover." The servicemen loved it, and she followed with "Praise the Lord and Pass the Ammunition." Then, she announced, it was time for something serious, and the room became silent as she played a Chopin nocturne followed by a Fritz Kreisler étude. She continued with a collection of the songs she had made famous, finishing with "I'll Be Seeing You," which had servicemen and their dates crying.

A dancer dressed as a footman delivered a dozen long-stemmed red roses, and she wandered through the room singing a tender song.

One by one, she selected a man in the audience, gazed tenderly at him, and handed him a rose (some had paid the headwaiter $50 to be included). Mostly she gave the roses to servicemen, leaving their cheeks marked with a red kiss.

Walter marveled at how Hildegarde maintained total control of her audience. She called admirals and gobs, generals and GI's onto the floor and had the officers salute the enlisted men. If a drunken customer became noisy, she played and sang, "Show him the way to go home." When a baby cried out, it was "Rockabye baby, shut your little mouth." The audience roared in appreciation. They also did when she brushed off the piano lid and sang, "Dust a song at twilight."

Just as the audience assumed a festival mood, she silenced them with her climactic number, a Gershwin medley or her arrangement of Irving Berlin songs. At the last note, the spotlight blacked out, and for a brief, magical moment the room was silent. Then there was the onrush of cheers and applause. Hildegarde returned to bow deeply, but Walter noted that she never played an encore. "Always leave them wanting it to go on," she counseled him.

Walter sought relief from the stultifying work as intermission pianist. He turned on his microphone and asked customers for request numbers. He was beginning to find a rapport with the audience, but the Plaza management wanted nothing to interfere with the sale of drinks, and he was fired.

He found other work in New York, filling in between the star attractions at nightclubs like Ruban Bleu, the Vanguard, and Spivy's Roof. While his work was politely applauded, his major function was to provide intermission music and sometimes accompaniment for performers such as Ella Fitzgerald, Imogene Coca, and the Revuers, which consisted of Betty Comden, Adolph Green, Judy Holliday, and Al Hammer. Walter's average salary was $175 a week.

Mae Johnston also booked Walter for stage shows at movie theaters and at supper clubs out of town. During an engagement at the Mount Royal Hotel in Montreal he was surprised when Mae appeared in the audience with three M.C.A. executives. After the show, Mae came to Walter's room with an extraordinary opportunity: "One of our most important clients, Eddy Duchin, is going into the navy. We think you'd be the perfect choice to take over his band. You'll be able to use his musicians, his arrangements. You'd be the new Eddy Duchin. Needless to say, the salary will be a lot more than you're getting here. How about it, Walter?"

The money and the instant fame appealed to him, but he said no. "I don't want to be another Eddy Duchin," he said. "I want to be myself."

The M.C.A. chieftains were angry with their young client's refusal of a golden opportunity, and Walter's engagements dwindled. Still, he never regretted passing up the Duchin replacement. He needed to establish his own identity, and he realized it would be difficult with the name Walter Liberace. In later years he maintained that Paderewski had suggested to the boy prodigy that he adopt a single name, declaring, "Where would I be with the name Ignace?" The more likely story: The suggestion came in 1942 in a chance encounter with Paderewski's onetime manager, Charles Perkins. From that time on, he was Liberace. But how could people address him in normal conversation? "You can call me Lee," he always said with a smile.

The single billing didn't help at all. Liberace felt the need to escape the disappointments of New York, and he remembered a friendly face from a Boston engagement. He was warm, outgoing Clarence Goodwin, a shoe manufacturer from California attending a convention. Goodwin had said: "If you ever come to Los Angeles, look me up." Liberace did, and he stayed with Goodwin and his wife for a year.

Clarence Goodwin realized the young pianist was at loose ends and needed the comfort and security of someone's home. "You have a rare talent," the shoe man insisted, "but what you need is a good manager. I'll do the job for you." To Liberace's astonishment, Goodwin declined the offers M.C.A. forwarded from New York. "You're worth more than that," Goodwin reasoned. "The more hard-to-get you are, the more they'll want you."

Goodwin was a member of the Lakeside Golf Club, and he took Liberace to lunch, introducing him to Bing Crosby, Don Ameche, Bob Hope, and other golfers. Liberace recounted such experiences in breathless letters to Mom.

One of Liberace's favorite places to visit was the Hollywood Piano Exchange. It was unlike any other piano store because it catered to the movie studios' need for instruments of every era. One of the store's pianos bewitched him. It was the biggest he had ever seen, covered in gold, even the stool. He looked inside the lid and saw four wires for every note instead of the usual three. The hammers were oversize, and when he struck a chord, the sound resonated, almost like an organ in a cathedral.

A salesman related the history of the piano. It had been one of a pair handcrafted before World War II by the famed piano maker Julius Bluthner. Its mate had reportedly been destroyed by Allied bombings. When Liberace raved about the Bluthner to Goodwin that evening, his host replied, "Then you must have it." The piano appeared in the Goodwin living room the next day, and Liberace couldn't believe it. "You can pay me for it out of your earnings," Goodwin said. "And with a piano like this, we'll have to demand more salary."

Liberace remained in Los Angeles at a time when the aircraft and movie factories were pouring out products for the war effort. Nightlife was booming; war workers with stuffed pockets and servicemen on their way to the Pacific demanded entertainment. Walter found work in clubs and bars in Hollywood and Long Beach. He also found compliant young men, both in and out of uniform, in search of an evening's pleasure.

Chapter 3

MAKING IT IN THE BIG TIME: ADVENTURES
WITH BUGSY SIEGEL, HOWARD HUGHES,
AND HARRY TRUMAN

After a year in California, Liberace decided that it was time to return to New York and make his bid for the big time. He realized he needed a gimmick to differentiate himself from the scores of other café pianists. One day it came to him: why not play duets with the masters? He bought records by Paderewski, Arthur Rubinstein, Egon Petri, José Iturbi, Vladimir Horowitz, and others playing familiar concertos and solo pieces. Working twelve hours a day for weeks, Liberace accompanied the recordings, perfecting his finger work until it coincided precisely with the music he heard. He truncated the numbers so they would intrigue his listeners but not bore them.

To be effective, the music had to resemble live sound. He devised a system of speakers that could be placed around the nightclub room so the sound would envelop the audience.

Liberace convinced the operators of the Persian Room to audition his new act. They were impressed, and they agreed to book him to follow Hildegarde at a salary of $900 a week. His highest salary before that had been $500 a week.

A vital and everlasting element was added to Liberace's act for the Plaza engagement. Liberace had thrilled over *A Song to Remember* when he saw it at a movie theater on Broadway. The affair of Frédéric Chopin (Cornel Wilde) and George Sand (Merle Oberon) had moved him to tears, and he had been overwhelmed by the piano work, recorded by José Iturbi. Liberace was impressed by the candelabra on the piano whenever Wilde pantomimed to Iturbi's playing. It seemed to create a mood of romantic elegance, exactly what Liberace was seeking. Just as important, it could be used at the beginning of the act to quiet the audience and create an air of anticipation.

One July night in 1945, a stagehand in a butler's costume carried a lighted candelabra into the Plaza's Persian Room and placed it atop a grand piano. An offstage voice introduced "the sensational new piano virtuoso, LIBERACE!" He strode onstage in white tie and tails, his wide smile exuding total confidence.

Liberace acknowledged the applause and sat down to play. With breathtaking pace he raced through "Twelfth Street Rag" and boogie-woogie. He played "duets" with Jesus Sanroma and the Boston Pops Orchestra's recording of "Rhapsody in Blue" and with Vladimir Horowitz's rendition of Tchaikovsky's B Minor Concerto, which had been popularized as the song "Tonight We Love." He gave chatty introductions to each number and invited a woman patron to join him in a duet;

when she admitted she couldn't play, he provided a florid accompaniment to her "Chopsticks." He played a Beethoven sonata and a Chopin nocturne and concluded with a thumping version of the Andrews Sisters hit "Beer Barrel Polka."

The sophisticated New York audience clamored for an encore, but Liberace politely declined. He retired to his dressing room supremely confident that he had at last found his show business niche.

The reviews reflected his feeling. For the first time, he was recognized in a New Act Review in *Variety*. Abel Green, editor of the show business paper, declared that Liberace "brings a nice style to big league nitery circuits with his legit and synchronized piano recitals." Green added:

> *Liberace looks like a cross between Cary Grant and Robert Alda (who plays Gershwin in the Warner picture [*Rhapsody in Blue starred Robert Alda, Alan Alda's father*]). He has a fetching manner on the floor, attractive hands which he spotlights properly, and withal rings the bell in a dramatically lighted, well-presented, showmanly routine. He should snowball into boxoffice which, at the moment, he's not, but definitely a boff café act.*

The successful opening at the Plaza brought a host of happy results. Fritz Mahler, conductor of the New Jersey Symphony, invited the young pianist to play a Liszt concerto. Mahler was pleased with the results, and he asked, "Do you play the 'Rhapsody in Blue'?"

"Oh, yes," Liberace said eagerly.

"Good. Morton Gould is looking for a soloist on his radio show."

Liberace gulped. He offered an abbreviated version of the Gershwin rhapsody in his act, but he had never learned the entire piece. He bought the sheet music and was astounded to see that it was thirty-seven pages long. By rehearsing ten hours a day for four days he was able to audition favorably for Gould, and the broadcast was well received.

The new attraction at the Plaza was being noticed by the cognoscenti. Liberace observed that every night at the late show, a small, mysterious-looking woman appeared at a back table. He found out who she was: Elisabeth Bergner, the Polish protégée of Max Reinhardt, who was starring on Broadway in *The Two Mrs. Carrolls*. One night Liberace sought her out, and she told him why she came nightly to the Persian Room: "Your music and these dimly lit surroundings are perfect for me after the theater. I can relax here as nowhere else. You play the music exactly as I want it."

When the Persian Room engagement came to an end, M.C.A. sent Liberace on a tour of the best hotel showrooms in the East and Midwest and into Canada. In Minneapolis he attracted the attention of the symphony conductor Dimitri Mitropoulos. "I like your boogie-woogie," the maestro told him. "By all means you must continue playing it."

In Montreal, a guest at the Liberace performance was Leonard Bernstein, then known as a rising conductor and knowledgeable guest on the radio quiz show "Information Please." Bernstein compared notes on the Liszt piano concertos and admitted to Liberace that he shared a fondness for boogie-woogie. Bernstein, who was making a guest appearance with the Montreal Symphony, said he was returning to conduct the following summer, and he invited Liberace to appear as soloist.

Liberace's travels returned him to Milwaukee, where he was treated as a hometown boy of growing celebrity. His mother was in the front row of the Pabst Theater for his sold-out concert, and Liberace employed his increasing number of tricks to captivate the audience. While complimentary in his review, the *Journal*'s Richard S. Davis noted that the young pianist had "turned his back on the concert platform and gone swaggering into nightclubs."

Friday night at the Pabst, the suave exponent of zip, sparkle and what is called schmaltz in pianism gave a packed house the time of its life. He played the classics and played them well. He did amusing stunts with popular music. He pounded away at boogie-woogie. He even tried a bit of singing with his pale little voice.

The critical tone had changed in his native city. No more the proud boosts for the Milwaukee youth of promise. The boy who had played Liszt with the Chicago Symphony had joined the forces of Tin Pan Alley. He couldn't be taken seriously anymore.

During the war years, Liberace heard from other performers about the gold to be found in Las Vegas. There were only two showplaces, the Last Frontier and El Rancho Vegas, both on a barren stretch of land outside the city, but they paid high salaries for entertainers who could appeal to the ranchers, cross-country tourists, and hard-bitten gamblers who patronized the dusty town that seemed a remnant of the Wild West misplaced in time.

Liberace had learned a trick from Sophie Tucker. At every new engagement, she sent handwritten penny postcards to talent buyers, members of the press, and others of influence in all parts of the country. Liberace did the same, mailing scores of postcards declaring: "Sold out every night here at the Statler in Boston." Or, "The Edgewater in Chicago wants to hold me over for two more weeks." The cards were always signed "Liberace (libber-AH-chee)."

The campaign succeeded. Maxine Lewis, entertainment director of the Last Frontier Hotel in Las Vegas, called Liberace while he was appearing at the Mount Royal Hotel in Montreal.

"How would you like to play Las Vegas?" she asked.

"I would love to," replied the excited Liberace.

"How much are you getting paid?"

"Seven hundred and fifty a week," he lied. His salary at the Mount Royal was $350 a week plus room and board.

"That's fine," Miss Lewis replied.

After appearing in some of the most sophisticated supper clubs in the country, Liberace was shocked by the Ramona Room of the Last Frontier. The chandeliers were wagon wheels mounted with replicas of kerosene lamps. The waitresses wore low-cut gingham blouses, short leather skirts, and cowboy hats. The show floor was scarcely large enough to accommodate a grand piano, and there was no backstage. Entertainers had to make their entrances through the tables.

On opening night, Liberace gazed over the shirt-sleeved audience and decided to forgo much of his long-hair repertoire. He concentrated on boogie-woogie, "Beer Barrel Polka," and other crowd-pleasers. The ovation was enthusiastic, punctuated by cowboy yells, and he returned to his room confident that he could succeed in the Ramona Room in Las Vegas as well as the Persian Room in New York.

Then Maxine Lewis summoned him to her office. He approached with foreboding, fearing his deception about the Montreal salary had been uncovered or the bosses disliked his act despite the audience response.

"There's only one thing wrong with your act," she announced.

"What's that, Maxine?" he asked warily.

"We're not paying you enough. We're going to tear up your contract and from now on you're getting fifteen hundred a week."

When Liberace marveled at his good fortune, the first time he had received a four-figure salary, she told him, "You'll get more; Sophie Tucker appeared here before you, and we paid her six thousand."

An oft-told Liberace tale concerns the first rehearsal in the Ramona Room. The showroom's facilities were primitive, and when it came time for rehearsal, he could find no one to assist him. Finally he spotted a tall, skinny man standing by the light switchboard.

"Oh, hi there," Liberace began. "Now here's my sheet of light cues. Basically, I want blues, pinks, and magentas when I'm doing a soft number. Then when I pick up the beat, bring up the color—lots of reds and whites. If I play 'Claire de Lune' be sure to give me a blue light. Y'understand?"

The man nodded as Maxine Lewis approached and remarked, "Oh, I didn't realize you knew Howard Hughes."

After serving four years with the Seabees, George Liberace left the navy in late 1945. Lee returned to Milwaukee for a joyous reunion with Mom, George, Angelina, and Rudy, a fifteen-year-old handsome enough to resemble his namesake, Valentino.

"What're you gonna do now?" Lee asked his older brother.

"I dunno," George replied. "Back to the road, I guess."

"Do you really want to?"

"No, I'm not really looking forward to living on bologna and Fig Newtons and avoiding restaurants with tablecloths because they're too expensive."

"Why don't you come with me, George? Be my manager?"

"What do you need me for? You got M.C.A."

"Yeah, but they just do the bookings. I need somebody to travel with me, arrange the publicity, check the showrooms, make sure the mikes are working. I can't do it all myself."

Mom Liberace was thrilled by the idea of her two boys traveling and working together. She worried about Walter's constant travels and the temptations he faced. George would be a steadying influence on him.

George, who realized he lacked the talent of his brother, agreed to submerge his own ambitions as a musician and assume the role of manager. George recognized that Walter had grown as a performer during the war years, and he agreed with Walter's assessment that with astute management and careful planning, the Liberace career could enjoy an unlimited future.

The arrangement worked well. George possessed no hint of brilliance nor was he blessed with imagination, but his brother provided enough of both. What George contributed was levelheadedness and careful attention to detail. The music sheets and props always arrived on time, the orchestra was properly rehearsed, Lee was always notified of celebrities in the audience. George's knowledge of the music business was an asset that few managers could provide.

With an age difference of eight years, the brothers had rarely quarreled as youngsters, George playing the fatherly role neglected by Sam Liberace. The relationship continued in show business. George tried to make Lee save his energies between performances and sought to protect him from the adoring young men who tried to reach him backstage.

The brothers' only arguments concerned Lee's extravagances, such as the Bluthner piano.

In 1946 Liberace was scheduled to perform in Long Beach, his first important concert on the West Coast. He decided to use the Bluthner piano, which Clarence Goodwin had been keeping for him. Not only that. He told George that he wanted to take the Bluthner on every engagement. He was tired of the pianos he had been forced to play across the country. More often than not, they had wretched tone and were poorly tuned. He wanted a piano that was both grand and reliable, one that would befit the aura of elegance he was striving to create. The piano was more important than ever in the act, since he no longer played to the accompaniment of Horowitz, Rubinstein, et al. The musicians' union had banned the gimmick on the grounds that it deprived musicians of work.

"For God's sake, be sensible," George answered. "How the hell are you going to haul a six-hundred-pound piano from city to city? It'd cost a fortune."

"I gotta have it."

When Liberace played the Bluthner in Long Beach, he believed that he had never exhibited such effortless style, such flawless playing. He wanted the performance to be his best effort, since M.C.A. had brought such celebrities as Barbara Stanwyck, Charles Coburn, Dennis Morgan, and Hedda Hopper. Most important, Mom was there. He had paid for her first trip to California, and he adored introducing her to the Hollywood figures who congratulated him after the performance.

Besides the Howard Hughes story, Liberace's other favorite about Las Vegas concerns a figure the town has tried to forget.

The Last Frontier had found Liberace to be an excellent attraction, especially for the wives of the high rollers, and he signed a ten-year contract with the hotel. In July 1947 he returned for another of his annual engagements. Opening night brought cheers from the audience, and afterward Liberace basked in compliments as he mingled with the crowd in the casino. All performers, and especially the showgirls, were required to appear in the casino after the floor show. It was a duty that Liberace enjoyed, since he liked to wager modest amounts on the craps table.

"Hey, kid, I want to talk to you." Liberace heard the gruff voice and felt a hand grip his arm. If there was anything he disliked from admirers, it was being handled. He turned and saw a man in an expensive glen plaid suit, with a dangerously handsome face that resembled George Raft's.

"Hey—don't grab me," Liberace said, pulling his arm away and hurrying to another part of the casino.

The man in the glen plaid suit pursued him and again clamped a hand on his arm. This time Liberace could feel the strength of the grip. "I want to talk to you," the man insisted.

"I've got to get ready for the second show," Liberace replied, heading for the exit. He stopped and asked the security guard, "Who *is* that creep over there, the one who looks like a gangster?"

"He *is* a gangster," the guard answered. "That's Bugsy Siegel."

Liberace's heart sank. Bugsy Siegel! He was the mobster from

Hell's Kitchen with a reputation for cold-blooded killings and conquests of famous beauties of New York and Hollywood. Now he was putting Las Vegas into the big time with his Flamingo casino, which he vowed would "make Monte Carlo look like peanuts." He had poured $6 million of the mob's money into the pink palace and had opened it at Christmas 1946 with a showroom bill that included Jimmy Durante and Xavier Cugat's Orchestra.

"Oh, my God, and I insulted him!" Liberace exclaimed.

After the second show he received a message that Mr. Siegel wanted to see him in the lobby. To his relief, Liberace found that the mobster wasn't angry.

"A classy act like you should be playing the Flamingo, not this cheesy dump," Siegel insisted. "How much are they paying you here? You might as well tell me the truth, because I'll find out anyway."

"Two thousand, Mr. Siegel," Liberace admitted.

"You can call me Ben. Two thousand is peanuts. I'll double that."

"But I'm very happy at the Frontier. They've been very kind to me."

"Bullshit. You don't owe them nothing. You come to the Flamingo and I'll show you what real class is."

Liberace fretted over the proposal for days. He didn't want to leave his friends at the Frontier, but he also didn't want to antagonize Bugsy Siegel. He told Maxine Lewis about his dilemma; she counseled him, "Only you can decide, Lee."

The decision proved unnecessary. Bugsy Siegel had incurred the mob's disfavor by overspending on the Flamingo and attracting too much attention to himself. On June 20, 1947, Bugsy was sitting with his friend Allan Smiley on the living room couch in the Beverly Hills home of his girlfriend Virginia Hill. An unknown marksman fired through the window, landing three bullets in Bugsy's skull.

In August 1947, Liberace was booked for seven months in the Empire Room of the Palmer House in Chicago. He was delighted with the assignment, the longest of his career thus far. For once he could settle down in one place. And Milwaukee was close enough so he could go home to visit Mom.

The Palmer House contract included a suite in the hotel. Liberace gazed around the living room of the suite and shook his head. "Those drapes have got to go," he decreed. "And those pictures—ugh." He shopped in Marshall Field's for brightly colored drapes to replace the maroon fake velvet of the suite. He removed the boring prints and hung paintings he had bought in an art gallery. He installed a coffee maker and set up a bar. In one of the bathrooms he created a make-shift kitchen where he could cook his favorite spaghetti at the end of an evening's performance. In the bedroom he installed a rack for his clothes and costumes.

George decided that his brother should have a press agent for the Chicago engagement to supplement the efforts of the hotel publicist, even though it might add $50 to weekly expenditures. Lee agreed wholeheartedly. A meeting was arranged at the M.C.A. office with the press agent the agency had recommended.

Lee liked Sam Honigberg immediately. He was a friendly, sincere little guy, not like some of the cynical press agents Lee had met on the road. Sam had worked eleven years for *Billboard* as nightclub and band reporter before opening his own publicity office. He admired show people and, for the most part, tolerated their idiosyncrasies.

Walking back to the Palmer House with Sam, Lee outlined some of the matters he was concerned about.

"My biggest problem is my name," he said.

"Your name?"

"Yes. People who don't know me call me 'Libber-ACE.' That's why I print on my stationery, my ads, and the cards I send to club owners and people all over the country: 'pronounced libber-AH-chee.' "

"Well, I can do that in my press releases. And I'll stress the pronunciation whenever I talk to press people."

"Good. George may have told you about my piano. It's the biggest in the world, and I ship it wherever I play. Costs a thousand dollars each time. You can say that it's insured for a hundred and fifty thousand, which isn't exactly true, but it sounds good."

"Is there anything else that might get us some feature stories in the papers?"

"My hobbies. I have a collection of 183 miniature pianos that might make a photo spread. One of them is a replica of my Bluthner piano with fifty little diamonds set in platinum. I had it made in Long Beach after I bought the piano. And I've got glass pianos and ivory pianos and one that actually plays three octaves."

"What other hobbies?"

"I paint ties and blouses. For instance, I did one for Hildegarde. It has all her trademarks: the waving arms, the upswept hair, the chiffon handkerchief. I'm doing one now for Dorothy Shay in the hillbilly theme. And I paint personalized ties for men. Another thing, I love to cook. I own a half-interest in a restaurant in Milwaukee where I cook special dishes."

Honigberg applied his press agent's zeal to the Liberace account. The *Daily News* ran a feature with Liberace as Cook of the Week. The *Tribune* did a spread on his miniature piano collection. *This Week in Chicago* offered a color photograph of Liberace on the cover, and he was pictured in a Pepsi-Cola ad.

Handwritten notes from George Liberace to Sam Honigberg reveal the publicity consciousness of the two brothers:

(August 5) "Lee told me to remind you if you can get some picture plants in the national magazines, like *Life, Time, Esquire,* etc. And here's a bit of news—Lee had a request for 'White Xmas' the other night, and it went over so tremendous that he's been getting requests to play it every night. 'The only pianist to play "White Xmas" in

August heat. The audiences claim it cools them off.' At least it's cool news, Sam."

(August 23) "A suggestion for a bit of news—someone stole Lee's pictures out of the lobby board yesterday. Lee says he's very flattered, and if someone wishes his pictures, he'll be glad to provide them, saving all the work of unscrewing them from the lobby frame. By the way, have you an idea when the painting spread will be in the *Daily News?*"

(August 31) "Lee has already told you about thumbs down on radio interviews, as the union says no. Seems all we have to work with are pictures and the press. I wonder if you could do something about getting Lee's special dishes in the 'For Men Only' column in the *Tribune.*"

Through the determined efforts of both brothers, the Liberace name was becoming more known in major cities. M.C.A.'s bookings were increasing in number and importance. In 1948 Liberace appeared at the Statler hotels in Boston, Detroit, and Cleveland, the Raddison in Minneapolis, the Park Plaza in St. Louis, the Fairmont in San Francisco, as well as in repeat engagements at the Last Frontier and the Palmer House. He made another triumphant return to Milwaukee at the Pabst Theater and also played concerts at Haddon Hall in Atlantic City and the Chicago Theater.

Astonishing things were happening to Liberace, things he hadn't conceived in his grandiose dreams. Like appearing before President Truman.

He never knew how the invitation arose. Perhaps M.C.A., with its network of power, had arranged it. At any rate, Liberace was listed with Betty Hutton, Dick Haymes, Gertrude Niesen, Billy DeWolfe, and Jack Carson as entertainers for the Press Photographers' Ball in Washington, D.C., in March 1949.

Liberace was met at the airport by Secret Service men who took him to his hotel for a briefing by a member of the White House staff. The instructions about the performance were thorough:

"Unless it is a regular part of your program, do not play 'The Missouri Waltz,' as the President has heard it too many times already. He much prefers the classics.

"Do not mention the name Truman or refer to Mrs. Truman or Margaret. When addressing the President, simply say, 'Mr. President.'

"The President is a modest man and would prefer that you directed your remarks and your performance to the entire audience.

"If you have any gifts for the President, do not present them personally, since all packages have to be first approved by the Secret Service." (Liberace did give him a hand-painted tie as well as miniature pianos and record albums for himself, Mrs. Truman, and Margaret.)

"Limit your performance to three numbers unless otherwise instructed during the performance.

"Do not refer to Mr. Truman's Florida vacation or the controversial pictures of him in bathing trunks.

"Do not make references to Mr. Truman's piano playing, since he wishes the public to forget the Lauren Bacall incident [in which she posed atop his piano], which he has for years regretted. He enjoys the piano but does not play it publicly.

"Do not make any appointments with the President for any future occasion as he does not have the final say-so regarding his social engagements.

"At the cocktail party preceding the dinner do not partake of any refreshments in the presence of the President. Have your drinks before his arrival.

"The President is here to have a good time. Please do not refer to controversial issues."

Liberace noticed at the cocktail party that some of the other performers were extremely nervous, even though Harry Truman sought in his homespun manner to put them at ease. As always, Liberace felt totally confident. Whether he was facing Las Vegas gamblers or the President of the United States, he always had faith in his ability to entertain.

The audience also included Gen. Dwight D. Eisenhower, Chief Justice Fred Vinson, cabinet officers, senators, congressmen, and movie executives. Jack Carson, as master of ceremonies, was so nervous that he grasped the microphone stand and broke it. He drew a huge laugh, and it took technicians ten minutes to repair the damage.

Liberace delivered his three numbers with total ease. He played the Liszt 14th Hungarian Rhapsody, a Gershwin medley, and then his boogie-woogie, always a reliable show-stopper. The climax of the number came when he finished a succession of crashing chords, then stopped playing. The audience, as instructed, shouted, "Hey!" Liberace always divided the audience, instructing the women to shout, "Hey!" first. Then he asked the men to give their version, and he often cited the male chorus of "Hey!" as proof that he appealed to both sexes.

Following his usual routine, he asked President Truman to respond. After the President's "Hey!" Liberace cracked, "That must be the shortest presidential speech on record."

More piano was demanded, and Liberace played three more numbers for a twenty-five-minute appearance, longer than any of the other performers. Afterward Harry Truman complimented Liberace and invited him to play in the White House after the renovation was completed. "I want Bess and Margaret to hear you," the President said. "They'll be so sorry they weren't here tonight."

Chapter 4

*LIBERACE DISCOVERS THE MAGIC OF BELIEVING
AND GIVES HIS CAREER A GIANT LEAP FORWARD*

Among the many listeners who were overwhelmed by the performance of Liberace at the Press Photographers' Ball was Nate Blumberg, the silver-haired president of Universal-International Pictures. He had risen to his position out of the hurly-burly of movie theaters, and he had a showman's appreciation of what captured an audience. When he returned to his New York office, he wired the studio: "Contact Liberace immediately. Give him a screen test and cast him in a picture no matter how the test turns out."

The casting office at Universal-International was in a quandary.

Who—or what—was Liberace? Inquiries were made, but no actor of that name could be found. Finally a junior member of the casting department remarked, "I read about him in Harrison Carroll's column. He's playing at the Mocambo."

Liberace was appearing nightly at Charlie Morrison's nightclub on the Sunset Strip, the favorite place of the movie crowd. A delegation of Universal-International executives attended a Liberace performance, and all agreed he staged an entertaining show. "But what are we going to do with him?" one of them asked.

The question was put to studio producers. Michael Kraike had a suggestion. He was producing a potboiler called *East of Java,* designed to exploit the studio's new star, Shelley Winters, who was being promoted as a sexpot. Perhaps Liberace could play a concert pianist on the bum in the South Seas, pounding piano in a waterfront bar for the sultry Winters. The script was rewritten to accommodate him.

East of Java, which was released as *South Sea Sinner,* starred MacDonald Carey as a Pacific vagabond who ends up on the island of Oraca with a doctor friend, played by Frank Lovejoy. Carey soon becomes entangled with the tempting cabaret singer Coral (Winters), incurring the enmity of the evil café operator (Luther Adler). The director was Bruce ("Lucky") Humberstone, who had turned out routine musicals at Twentieth Century–Fox.

Liberace could not believe his luck in being cast in a movie. From his earliest years the illusions on the screens of Milwaukee theaters had provided escape from the discord of his home life. He thrilled over the operettas of Jeanette MacDonald and Nelson Eddy, the musicals of Fred Astaire and Ginger Rogers, the operatic romances of Grace Moore. He approached his first acting role in a movie with great anticipation.

Universal-International, Liberace discovered, was no Metro-Goldwyn-Mayer. After decades of being one of the three minors (along with Columbia and Republic) competing with the major studios, it was struggling for respectability. But there was still a threadbare appearance to the studio, with its rickety sound stages and buildings that dated back to the founding days of "Uncle" Carl Laemmle.

Liberace was interviewed by a member of the publicity department, who agreed to emphasize in press releases that his name was pronounced Libber-AH-chee. The basics were included in the studio biography: the anointment by Paderewski; the debut with the Chicago Symphony Orchestra at sixteen (actually, twenty); the Bluthner piano. The pianist was quoted: "Hollywood is definitely a city of longhairs. Filmland personalities request the classics twelve to one. I was indeed surprised."

When Liberace was introduced to Shelley Winters, he was astonished, and somewhat frightened, by her forthright personality. "Have you ever in your life read such a piece of shit as this script?" she demanded. Liberace admitted that he had never read *any* script before.

"This bastardized version of *Rain* is so bad even Yvonne DeCarlo wouldn't do it," Winters ranted. She poured out her vitriol against the studio bosses. She had been nominated for an Academy Award for *A Double Life* and now U-I was trying to make her into Tondelayo, the tropics siren played in dark-face by Hedy Lamarr in *White Cargo*. She had dieted and sweated her ample figure down to 118 pounds, and the ordeal had contributed to her bad temper. She was further incensed because MacDonald Carey, on loan from Paramount, was receiving top billing.

Liberace was required to accompany Winters as she strutted and slunk around the piano singing such tunes as "It Had to Be You" and "I'm the Loneliest Gal in Town." He asked for the chance to perform something from his own repertoire, and he was allowed a scene in which the island drifter imagined he was back in Carnegie Hall. He played an abbreviated version of the Liszt Concerto in A Minor. Despite the South Seas locale, the director allowed Liberace to place a candelabra on the piano.

The studio boss, William Goetz, feared that Liszt was too highbrow for a movie like *South Sea Sinner,* but the number played well at the preview and it remained in the final version. Although the studio had no illusions about the quality of the film, it seemed exploitable on the basis of Shelley Winters's growing popularity. The publicity department plotted a twenty-city tour for the star through the American heartland, where the unsophisticated natives might prove more receptive to a movie like *South Sea Sinner.*

Since Shelley's musical talent was limited, U-I decided to send along competent backing for her appearances at the theater openings. The Bobby True Trio, a popular combo at Sunset Strip clubs, and Liberace were enlisted. George Liberace accompanied the tour, which proceeded by train through the Midwest.

Shelley, who could be a funny, convivial companion away from the pressures of her career, made friends with all the musicians—except Liberace. He remained as frightened of her as he had been during the filming.

Early one morning at the Muehlebach Hotel in Kansas City, Shelley found she was too stimulated by the evening's performance to sleep. It was 3 A.M. and she was hungry. She took the elevator down to the coffee shop where she found Liberace sitting before a coffee cup at the counter. She sat down beside him.

"Insomnia?" she asked.

He nodded.

"Happens to me all the time. I start thinking about things and I can't stop. You know what I'd like?"

"What?"

"A hot fudge sundae. I've been starving myself for a year, and I say to hell with it."

He grinned. "Me, too. Let's grow fat together."

Shelley and Lee often met for early-morning consolation over hot fudge sundaes. They also joined with Bobby True and his musicians in ribald sessions aboard trains. While they were en route from

St. Louis to Chicago, a porter entered Shelley's compartment and smelled the air. "You kids can get in trouble smokin' that stuff," he warned.

"What stuff?" Shelley asked. She looked at the musicians' cigarettes and the happy expressions on their faces. "You mean that isn't tobacco? Oh, my God! Get rid of it. You know what happened to Mitchum." Robert Mitchum had served a jail term in 1949 after being arrested while smoking marijuana with a starlet in an apartment.

Although Liberace was well reviewed in his hometown, Shelley Winters and *South Sea Sinner* were not. Commenting on the personal appearance at the Riverside Theater, the *Milwaukee Journal* reviewer commented that the "not so bashful blonde sang (?) the usual sexy song ('I Want to Get Married') in an unusually unpleasant, off-key voice."

> *However, while Shelley played the star, it was our boy Walter Liberace who shone like one. The breakneck pianist, who played his way from West Milwaukee High School and Milwaukee night spots to the White House and the Waldorf-Astoria, staged a tingling display of the classics, boogie-woogie and jazz that had the customers beating their palms in approval.*

The reviewer termed the movie "a masterpiece of misunderstanding" and cited Winters as a "streamlined, poor man's Mae West." He added: "Oh, yes—Liberace has a Hoagy Carmichael type of role as a waterfront saloon piano player, and he comes through nobly."

The tour was mostly a success, but *South Sea Sinner* sank of its own ponderous weight. Shelley and Liberace didn't meet again until many years later in Las Vegas. She found he was still uneasy around her.

"Hello, Mom. It's Walter." Liberace's mother received the telephone call at the ice cream franchise store she operated in Milwaukee.

"My goodness, where are you?"

"I'm in Chicago, playing the Palmer House. Look, I want you to come down here."

"Well, I don't know if I can leave the store."

"Please. It's important. George would like to see you, too."

"I suppose I could get someone to watch the place. Yes, I'll come."

Frances Liberace Casadonte welcomed the chance to see her much-traveled sons and to escape the daily grind of running an ice cream parlor. As always, Walter had her hotel room filled with flowers, but he seemed especially excited when he greeted her.

"Mom, I bought a house in North Hollywood," he announced. "It's a nice little house, and it's on a street called Camellia."

"Oh, I'm so glad you're settling down," she said.

"Well, I don't know about that. But at least I'll have a place to come home to. And you know what, Mom?"

"What?"

"I want you to be there. Sell the ice cream store and come to California. You'll love it out there, I know you will."

Mom was startled by the proposal. She had spent most of her life in or near Milwaukee, and she expected to end her days there. But now Angelina was married and raising her own family, and Rudy was on his own. The prospect of living with Walter and sharing the excitement of his career seemed exciting. Within a week she had sold the ice cream store and moved her belongings to California.

From his earliest days in the honky-tonks of Milwaukee, Liberace had never lacked total confidence in his capacity to entertain. He never suffered the agonies of stage fright or what show biz calls flop sweat (the fear of flopping) that afflicted other performers. Partly that was due to his symbiotic relationship with the piano, his total assurance that he could use the instrument to please, charm, amuse, and excite his listeners.

His thirtieth birthday prompted Liberace to reassess his career. Yes, he was earning big money now—$3,000 a week—but he felt a vague dissatisfaction. The failure of *South Sea Sinner* contributed to it. So far he had not been able to reach a mass audience. Mostly he played to conventioneers and expense-account spenders in hotel supper clubs. He wanted to reach a wider public. In a rare moment of self-doubt, he wondered if he had the drive and the will to achieve such a goal. Amazingly, he found his resolve in a book.

Claude M. Bristol was a West Coast newspaperman and a veteran of World War I who discovered the self-help industry before others were purveying positive thinking and success through intimidation. As a reporter he was fascinated by the persuasive power on human minds of Mormonism, Christian Science, Holy Rollers, and evangelists like Billy Sunday and Aimee Semple McPherson.

"Belief is the motivating force that enables you to achieve your goal," Bristol concluded. "If you are ill and the thought or belief is imbedded deeply within you that you will recover, the odds that you will do so are all in your favor. It's the belief or the basic confidence within you that brings outward or material results."

Bristol embodied his beliefs in a booklet, *T.N.T.—It Rocks the Earth,* and he traveled the country spreading his positivism to gatherings of business executives, doctors, lawyers, and others. In 1948 Prentice-Hall published his book *The Magic of Believing,* and it became an instant best-seller. Among the thousands who bought a copy was Liberace.

He pored through the book with astonished eyes. In these pages was his own personal philosophy, and more. The revelation was breathtaking. All he had to do was follow the author's precepts, and success—nay, triumph—was his.

How many times have you heard it said, "Just believe you can do it, and you can!" Whatever the task, if it is begun with the belief you can do it, it will be done perfectly. Often belief enables a person to do what others think is impossible. It is the act of believing that is the starting force or generating power that leads to accomplishment.

"Come on, fellows, we can beat them!" shouts someone in command, whether in a football game, on a battlefield, or in the strife of the business world. That sudden voicing of belief, challenging and electrifying, reverses the tide and—Victory! Success! From defeatism to victory—and all because some mighty believer knew that it could be done.

The Magic of Believing permeated Liberace's life ever afterward. He memorized key portions of the book and applied them to everyday experiences. He avoided becoming moody or depressed. (" 'I am strong,' 'I am happy,' 'I am convincing,' 'I am friendly,' 'Everything is fine,' are a few simple affirmations you can use to change your mental point of view for the better.")

If a musical conductor had a pessimistic attitude, he was banned from the Liberace dressing room before a performance. ("When you permit negative thoughts of doubt and fear to enter your consciousness, it is obvious that the forceful, positive, creative thoughts will have to give way, and consequently you lose your positive state.")

Reporters visiting the Liberace residences often noted the abundance of mirrors. This was not pure vanity. A prime element of the Bristolean theory was the mirror technique. The author observed that Winston Churchill, Woodrow Wilson, and Billy Sunday, as well as other statesmen, orators, preachers, and actors, practiced their craft before mirrors.

As you stand before the mirror, keep telling yourself that you are going to be an outstanding success, and nothing in the world is going to stop you. Does this sound silly? Don't forget that every idea presented to the subconscious mind is going to be produced in its exact counterpart in objective life, and the quicker your subconscious gets the idea, the sooner your wish becomes a picture of power.

When Liberace decided late in his career that he wanted to appear at Radio City Music Hall, his advisers were strongly opposed. He persisted, and the engagement was a triumph. ("Jimmy Gribbo, well known to sports fans as a manager of prizefighters, has made winners of many boxers by teaching them how to visualize themselves as winners—and they became winners.")

When Liberace began wearing outlandishly lavish costumes on-stage, critics ridiculed and berated him. He responded by dressing even more garishly. ("You have seen in movies and plays how a badly dressed ordinary-looking girl can be transformed into a most attractive woman by beautiful clothes and the latest style of hair-do. You can do the same thing—and you will speed up the process if you continue to hold the mental picture of your new self and never relax for a second.")

After he had become a national figure, Liberace acknowledged his debt to *The Magic of Believing* by sponsoring a Special Liberace Edition of the book. His picture was featured on the cover, and he wrote an introduction citing how Bristol's teachings had changed his life as he stood on the brink of fame. The verities as interpreted by Liberace:

To experience happiness, one must express happiness.
To find love, one must give love.
To possess wealth, one must value wealth.
To acquire health, one must live health.
To attain success, one must positively think success.

Armed with his newfound knowledge, Liberace contemplated how he could attain far greater success than he had yet known. He came to one inescapable conclusion: he needed better management. George was perfectly capable of arranging transportation and checking spotlights, but he was no strategist of the Liberace career. M.C.A. was expert at arranging dates and making contracts, but it had no concern for Liberace's future.

Liberace wanted to make the change without hurting George's feelings. He found a way.

"I need you to devote full time to the music, George," he said. "It would be a great help to me if you would conduct the orchestra on all the dates. Pick out new arrangements, too, and hire the musicians. Then I think we should get a management company, out of either New York or Los Angeles, people who can give us the kind of attention we need."

George received the proposal with enthusiasm. He felt much more comfortable with music than with business. He began asking bookers to recommend management firms, and the name that kept recurring was Gabbe, Lutz and Heller of Hollywood.

They had all sprung from the big-band business. Dick Gabbe had managed Jimmy Dorsey, Sam Lutz was Lawrence Welk's manager, and Seymour Heller had represented various bands. They had formed a management company after the war, with Gabbe directing the New York office and Lutz and Heller operating from the West Coast. Within a brief time, they had developed an impressive roster of musical talent, including Lawrence Welk, Frankie Laine, Mel Torme, Al Martino, the Andrews Sisters.

George Liberace began sending notes and postcards to Gabbe, Lutz and Heller: "Lee sold out all seven nights at the Baker Hotel in Dallas"; "Standing ovations every night at the CalNeva Lodge here at Lake Tahoe."

One day George walked into the offices of Gabbe, Lutz and Heller over the *Daily Variety* office on Vine Street, just north of Hollywood

Boulevard. "So you're the guy who sent us all those postcards," said Sam Lutz, an amiable but blunt-spoken man.

"My brother's playing at the Orpheum Theater downtown," said George. "I wish you guys would come down and see his act."

"After all your buildup, I guess we should," said Seymour Heller, a man with shrewd eyes and balding head.

Lutz and Heller agreed to make the pilgrimage to the Orpheum, and they were unimpressed by Liberace's performance. The cavernous old movie cathedral was sparsely occupied by Latinos and women shoppers resting their feet. All of Liberace's usual endearments failed to evoke a response, and he finished to faint applause.

Backstage, George offered excuses for the disappointing performance, to no avail. Lutz and Heller tried to avoid any real assessment of the act, but their message was clear: "We just don't think we can do anything for you at this time."

"That's all right," Lee said cheerfully. "Maybe someday you will."

Three weeks later, George returned to the Gabbe, Lutz and Heller office. "You didn't get to see Lee under the best conditions," George said. "He's opening at the Hotel Del Coronado next weekend, and I guarantee you he'll be a sensation down there. I'd like you to come down there as our guests."

"No need," Sam Lutz said. "I was planning to take my family down there anyway."

On Saturday afternoon, Sam Lutz was sitting on the beach in front of the elegant Victorian Hotel Del Coronado, watching his children play in the surf. His companion was Leo Robin, lyricist of "Thanks for the Memory," "Love in Bloom," and scores of other movie songs.

"Why don't you come to the jai alai matches in Tijuana tonight?" Robin suggested.

"Thanks, but I gotta catch an act in the Circus Room tonight," Lutz replied. "Liberace."

"What's a Liberace?"

"He plays piano. Do me a favor. Skip the jai alai matches. You and your wife come with us tonight and hear the guy. He wants Seymour and me to manage him, and I'd like to get your professional opinion."

Robin agreed. During the middle of Liberace's show that night, Lutz glanced over and saw sweat on Robin's forehead. "This guy is amazing," the songwriter said. "He does some trick of modulation on the piano that I've never heard before. Sign him, Sam."

On the following Monday the Liberace brothers appeared at the offices of Gabbe, Lutz and Heller to sign a seven-year management contract.

Sam Lutz and Seymour Heller plotted their strategy for the career of Liberace. As an entertainer he had reached the limit on the supper club circuit. The only way to enhance his career, and hence justify their performance as managers, would be to introduce him in a mass medium. *South Sea Sinner* seemed to prove that movies were not his forte. Network radio was dying. Why not break into television, which in 1951 had captured the nation's attention?

Liberace had already appeared on such network television shows as "Texaco Star Theater" with Milton Berle, "The Kate Smith Show," and "The Spike Jones Show." The directors on each show were convinced that solo piano playing was too static for television. One director placed the camera twenty feet from Liberace and panned through a group of musical instruments mounted on pedestals; by the time the camera reached Liberace he had completed his three-minute selection. On another show Liberace was surrounded by ballet dancers and a chorus, who shared camera time equally with the soloist.

"It's too bad you don't play a clarinet instead of a piano," a director told Liberace. "With a clarinet we could get some movement."

The directors didn't realize that television was the perfect medium for Liberace, who communicated best in intimate situations, not in big theaters like the Orpheum. His new managers placed a call to Don Fedderson, general manager of KLAC-TV, Channel 13, in Los Angeles.

"Sure, I know Liberace," Fedderson said. "As a matter of fact, I caught his show at the Waldorf when I was in New York on my annual visit to the ad agencies. When I stopped in Chicago, he was appearing at the Palmer House, so I saw him again. He's good." Fedderson agreed to watch Liberace one more time at the Hotel Del Coronado.

Tall, with handsome, strong features, Don Fedderson had the imagination and decisiveness requisite for the booming new medium of television. He was managing radio station KYA in Denver for Dorothy Schiff, owner of the *New York Post,* when he heard that a second-rate station, KMTR, was up for sale in Los Angeles. Mrs. Schiff took his advice and bought it for $330,000, placing Fedderson in charge. He changed the call letters to KLAC, hired the city's most popular (and the nation's first) disc jockey, Al Jarvis, away from KFWB, and instituted an all-music policy with news on the hour. It had never been done before, and soon KLAC was the number-one station in Los Angeles, earning Mrs. Schiff $500,000 in its first year.

When Mrs. Schiff was granted the last UHF channel in Los Angeles, Fedderson called it Lucky Channel 13. Facing the tough competition of the network-owned stations, he acquired rights to baseball games of the Hollywood Stars and Los Angeles Angels and the football games of USC and UCLA. While other channels remained dark in the afternoon, Fedderson scheduled Al Jarvis in a talk and music show with a secretary-assistant, Betty White. Stars like Bing Crosby and Nat King Cole dropped in to plug their new records, and the show attracted a large audience.

"The Al Jarvis Show" was televised from a former movie theater, the Music Hall, in Beverly Hills. Fedderson had been looking for other shows to occupy the theater.

In Coronado, Fedderson confirmed what he had suspected in New

York and Chicago: that Liberace had a television potential. They met after the show, and the station manager remarked: "I think I may have a spot for you with a weekly show. I've seen your show three times now, so I'm familiar with what you can do. The thing you do best is communicate with your audience. You make them feel you're playing just for them. That's what television is all about. You won't be entertaining a crowd of people, as you do in a nightclub or theater. You'll be playing to individuals, maybe one lonely person in front of a television set, maybe two or three. Think about that and you'll be a success in television."

Elated over the prospect of a major career change, Liberace began his next engagement with great enthusiasm. He returned to Ciro's on the Sunset Strip in West Hollywood, where he had been well received by the movie crowd two years before.

On opening night, Liberace lavished a forty-five-minute performance on his listeners. Afterward, the bull-like proprietor of Ciro's, Herman Hover, stormed into the dressing room. "Dammit, I told you to play half an hour!" Hover ranted. "Do you know how much that extra time costs me in bar sales?"

Liberace continued shows of forty-five minutes or longer, while Hover raved. "I'll sue you for twenty-five thousand dollars," he threatened. "That's how much you're costing me." But when Hover added up his receipts, he saw that Liberace was attracting more customers and they were spending more. The threats ended.

Don Fedderson was a regular patron at Ciro's, and he studied the Liberace technique and repertoire with great care. One afternoon, after concluding a planning conference at the KLAC-TV studios in Hollywood, Fedderson invited Liberace for an automobile ride. First they drove through the side streets of Hollywood, past dilapidated bungalows and house trailers parked in driveways. "Now I want you to study these houses carefully and tell me what you see," said Fedderson.

"Well, I see a lot of old wooden houses with weeds and bicycles in the front yard—and television antennas on the rooftops," said Liberace.

Fedderson continued his tour toward the west, and he cruised down Roxbury Drive and Bedford Drive and other streets of Beverly Hills. "Now tell me what you see," Fedderson said.

"I see grand houses with manicured lawns and Cadillacs parked in the driveway and tile roofs and—no television antennas," Liberace said.

"Remember that. Maybe these people will pay to see you in night-clubs or concerts, but they won't be your television audience. Those folks in Hollywood will be, and there are lots just like them. Capture enough of them and you'll be a winner."

As Liberace approached the start of his television series, he reread *The Magic of Believing* every night. Television, he realized, would be the true test of Claude Bristol's teachings. Liberace did not merely need to entertain his viewers. He had to *win* them.

Liberace realized he needed other help as well. There was the problem of teeth. Orthodontia had been an unthinkable expense for the Liberace family, and his teeth had grown in haphazardly. They were not so important in nightclubs and concerts, but the television camera would come within inches. Liberace had his teeth filed down and capped.

He also realized that some members of his audience had considered him young and a trifle callow. To give himself maturity—and not incidentally to appeal to mature women, who had long comprised the bulk of his following—he sprayed gray at his temples. He scoffed when reporters asked if he did so. Only in his late years did he admit it.

At the first rehearsal in the Beverly Hills Music Hall, the director said to Liberace: "No, no, no, Lee, don't look into the camera; we don't do that in television."

"I do," Liberace replied. He insisted on directing all his songs and his comments directly to the camera. Soon he adopted an almost mystical relationship between himself and the camera lens. It became his Nirvana, his conduit to the hearts of those on the other side of the Orthicon tube.

"Liberace" made its debut on KLAC-TV in January 1952 to little notice. Newspaper reviewers ignored the show, which was sustaining, meaning it had no sponsor. Liberace received $1,000 per show, and from that he had to pay George and a five-piece orchestra.

The public reaction was everything that Don Fedderson had hoped for. Viewers telephoned the station with compliments, and within four weeks Fedderson convinced Citizens National Trust and Savings Bank to sponsor the show.

On the morning after Citizens' first sponsorship of "Liberace," the manager of the bank's branch in Van Nuys saw a horrifying sight when he went to work. Almost one hundred people stood in line, waiting for the opening. A run on the bank! But no, he soon learned what the people were waiting for. Liberace had announced on his show that anyone opening a new account at Citizens with a minimum of $10 would receive one of his records.

Within three months, new depositors had handed over $600,000 to Citizens Bank in exchange for records. One elderly woman deposited $100,000 of her savings, declaring, "Any bank that puts Liberace in my home is a friend of mine."

"Liberace" looked deceptively simple. The star appeared in a plain tuxedo at the Bluthner piano, on which stood the candelabra. Liberace spun a little story about each number, a historical note or a reminiscence. He played classics and pop and sang a song or two. He introduced George and carried on a one-sided conversation. George never spoke, and it became a running gag. At the end of the half-hour, Liberace thanked his viewers for watching and said good night with a sincere wink.

The classics were given in "a *Reader's Digest* version." Liberace required three minutes to deliver a movement of Beethoven's *Moonlight Sonata* that took Horowitz eight minutes. As Liberace explained:

"My whole trick is to keep the tune well out in front. If I play Tchaikovsky, I play his melodies and skip his spiritual struggles. Naturally I condense. I have to know just how many notes my audience will stand for. If there's any time left over, I fill in a lot of runs up and down the scale."

His approach appalled the purists, but Liberace had long since learned to ignore them. Nor was he upset by the critics and columnists who began taking notice of the Liberace phenomenon, often with snide and caustic comments. His endorsement came from the delighted sponsor, the pleased viewers, and then, surprisingly, from the Academy of Television Arts and Sciences.

At the Los Angeles area awards in February 1953, Liberace was named Most Outstanding Male Personality of the Year and "Liberace" won as Best Entertainment Show of the Year. He had never won an award before, and Liberace was overwhelmed.

"I want to thank my mother, who made all this possible," he said. "And George, who is my strong right arm, even if he can't talk. I thank Seymour Heller and Sam Lutz for their extraordinary vision, and Don Fedderson for having the guts to put a piano player on television. And I also thank Citizens National Bank, whose product I admire."

The KLAC-TV show brought a wave of popularity that neither the station, Liberace, nor Gabbe, Lutz and Heller had anticipated. The Hooper ratings were the largest ever registered by an independent channel in Los Angeles. Women were reported to have paid up to $50 apiece for tickets to the show, which had no admission charge. When Liberace announced on the air that he would appear in concert at the Pasadena Civic Auditorium, tickets were sold out within forty-eight hours.

Seymour Heller and Sam Lutz saw the need for a publicist to control and contribute to the fast-rising public interest in Liberace.

They chose Red Doff, a stubby, hyperactive young army veteran with an old-time press agent's imaginative flair. Doff's clients included Al Jarvis, KLAC-TV, Frankie Laine, Margaret Whiting, Steve Allen, and others. One of Doff's stunts was putting Steve Allen, then a late-night personality on local radio, in the window of Music City at Sunset and Vine to see how many songs he could compose in twenty-four hours.

"You're going to Vladimir Horowitz's concert at the Philharmonic Sunday afternoon," Doff announced to Liberace.

"I'd love to hear Horowitz play, but Sunday is Mother's Day, and I have plans with my mother," Liberace replied.

"Cancel them. This is more important."

Liberace followed Doff's directions. He waited until just before the recital began, then he and his mother walked down the aisle to seats in the center of the orchestra section just before the lights dimmed. "It's Liberace!" a voice exclaimed, and the crowd rustled, then applauded.

Reporters, who had been tipped off by Doff, reported the upstaging of the virtuoso by the pop pianist. Mr. Horowitz was not pleased.

In San Diego to hype a forthcoming Liberace concert, Doff decided on a means to attract immediate attention. He reported that a hundred Liberace record albums, intended for critics and disc jockeys, had been stolen from the trunk of his car as it was parked near the El Cortez Hotel. Then he alerted the newspapers of the alleged theft, knowing they would check police records before printing the story. The news reports were picked up by AP and UP and sent across the country.

Doff produced more space when he took Liberace to court and had his single name legalized. No more Wladziu Valentino.

Liberace found he enjoyed the hoopla that Red Doff created. He listened carefully to the publicist's hints on how to conduct an interview that would make lively and provocative articles. "Whatever you say better be what you want to see in print," Doff warned. "Tell the truth as long as you can live with it. Honesty is the best policy. If you don't lie, you don't have to remember the lies you told."

In the summer of 1952, Liberace was chosen as the summer replacement for Dinah Shore's fifteen-minute NBC show on Tuesdays and Thursdays at 7:30 P.M. He performed a shortened version of the KLAC show, with George, the candelabra, and the simple set. The series lasted only eight weeks, but the impact of Liberace's first national exposure was startling. Before the series, he had appeared at a Kansas City nightclub, where he was lucky to fill the 150-seat room. After the summer telecasts, he returned to play two sell-out performances at the Kansas City Municipal Auditorium, with a capacity of 14,000.

Clearly "Liberace" was destined to be more than a local television program. This was recognized by Reub Kaufman, a man whose bland face and glasses made him look like an accountant, but who possessed the instincts of a riverboat gambler. He had leaped into television with his Guild Films, supplying odds and ends to product-hungry local stations across the country.

Kaufman sold Don Fedderson on the idea of syndicating the "Liberace" show, and a contract was signed between Guild Films, KLAC-TV, and Liberace on January 9, 1953.

Now Reub Kaufman was faced with finding enough sponsors to finance the syndicated show. He began in Chicago, where he had been a whiz in the advertising trade. But the Liberace craze was considered merely one of those fads for which Californians were famous. And who wanted to see a guy with wavy hair and an unctuous smile playing the piano when television offered wrestling, Hopalong Cassidy, and other delights?

His Chicago mission a failure, Reub Kaufman found himself

stranded without funds. He used his air-travel credit card to fly to Tucson, where his brother operated a prosperous haberdashery.

After hearing Reub's plight, the brother asked, "What can I do for you?"

"You can introduce me to your banker," Reub replied.

He showed the banker a sample program and painted a glowing picture of Citizens National Bank's bonanza with "Liberace." "I'm not sure banks should be advertising on television," the banker said, "but I'm willing to take a chance. When can I start broadcasting the shows?"

"As soon as I get the financing. You can help by giving me letters to twenty other banks in the Southwest."

Kaufman sold fourteen out of the twenty, and he returned to California with enough financing to start the series.

The first season of "Liberace" had been shot with video cameras and telecast live. The show would continue to be live in Los Angeles, then would be filmed so it could be shipped to other parts of the country. Jim Hobson would continue to direct the KLAC-TV show. For director of the filmed show, Kaufman chose Duke Goldstone. He was a veteran of the movie trade who had risen out of the Poverty Row of cheapie filmmakers. Kaufman admired the no-nonsense, professional style with which Goldstone had directed dozens of three-minute musical shorts that supplied a kind of visual jukebox in bars and cafés.

The first filmed show of the new season proved to be a triumph for all concerned. Dripping with sweat and highly elated, Liberace praised Goldstone and suggested a celebration. Goldstone mentioned a favorite place, the Silver Dollar Bar, on Doheny at Burton Way, a few blocks away. "Fine," said Liberace. "I'll meet you there after I have a shower and sign some autographs."

When Liberace arrived at the Silver Dollar, he inquired what Goldstone had been drinking. Goldstone had consumed two double Gibsons and was about to reorder. "Then I'll have to catch up," Liberace said. "I'll have three double Gibsons, bartender."

Later Goldstone suggested dinner at his favorite restaurant, Lucey's, on Melrose Avenue. After another round of Gibsons, they ordered dinner: marinara salad and Chateaubriand. In the middle of the salad course, Liberace excused himself from the table. After a lengthy absence, he returned looking pale and ill.

"I'd better drive you home," Goldstone suggested. On the way to North Hollywood, Liberace stuck his head out of the window and lost his dinner. Goldstone parked his car before the Camellia house and assisted his ailing star to the door. Liberace's mother greeted them with a stern face. Goldstone made a quick exit. As he drove away, he saw Liberace rush outside and throw up in the bushes.

It's over, Goldstone concluded. The situation was classic: evil director brings home drunken star to furious mother.

Goldstone warily approached rehearsals a few days later, entering the Music Hall from the front door. Liberace was on the stage, and he rushed down the stairs to meet Goldstone, apologizing profusely for his behavior. Their relationship was smooth ever after.

The incident caused a blind item in the entertainment column of a Los Angeles daily: "What local television star caused a disturbance in the men's room of Lucey's the other night?" It was a two-edged item, a forerunner of the innuendo about Liberace that would follow.

Liberace had not spoken to his father in thirteen years. Then one day in October 1953, the two met again.

Lee never forgot his ties to Milwaukee. Whenever he played a concert in his hometown, he invited old chums to visit him backstage, particularly musicians who had started in the business with him: Joe Zingsheim, Del Krause, Carl Lorenz. Also Steve Swedish, the musician who had encouraged Sam Liberace to seek treatment for his son's speech difficulty. Lee appointed Swedish his Midwest musical contractor, with the duty of hiring a forty-eight-piece orchestra for the concerts.

Having heard Liberace's record albums, Swedish knew that the arrangements were heavy with French horns. So why not hire Sam Liberace? Swedish had long believed that Walter was wrong in taking his mother's side in the divorce to such a degree that he cut off all contact with his father.

Swedish telephoned Sam at his home in Middleton and told him of the job but didn't mention the same of the star performer. Swedish had planned to keep Walter in the dark, too. Then he began to lose his nerve.

When Liberace arrived in town, he was entertained at a big reception by Fred Miller at the Miller brewery. As he watched Liberace greeting old friends and civic dignitaries, Swedish decided to divulge his plot. He invited Liberace into a corner.

"Walter, I've done something you may not approve of, but *I* think I've done the right thing," Swedish began. "I've hired your father for the horn section."

Tears began to well in Liberace's eyes as memories tumbled through his mind. Then his face hardened. "Damn you!" he shouted. "How could you do such a thing? You have no right to interfere in our family matters."

"Goddammit, Walter, he's your father!" Swedish shouted back. "He's the man who fed you, taught you how to play the piano, got you the right kind of training. You can't just treat him like he doesn't exist. He's an old man. He needs his son's love."

Liberace wavered between anger and tears. "All right," he said. "He can play in the orchestra. But I won't be at the rehearsal. Bring him to my hotel room afterward."

Sam Liberace arrived at the auditorium ten minutes before rehearsal time, a small man who had to hold his horn case off the floor when he walked. Swedish greeted his old friend and then broke the news: "Sam, I didn't tell you who is appearing with the orchestra. It's Walter."

Sam was sobbing so much he could hardly play in rehearsal. Afterward Swedish invited him and two other musicians to visit Liberace at the Schroeder Hotel. The door to the suite was ajar, and Swedish looked in and saw Liberace, handsome in a red silk robe. As father and son studied each other, Swedish pushed the other two musicians out of the room and closed the door. Twenty minutes later, Liberace and his father emerged, emotionally spent, thirteen years of bitterness ended.

At the Milwaukee concert, Mom occupied her customary position in the front row, and Liberace introduced her during the performance. At a reception afterward, she remained by his side, and Sam Liberace contemplated whether to try for a reconciliation. Finally he tapped her on the shoulder.

She turned around and stared at him icily. "I'm a star now," she declared. "I don't need you anymore."

Sam Liberace had the last word. A few months later, Mom decided she wanted to take back Liberace as her legal name instead of Casadonte. She petitioned the Los Angeles Superior Court for the change, explaining that she wanted to avoid confusion.

Her former husband exploded. Now the woman who had reviled him and estranged him from his own children wanted to take back his name! "To hell with her!" he exclaimed. Sam hired an attorney to fight her petition, and he told the press he objected to her capitalizing on the name. Frances Casadonte quietly abandoned her suit.

Chapter 5

*LIBERACE ACHIEVES NATIONAL FAME AND
DISCOVERS FIRSTHAND THE TRAVAILS PERTAINING
THERETO*

Liberace stood before the bathroom mirror for his daily exercise in The Magic of Believing. As always, he spoke to his reflection in a stern, prosecutorial manner, demanding answers of the sometimes proud, often self-satisfied image.

"Liberace," the inquisitor asked, "are you as good a pianist as Horowitz?"

The question required some thought. "No," Liberace admitted. "But I'm probably better than him in some respects."

"About your new television show. Do you really think it's as good as 'I Love Lucy'?"

Another pause. "Well, if I'm never too self-important to bring entertainment to everybody, I don't see why it couldn't be."

Because of the salesmanship of Reub Kaufman, "Liberace" was beginning to reach everybody. In April 1953, only thirty-five stations had bought the films, but by September the list had grown to one hundred. Soon the total would be 180 stations, more than carried "I Love Lucy."

The success stories of Liberace sponsorship helped increase Kaufman's sales. In Cleveland, the Society for Savings amassed $9,216,000 in new and old accounts over a seven-month period as a result of an offer for a Liberace phonograph record. In Corpus Christi, a Denver-based company advertising canned crab meat on "Liberace" sold out a two-year supply, despite the fact that fresh crab was available in Corpus Christi ten months out of the year.

Don Fedderson resisted urgings by ad agencies to spice up the show with a chorus line, guest stars, and other trappings of television variety shows. "Lee has a terrific nightclub act," Fedderson reasoned. "It works in clubs, and it works on television. Why change it?"

The formula remained the same: the intimate set; the lighting effects; introduction of the mute George and of Mom; the chatty talk directly to the viewers. During most of the show, the screen was filled by Liberace and his piano.

Because of the tight budget, the "production number" required ingenuity. If Liberace decided to play "Tales from the Vienna Woods," crew members would be asked to stop in Coldwater Canyon as they drove from the valley and collect branches for the set. For a "Kitten on the Keys" number, a stagehand searched the alleys of Beverly Hills and found a cat to trip over the piano keys.

At one show Duke Goldstone peered into the audience and saw a group of priests and nuns. He asked one of the nuns if she would be willing to appear onstage. "What do you want me to do?" she asked in surprise. "Just kneel down and pray," he instructed. When she agreed, the director told Liberace, "We're gonna put 'Ave Maria' into the show."

The $10,000 budget allowed no frills. Duke Goldstone received $1,500, Liberace $1,000 (he also shared in the profits). George, the musicians, crew (which included a young man from Fresno, Sam Peckinpah), cameras, film, and theater rental had to come out of the remaining $7,500. To save money, Goldstone cut from the original three cameras to one basic camera with another for partial use.

Goldstone used all of his directorial skills to enhance the production. Motion picture spots, instead of the flat lighting of most television shows, gave the program clear whites and rich blacks for a sophisticated look. For a Mother's Day show, Goldstone featured a framed portrait on the piano. When Liberace came to the climax of his boogie-woogie, the portrait came to life and Mom shouted, "Hey!"

For "Danse Macabre," Goldstone employed a skeleton puppet. As an added effect, he reversed the film to negative. Engineers at some local stations thought the negative was a technical mistake and changed the polarity, thus wiping out the picture.

By splitting the screen for two images, Goldstone could have Liberace play a duet with himself. Or he could materialize Liberace ghostlike by double-exposing a blank curtain, then Liberace against the curtain, fading him in slowly.

Liberace reported to the Music Hall at 9 A.M. to begin rehearsals, and he worked straight through the day, pausing only for the lunch that Mom had packed for him, George, and Goldstone. It was always hearty food with a Polish touch, and all three men were chronically overweight. Even though the show was on film, Goldstone tried to shoot without interruptions, retaining errors and miscues to preserve the spontaneous atmosphere. Mom, wearing an orchid corsage, always led the applause from her front-row-center seat.

Goldstone was amazed by his star's inexhaustible source of material. For each new show Liberace offered a wealth of numbers to choose from. One day the program was short, and he suggested playing "All Alone."

"Good idea," said the director. "We'll put the picture of a girl on the mantel, and you can talk about how you haven't seen her in a long time. Then go into the song."

Liberace listened intently to the direction, as he always did. "Okay, let's try it," he suggested. When he finished "All Alone," Goldstone and members of the crew were in tears.

The Liberace craze began its inexorable sweep across the nation.

Fan clubs, composed largely of gray-haired women, sprang up everywhere. Fan mail amounted to five thousand pieces a week, and Mother's Day brought a flood of greetings to Mom. When Lee mentioned on the air that his brother Rudy, serving with the army in Korea, wasn't getting much mail, the overseas post office received an avalanche of cards and letters addressed to Rudy Liberace, Korea.

The most visible evidence of Liberace mania came when he went on the road to play concerts and promote his television sponsors.

In Miami, Liberace appeared at the opening of a branch of the First Federal Savings and Loan Company. Many women fainted, several were bruised, and one small child suffered minor injuries. A police sergeant was asked how many people were in the crowd. "Damned few," he grumbled. "But there were about ten thousand wild animals."

The Denver National Bank offered to give customers personally autographed photos of Liberace. He signed his name for three hours until the supply of photographs was exhausted. The bank mailed 2,500 photos to fans who had waited in vain.

Back home in Milwaukee, Liberace made an appearance for his Ford sponsors. The crush of admirers at an autograph party was so great that Seymour Heller told the police: "We've got to get him out of here. I've seen this happen before."

Cleveland's Society of Savings had profited so much from its Liberace sponsorship that it was able to buy a chain of banks. To celebrate the occasion, the Society brought Liberace to Cleveland for an hour's television show attended by a huge crowd, including the mayor and the governor of Ohio.

During the summer hiatus from filming the television show, Liberace appeared in concert halls, arenas, and stadiums. A historically important occasion was his first Hollywood Bowl appearance in 1952. His advisers were concerned about drawing a respectable crowd at the eighteen-thousand-seat Bowl. Not Liberace. His only worry was whether patrons in the highest reaches of the Bowl would be able to distinguish him against the orchestra's sea of black tuxedos.

"Do you think it would be too much if I wore white tails—I mean all-white?" he asked Don Fedderson.

"Sounds like a great idea," Fedderson advised.

Liberace's favorite tailor, Sy Devore, created a stylish suit of white tails, and then a duplicate, because Liberace would sweat through the first one. It was the first time that Liberace had appeared in concert wearing anything but traditional black, and it would set a precedent for things to come.

Florence Bettray Kelly came from Milwaukee to help her onetime pupil prepare for the important concert. Angelina arrived in California, and both women were astounded at Lee's calmness on the day of the big event. He spent his time building a window planter and playing with his poodle, Suzette.

In midafternoon, the radio carried news reports of a traffic jam already forming in the Hollywood Bowl area. "Oh, dear," said Mrs. Kelly. "I think I'd better go early so I'll be on time. You should, too, Walter."

"Don't worry, I'll get there," he said airily.

Despite his sister's urgings, Lee didn't leave the house until eight o'clock. Somehow he managed to penetrate the near-gridlock surrounding the Bowl. He donned his white tails and strode confidently onto the huge stage after George had led the Los Angeles Philharmonic Orchestra in a Bizet overture. The crowd was the largest in Hollywood Bowl history, and Liberace was cheered by the audience, though not by the critics, who berated his kitschy repertoire as well as his white tails.

Liberace returned to the Hollywood Bowl to face another sellout crowd the following summer, and the year brought two other important events.

Once again Liberace was invited to entertain at the White House Photographers' Dinner, this time for President Dwight D. Eisenhower. George Murphy was the master of ceremonies, and the other entertainers were Ezio Pinza, Jane Froman, and Danny Kaye. Liberace was accompanied by the NBC Symphony Orchestra, and he also played solos, including boogie-woogie. Again he invited presidential participation.

He delivered his hard-driving, crowd-pleasing boogie-woogie, stopping for an occasional "Hey!" in chorus. Liberace paused and inquired: "I wonder, Mr. President, if you would care to commit yourself as a real fan of boogie-woogie." When the cue was given, Eisenhower shouted a military-like "Hey!" to the whoops and laughter of the throng.

Then on September 23, 1953—Carnegie Hall.

Again the Liberace advisers cautioned against it. The long-hair critics would have their stilettos sharpened, ready to puncture the TV piano player who had the audacity to occupy the hallowed stage of the world's great artists.

"Forget the critics!" Liberace replied. "They're never going to like me anyway. It has been my dream to play Carnegie Hall since I was a hungry kid in New York back in 1941. I'm gonna do it."

With a symphony orchestra behind him and the candelabra on the Baldwin grand, Liberace raced through his repertoire of classic, pop, and boogie-woogie before a wildly enthusiastic capacity audience. The cheers were deafening when he introduced Mom, queenly in her mink and orchids, sitting in the first-tier box.

As Liberace predicted, the New York critics wrote savage reviews. Said the *Times* man:

> *Like Solomon, Liberace scorns a given name, but resemblance between the two artists stops there. . . . Liberace displayed good fingers and prodigious skill at taking brilliant runs up and down the keyboard. He has two styles of playing: fast, loud and energetic; and slow, with sentimentally exaggerated retards and accellerandos. It is a type of piano playing frequently heard in cocktail lounges and is very pleasant to go with cocktails.*

The *Times* review followed the pattern established from the beginning of the Liberace phenomenon. Never in show business history had any successful performer evoked such an outpouring of scathing—and occasionally vicious—reviews.

John Crosby of the *New York Herald Tribune,* the most read and most influential of television reviewers, wrote: "If women vote for Liberace as a piano player—and I'm sure they do—it raises questions about their competence to vote for anything. I'm not suggesting that we repeal the 19th Amendment, exactly, just that maybe we think about it a little. . . .

"Sometimes a man wonders . . . whether the women of this fair land are people or whether some other designation ought to be given them—say, plips—to distinguish them from the rest."

The column was designed to arouse the female populace, but even Crosby was astonished by the violence of the reaction.

"The roof fell in," he wrote in a subsequent column. "Brother, there hasn't been vituperation like this since Cicero delivered the Philippics in the Fifth Century B.C. The nicer letters started out: 'Drop dead.' The not-so-nice letters—well, never mind."

The *Indianapolis News* printed the "plips" column on page one. Telephone protests poured into the newspaper that day, then hundreds of letters. ("John Crosby is the most terrible writer I have ever read. He is rotten, disgusting.") A man listed as John Crosby in the Indianapolis telephone book received ten threatening phone calls before having his number changed.

The *News* editorialized: "A word of advice to budding politicians. Don't run on lower taxes or higher Social Security. Run on Liberace. Say you think he's terrific."

The Indianapolis experience was repeated in Boston, Philadelphia, South Bend, Memphis, and other cities where Crosby's column was syndicated. He remained unrepentant: "I still think Liberace plays piano as if he were wearing boxing gloves. I could phone Local 802 of the musicians' union and dig up 100 piano players I would rather listen to."

The Crosby incident encouraged other columnists and critics to take potshots at Liberace, certain that the reaction would be swift and vocal. Even the *New York Times* joined in.

The *Times* assigned Howard Taubman, who normally reviewed the likes of Yehudi Menuhin and Pablo Casals, to write a critique of the Liberace television shows and record albums. His Sunday magazine article was titled, "A Square Looks at a Hotshot."

Taubman made sardonic comments about the television show, citing the candelabra "standing in refulgent solitude on the piano," the ring ("even in black and white television you have the sensation that it must hold rare gems"), the smarmy monologue ("Liberace is telling about a sweet old lady in New England who writes him all the time).""

The record albums received no better treatment: "Liberace creates—if that is the word—each composition in his own image. When it is too difficult, he simplifies it. When it is too simple, he complicates it."

Taubman's conclusion:

What kind of pianist is Liberace? Don't ask a square with Horowitz and Rubinstein on the brain. He'll say that Liberace is not much more than a parlor pianist who ought to be kept in someone else's parlor. Such a bilious critic will point out a lot of flaws—slackness of rhythm, distorted phrasing, and an excess of prettification and sentimentality, a failure to stick to what the composer has written.

In March 1954, the *Los Angeles Mirror* printed four articles dealing with Liberace. The series by Roby Heard began:

One of the strangest roles in the strange world of show business is being enacted today by a dimpled, curly-haired piano player who loves his mother—and tells the world about it.

His popularity raises speculation over the sanity of the nation's women—particularly those in their middle and late years—who idolize him. . . .

Heard wrote exhaustively about "the Candelabra Casanova of the Keyboard, the musician-actor who makes millions out of Momism." Everything about Liberace was explored: his life story, loves, music, family, fans, the music critics, etc. Most of it could have been printed in fan magazines, except for a recurring tone of cynicism.

Liberace's ever-protective lawyer, John Jacobs, was prompted to dispatch to the *Mirror* a ten-page letter refuting certain elements of the series. Among his complaints:

There is much derision made about Liberace's devotion to his mother. He is accused of "Momism," a term invented by a notorious woman hater, Philip Wylie. The term is used as an expletive like Communism or Nazism. It is given a sinister connotation. Liberace does love his mother . . . he vividly recalls when she nursed him through double pneumonia and the time she saved his finger from amputation by the application of an old-time poultice remedy after doctors recommended surgery. . . .

There is an allusion in the series to the fact that youths find Liberace "silly and affected." How can I believe that when I see hundreds of letters every day addressed to Liberace from teenagers who revere him?

You state that Liberace's mother said as a child he preferred sewing. Did you ask Liberace's mother if that was so? Well, I did, and the answer was an emphatic no. . . .

I played seven years of football and boxed in college, yet I would hesitate to challenge Liberace to any feat of strength. He is in perfect trim, almost six feet tall, and weighs 180 pounds. His tastes, however, are gentle. He does not hunt or fish because he will go to any extent to protect his hands, the hands which make his music. . . .

Liberace was hurt by all of the bad notices and derogatory articles. But he had learned in the barrooms of Milwaukee, where he was subjected to the abuse of roaring drunks, that the best defense for such attacks was a wisecrack. He found the classic remark when he told the audience in San Francisco one night: "I don't mind the bad reviews, but George cries all the way to the bank." In time, the crack made its way into *Bartlett's Quotations.*

The first time Paul Weston saw Liberace, both were appearing at a charity telethon in Los Angeles in the early 1950s. Weston, a composer, arranger, and conductor of record albums and radio shows, had known Liberace as a television personality but had never seen him perform.

Weston was dumbfounded. With nothing but a piano and a smile, Liberace transformed an inattentive audience into enthralled listeners. Especially the women. Weston, who was also West Coast representative for Columbia Records, asked if the pianist would be interested in making some recordings. Indeed he would. He had recorded for Decca and smaller companies, but promotion and sales had been meager.

Ideas that emanated from the West, Weston had learned, lost their potency with every mile eastward; by the time they reached New York, they were virtually devoid of life. "Who's Liberace?" demanded Goddard Lieberson, majordomo of Columbia Records.

Weston tried to explain the amazing hold that Liberace wielded over an audience. He described Liberace's great success in television. Lieberson was unswayed.

"At least let me make some ten-inch albums with him," Weston proposed. Lieberson reluctantly agreed.

With George Liberace as conductor and Gordon Robinson providing the musical know-how, Liberace wove his repertoire of pops and classics into albums such as *Liberace by Candlelight, Liberace at the Piano,* and *An Evening at the Piano.* Executives at Columbia Records were flabbergasted when each of the albums placed among the top five best-sellers in the country. Weston was able to convince Lieberson to record a twelve-inch album of concertos. Weston himself conducted and Liberace played his *"Reader's Digest"* versions of Grieg, Addinsell ("Warsaw"), Rachmaninoff, Rozsa ("Spellbound"), etc. By the time the album was released, the "Liberace" show had become syndicated nationwide, and sales impressed even Goddard Lieberson.

Then came the Carnegie Hall concert.

"I think everyone from Columbia Records should be out in force," suggested Paul Weston.

"I couldn't possibly go to a Liberace concert," Lieberson said.

"Why not?"

"When I go to Carnegie Hall, I go for Sir Thomas Beecham, Koussevitzky, Stokowski."

"Goddard, you must go. Liberace is an important artist for Columbia Records, and he will expect to see you there. He will be insulted if he doesn't."

The Columbia Records contingent occupied a box next to Liberace's mother. Goddard Lieberson sat at the far rear of the box, desperate not to be seen.

On a brisk day in February 1954, I paid a visit to Liberace's new house.

It wasn't hard to find. It stood on a corner lot on two broad streets a short distance from the busy intersection of Sepulveda and Ventura Boulevards in Sherman Oaks. The front yard was filled with mounds of red and white gravel, topped by plants that resembled abstract sculpture. The Liberace signature and a piano were inscribed on the mailbox. The signature was also perforated on large brass plates at each side of the door. The doorbell chimed the Liberace theme, "I'll Be Seeing You."

Liberace greeted me with his wide smile. We had met three years before, when a movie magazine gave a reception at Ciro's for its choice of future movie stars. Liberace, who was appearing at Ciro's at the time, was also invited. He mingled with Rock Hudson, Natalie Wood, Tony Curtis, Piper Laurie, and other young studio players, then someone asked him to play the piano. As always, he obliged. But no one listened. The actors were too busy talking about their latest pictures, and Lee couldn't compete with the din. He gave up trying.

"Come into the den and have some coffee," Liberace urged. "Mom has made some wonderful banana cream pie."

Along with Seymour Heller and a man from Columbia Records, I had some of Mom's pie and coffee while Lee talked about his new home.

"I hunted and hunted for a new house, because the one on Camellia just wasn't big enough," he said. "But all of the places fell short of what I wanted. So I decided I would have to build my own house. I found an architect I liked, Al Dingman, and I told him my needs. I wanted large, airy rooms, I wanted living space for me and Mom. I needed a soundproofed room where George and I could practice. I wanted a big, modern kitchen for Mom. And I wanted a swimming pool, because I always dreamed of having one.

"Then Al asked me my preferences. I told him I like comedy and I like drama. I enjoy classical music, but I have a fondness for jazz. He went to work with that in mind, and I contributed my own ideas all the time. I made little sketches of the things I wanted. I picked out everything, from hardware to furniture. What you see is what I had in mind. The house has drama, but it also has touches of humor. It's classical, but it's modern, too. Would you like to see it?"

It was—well, pure Liberace. Candelabras everywhere. The color motif: black and white, like the piano. The living room was huge, necessarily so to house the Baldwin grand piano, which was six inches longer than normal size. A large, glass-topped planter was piano-shaped, and pianos were etched into the bottoms of the lamps. The bookends were shaped like pianos. Shelves displayed a collection of miniature pianos and pictures, each with a printed card of explanation: "Liberace as seen by a young fan"; "Hand-painted portrait of Liberace; plays Brahms's Lullaby"; etc.

"I started the collection when I was eight years old," Lee remarked, holding a miniature. "It was given to me by Paderewski, who was a friend of the family. I guess he was my idol."

The tour continued through the dining room with its music-scroll-backed chairs, and to the bedroom, dominated by an immense bed covered with a satin spread emblazoned with a large script *L* intertwining a piano. More piano lamps, a large oil painting of Liberace on the wall. The large bathroom was done in black and mirrors. No pianos.

"The sunken bath was my idea," Lee explained. "When I was making a musical short at RKO, I wandered over to the set where they were shooting *Androcles and the Lion.* An actor was sitting in billows of suds in one of those Roman baths, and it seemed to me the height of luxury."

He saved his greatest pride for the end of the tour. The swimming pool. It was shaped like a piano top, with eighty-eight keys painted in black and white on the cement deck at the wide end. The towels were hemstitched with titles of all the songs Liberace had recorded: "Laura," "Liebestraum," "I Don't Care," etc.

After the tour we returned to the den, and I questioned Lee about the wave of criticism in the press, especially the John Crosby attack.

"Since Crosby wrote that about me," he said cheerfully, "I have had thousands of letters from men, apologizing because they never took the time to write me. They said they had always enjoyed my TV shows and my concerts, but they had let their wives do the writing."

He shrugged off Taubman and other highbrow critics: "Naturally I condense. I have to know just how many notes my audience will stand for."

Far from retreating from the critics, he was planning to face them May 26 in the biggest arena yet: Madison Square Garden. "Did you know there has been only one other pianist to give a recital in the Garden?" he asked. "You know who it was? Paderewski!"

Before I left, Lee insisted that I sign the guest book. It was shaped like a piano.

The Garden had never seen such a crowd. They came from Scarsdale and Larchmont and Stamford, as well as Newark and Staten Island and the Upper East Side, too. They wore muskrat stoles and fox boas and rimless glasses, and many had hair the shade of pale blue. Some were accompanied by husbands who grumblingly consulted ticket stubs as they searched for seats in the arena where Joe Lewis defended his title and Gargantua the ape headlined the circus. There were fifteen thousand of them, and they snapped up dollar programs that offered photographs of Liberace as a boy, with George in concert, with Mom in the kitchen, and rising out of the piano-shaped pool.

The Garden, smelling only faintly of athletes' sweat and elephant dung, was draped with American flags and red, white, and blue bunting. At the west end stood a bandstand with a huge piano. Above it was a huge turquoise wall hanging adorned with a piano symbol.

Liberace's entrance was described by the *New Yorker*'s man Stanley:

"Tense moment. No sound in the entire Garden, other than heavy breathing. The entrance! Liberace! Himself! A poem in white tie, tails, white shoes, and pancake makeup. Auditorium beside itself. Scenes of pandemonium. Ladies waved handkerchiefs, chirped greetings, shouted welcome. Cries of joy! Great happiness! Liberace smiling like a well-fed baby. His dark curls gleamed under spotlights. 'It's a dream come true,' he said. 'Playing here tonight! Did you count them, George?' "

He sat down at the piano and raised the piano stool higher, explaining: "This is a pretty high-class number." Much laughter. He began with "Cornish Rhapsody," followed with truncated Chopin and a brief version of Debussy's "Claire de Lune," with five Garden spotlights simulating the moon.

Liberace raced through his fail-proof repertoire: "The Rosary," "Cement Mixer (Put-ti Put-ti)," "Beer Barrel Polka," "Twelfth Street Rag," a Mexican number (with George shaking the maracas), the standard boogie-woogie with the crowd-pleasing "Hey!" He introduced Mom in a side arena box to a roar of applause. He mentioned the names of all fifty musicians and talked about his television sponsors. He did a soft shoe, a hillbilly number in farmer clothes, and returned in a gold lamé jacket to play requests.

Of his piano style, Stanley reported: "Strong fingers, this fellow. Loves to run them up keys, back again, then up again. Series of runs and flourishes. Pedal work difficult to analyze. Keeps pumping feet up and down and sidewise, as though he were on an electric horse."

After two and a half hours of playing, he told the audience, "I'm not tired if you're not." A roar of approval. He remained for another half-hour. "You overwhelm me!" he exclaimed. "I got goose pimples." Next year, he said, he might try Yankee Stadium.

Liberace could smile en route to the bank. His payment of $138,000 for the Garden concert was to be forever enshrined in the Guinness Book of Records as the highest single salary every paid a pianist.

The television era brought with it the creation of instant pop folklore. None was more pervasive than Liberace.

By 1954, the "Liberace" show appeared on 184 channels, reaching virtually every household that contained a television set. For New Yorkers who couldn't get enough of Liberace, WPIX offered his show ten times a week.

Comedians found rich material in Liberace, his costumes, the candelabra, the swimming pool, Mom. From a Bob Hope monologue:

"You have to admire that Liberace, he's such a colorful guy. He's the only fellow I know who leaves a chartreuse ring around his tub. . . . The older women really go for him. When he makes a personal appearance, you can hear the corsets snapping all over town. . . . Did you ever see such a smile? He's got so much ivory in his head, when he takes a bath he and the soap float together. . . . But it isn't his fault, really. You see, he was such a delicate baby that instead of slapping him, the doctor patted him with a powder puff, and he's been smiling ever since."

Liberace went along with the gags. On Jack Benny's television show, the ornate set purporting to be Liberace's home was filled with candelabras of all sizes, and servants were kept busy lighting them. When the gardener entered and placed his rake against the piano, a servant placed candles on the tines and lighted them. When Liberace suggested a duet, Benny produced a violin on which shone a tiny lighted candelabra.

Some of the Liberace jokes, the ones told in bars and locker rooms, were not so polite. No one enjoyed telling them more than Liberace. One of his favorites:

Liberace has a piano-shaped pool, he's got pianos on his napkins, pianos on his sheets. Do you know what he's got on his toilet paper?

Pianos?

No—shit, just like everyone else.

One of the biggest song hits of the 1950s was "Mister Sandman," as recorded by the McGuire Sisters. As they pleaded with the Sandman to send them a dream, they specified:

> *Give him a lonely heart like Pa-gli-acci*
> *And lots of wavy hair like Liberace!*

In Chicago, the National Pickle Packers Association bestowed on Liberace the title of Pickle Man of the Year. The reasoning: "Some people find his piano playing sweet; others, rather sour." The association planned to send Liberace a "pickle-abra," a candelabra stuffed with pickles.

In Duluth, a Methodist minister preached that behind Liberace's famous smile "lurks an ancient evil which eats at the foundation of homes throughout the United States." The reason for his outburst: one of Liberace's television sponsors was a brewery.

At the International Livestock Show in Chicago, Liberace was memorialized by a statue in lard. It depicted a dozen porkers sitting around a piano while another one, smiling broadly through a candelabra, played for them.

The head of the Steinway piano company said that Liberace's

success had sparked a boom in piano sales. He noted with regret that Liberace played only the Baldwin.

When Liberace returned to Milwaukee to appear before a sold-out audience, he reflected on his Depression days when he wheeled his coaster wagon to the relief office to collect groceries for the family table. A county official made news by sending Liberace a letter informing him that "relief is recoverable under Wisconsin law. Our records show that your family received relief amounting to $100.43. Your check can be made payable to the Milwaukee County Department of Public Welfare." More news was made when Liberace forwarded his check.

Liberace's fame even reached the Soviet Union.

The Soviet satirical magazine *Krokodil* decided that Liberace was no genius. He was assailed as a "gravedigger of art," whose one great gift was "a beautiful thick mop of hair."

Krokodil related the turning point in the career of the pianist whose name somehow translated as Leeberice (rhyming with ice):

> *Once when Leeberice was about to begin a scheduled concert, the hall seemed empty. The self-loving youth became melancholy, but suddenly a great idea occurred to him. He began to chat with the audience. Wladziu sent into the gloomy, empty expanse his sugary smiles and told tasty anecdotes. The casual listener might have been proud at that moment to be at the birth of palpable genius.*

The magazine then unleashed the party line:

> *What was the secret? America actually has talented and great masters of musical art. But the very law of American life which permits bestial comics to train youthful sadists and murderers and dislodged better work of progressive writers and artists from*

*the book markets, which long permitted gangster films to occupy
all the screens of the country, helped to eminence the pretty youth
with the luscious smile.*

*Reaction, which rages in the U.S.A., had entered into an alliance with vulgarity. Indeed, it is a strong poison by which the
minds and hearts of millions can be dispatched.*

Leeberice was amused.

"I'm not worried," he commented. "I had not intended to include
Russia in my world tour, and I think I'm here to stay and they're not."

Liberace's lawyer, John Jacobs, was not amused when Al Capp
suggested a spoof in his "Li'l Abner" comic strip. Capp had written
Liberace: "I was sure that you would someday become famous
enough for me to kick around in 'Li'l Abner.' . . . Since you are now
a household word, it is up to all the Yokums and all the Capps to kid
the daylights out of you, your piano, your curly hair, and your adoring
fans. I plan to do a Sunday-page sequence about a pianist named
Liverarchy. Any resemblance to you will be deliberate."

Absolutely not, thundered Jacobs. So Capp invented another character, Loverboynik, who differed from Liberace only in being blond.
Capp maintained that the two did not match "because Loverboynik
can play the piano quite well and he doesn't giggle hysterically." He
added, "I don't think he's as funny as Liberace."

In Tallahassee, a woman claimed Liberace as the father of her baby.
She said he impregnated her with his penetrating wink.

Chapter 6

LOVE FINDS LIBERACE—AND LOSES HIM AGAIN

THE GIRL I'LL MARRY
BY LIBERACE

I have been engaged three times and in each instance I felt I was very lucky to have had the experience. Later on, as each romance in turn did not seem to work out, I felt I was fortunate that it did not culminate in marriage. There were different reasons in each case for the breakup. All three of the girls had sex appeal, too, and yet this rather intangible quality figured in our romantic problems. . . .

Thus a 1954 fan magazine story bearing Liberace's byline and strong evidence of ghost-writing. He went on to analyze the elements of sex appeal ("The exciting woman is the one who makes a genuine effort to take her natural beauty and enhance it by proper use of cosmetics, makeup, girdles, or bras").

Liberace described his three "engagements." The first was an adolescent, a ballet dancer who "had all the qualities of sex appeal for which a man could ask." She wanted to marry immediately, but it was during the Depression and young Walter wanted to establish himself first. The first time he took an out-of-town job, she married someone else.

Next came a singer, also very sexy. She was a girl who just wanted to have fun, and she thought nothing of canceling an appearance so she could attend a party. She expected Lee to do the same. The crisis came when she wanted him to go to a beach party on the night of his Hollywood Bowl concert. "I realized that a lifetime involving an irresponsible attitude toward my work was not for me, and the engagement was over."

Finally, a woman of independent means and spirit. She took everything for granted, including their engagement. Finally Lee got a word in, and it was no. They decided to see if they could stand being apart. They could.

Liberace declared that he didn't regret the relationships because they increased his awareness of women. But by depriving himself of marriage, he was able to devote his total energies to his career. Now he was ready for marriage, and the ideal wife would have sex appeal but also the element of faith that meant so much to him ("Everything about the success of my 'Ave Maria' record I attribute to faith—my own and other people's").

The article was standard fan-mag stuff that bore little relationship to known fact. If Liberace had been through three engagements, they were secret ones indeed. None of his Milwaukee friends nor his career associates were aware of any relationship with women. He was sometimes seen at Hollywood events with a date, but that was for publicity purposes. When he and Betty White were the principal stars of KLAC-TV, they sometimes paired for public appearances. One night they arrived in a limousine at the premiere of a new movie just as a windstorm kicked up. He emerged from the car first. Betty was dressed in a bouffant gown, and she was hoping that he would help her control it as she stepped out. But he was busy holding onto his hair.

Despite all the innuendo and all the fag jokes about Liberace, no one working closely with him saw any evidence of homosexuality. Duke Goldstone, who directed Liberace for long hours daily and traveled across the country with him, saw nothing. Nor did Paul Weston, who worked intimately with Liberace on record albums. There were no willowy young men in his entourage, nothing like that. Everyone simply thought he was a mama's boy. Certainly no one had ever been so publicly devoted to his mother, nor had reaped such rewards because of it.

In fact, Liberace was confused about his sexual identity. His introduction to sex with the wanton blues singer had obliterated any boyish notions he had about romance. Alone in big cities, he found himself drawn to overnight relations with other men. It was a dangerous game, he realized. A homosexual scandal could destroy a career; film stars like William Haines and Ramon Novarro had discovered that. As his fame grew, Liberace suppressed the homosexual side of his nature. He had worked too hard for too many years to have his achievement wiped out by a few moments of pleasure.

Meanwhile, he continued telling interviewers about his "engagements," explaining: "Resentment of my women fans ruined each of them. None of my fiancées could understand or accept the adulation of my fans, an understanding that is so important in a complex career like mine."

He continued: "I keep my eyes open every day. And any minute I might walk into a hotel lobby and find her sitting there."

As it turned out, Liberace found his only publicized romance across the street.

Her name was Joanne Rio, and she lived across Camellia Avenue when Lee moved into his North Hollywood house. She was eighteen, and she had grown up in a show business family. Her father, Eddie Rio, had danced with the Rio Brothers in vaudeville and Broadway musicals and had given up performing to head the Los Angeles office of the American Guild of Variety Artists. Her mother had been a Chicago blues singer known as Mildred LaSalle. Joanne had taken singing and dancing lessons and had played small roles in movies.

Joanne took notice of the dark stranger who had moved into the neighborhood. Soon his mother came to live with him, but she noticed no other women at the house. Through the open window she could hear him playing the piano, and she thought she could sense his moods through the music he played. "When he was tired or perhaps unhappy," she recalled later, "he would play somber, serious pieces, and when he was happy, the piano would come alive with gay, titillating tunes that would seem to make the street lights dance."

Some days Joanne played baseball in the street with her younger brother, Eddie Jr., and the neighborhood boys. She insisted on playing outfield so she would be close to Lee's house and he might notice her. He didn't. But Joanne's father knew of Liberace, and the two families met after Sunday Mass at St. Charles's Church.

Lee and Joanne met a few times on the street when he was walking his poodle, Suzette. Then he moved to the piano-pool house in Sherman Oaks.

When Joanne was twenty-two, she was hired for a chorus job at the Moulin Rouge, formerly Earl Carroll's Theater, in Hollywood. Liberace frequented the Moulin Rouge shows, and one night she spotted him at ringside. Along with the other chorus girls, she was performing bumps and grinds in a scanty negligee while ringing bells in accompaniment with the orchestra. She sent him a note: "You can ring my bell anytime."

Lee invited her to his table for a drink and was surprised to recognize that she was the girl who had lived across the street. He drove her home. "He walked me to the door and shyly asked to see me again," she recalled. "Then he bowed and squeezed my hand. It was like a caress."

They began dating. Pizza at Casa d'Amore in Hollywood. Barbecues at Lee's house. She was unable to attend his Hollywood Bowl concert because she had to dance at the Moulin Rouge. But she hurried to the reception he held afterward at his house. He stayed by her side amid the crowd of celebrities and socialites, and at the midnight supper he seated her next to Mom.

Joanne later related her memory of how the evening ended. She was the last to leave the party, and Lee escorted her to her car, the poodle tagging along. "Give me a kiss, Suzette, because if you don't, your master won't," she said. And then: "Lee took me in his arms and kissed me soundly. Wow! I blushed. But in the back of my mind I knew that was exactly what I wanted."

The next evening Joanne cooked lasagna and chicken cacciatore for Lee and his sister, Angie, at the Rio house. Other guests were family friends—Rosemarie and Danny Thomas, and Virginia Mayo and Michael O'Shea. Joanne's cooking was extravagantly praised, and after dinner Lee sat down at the spinet piano, Eddie Rio Jr. played drums, and several of the guests performed vaudeville turns. A week later Lee took Joanne to a party at the Thomases' house, and Danny taught him how to play pool—Lee had never learned. Lee accompanied Frankie Laine and other performers, and after a good-night kiss he told Joanne it had been one of the nicest evenings he could remember.

Lee began escorting Joanne to premieres and publicity parties, delighting the fan magazine photographers. The gossip columnists took note of their frequent dates. Soon there were rumors of a forthcoming marriage. Lee's office issued a statement to calm his anxious fans: "Mr. Liberace is not engaged and is not married."

The rumors would not die.

"I'm not ready to get married," Lee told me at his house one day. "There are too many things I want to do. I want to play Europe, and I want to make movies. My kind of schedule won't leave any time for marriage."

He continued: "I'd known Joanne long before the rumors began. When she was young, I used to see her and her brother playing in the street, and I also saw her at church. She seemed like a very nice girl. Of course when you're dating, you don't want a goody-goody girl. You want someone who is fun and has sex appeal. I realized that when I saw her at the Moulin Rouge. By the way, we still go to church."

"The question of marriage has not been discussed," Joanne insisted to me. "We are fond of each other, but it hasn't become any more serious than that. Lee is a very busy man, and I have my career to think of, too. Besides, he is leaving on a five-week concert tour."

Joanne told another reporter that Lee was "the perfect all-around man any woman would be thrilled to be with." She gushed: "He's so considerate on our dates. He's just the end. He never forgets the little things that women love. He brings me orchids. He lights my cigarettes and he opens doors. He makes you feel that when you are with him, well, you really are with him."

Their dates resumed after the concert tour, and so did the rumors. Finally Lee announced that he and Joanne would be married in a year—"if she really loves me and is willing to wait for me." The year's wait was necessary, he said, because he had to fulfill his commitments, "and I don't want my career to interfere with my marriage like those Hollywood couples such as Marilyn Monroe and Joe DiMaggio. I want a wedding with the full Catholic commitment. It must be a lasting thing."

Joanne agreed. "If it's God's will that Lee and I get married, then we will," she said. "I'm leaving everything in God's hands." She added that Lee's mother had given her approval to the match.

That much was true. Frances Liberace Casadonte had long wanted Lee to marry, though not as often as George, who had taken his third wife. Mom was genuinely fond of Joanne, a nice Catholic girl who might make Lee settle down and could provide him with beautiful children. Mom had worried over the fact that Lee had never known a serious romance, and she distrusted some of the male companions that he sometimes brought home with him. She was delighted to think that Lee and Joanne might get married.

The Lee fans were not. On the day news broke of a possible wedding, the fan mail was flooded with calls from all over the country. "Is it true?" women asked, and when the news was confirmed, they broke into sobs. The outpouring of dismay overwhelmed the secretaries who handled the six thousand weekly letters sent to Liberace. Eighty percent of the writers were adamant that Liberace should remain a bachelor. They argued that (1) Liberace would love his mother less if he married Joanne, (2) his career would suffer from the loss of his most devoted fans, (3) he would suffer the same kind of personal tragedy that hit Joe DiMaggio.

An aged widow in St. Paul wrote: "I feel sorry for your mother. Now she will have to share the adoration you give her." A woman in Detroit inquired: "How can you think of marriage? You belong to us." A Monroe, Louisiana, fan reasoned: "Everything a man is, he owes to his mother. A wife would never make the sacrifices a mother would." A Gardena, California, woman wrote: "Your appeal is the fact that you're single. If you have to get married, pick a plain type, not a glamour girl."

The reaction alarmed the Liberace brain trust. Serious erosion of the solid core of his popularity—over-forty females—could prove disastrous. Liberace himself attempted to shore up the damage.

"I think anyone who sacrifices his personal life is foolish," he told reporters. "I'm sure the public wouldn't want that. Actually, women adore a lot of male performers who are married.

"I'm reading a book on Rudolph Valentino, my namesake. When he married, there was a tremendous reaction against it. But when he took his wife on tour, people came out even more. The reaction of fans just goes in a different direction, that's all."

But the uproar did not diminish, and it caused Liberace to reevaluate his position. Did he really want to marry and thus endanger his career? More important, did he believe that he could play the role of husband? Or would Joanne become like the wife of Cole Porter and other public figures, providing disguise for a homosexual husband?

Lee was rescued from his dilemma by Joanne herself—and her father.

The engagement to Liberace provided Joanne Rio with a profound lesson in the power of publicity. Suddenly she was being sought for roles in B movies and for television commercials. Fan magazines and columnists sought her for interviews. She was being recognized in beauty salons and supermarkets. Heady stuff for a twenty-two-year-old.

Motivated more by ambition than sense, Joanne allowed her name to be signed to a series of three ghost-written articles in the *Los Angeles Mirror* about her romance with Liberace. In gushy movie-magazine style, she related her crush on "the handsome stranger across the street," their first date, their kisses in the dark.

"Am I upset because 5,000 to 6,000 women write him fan mail (including many proposals of marriage) each week?" she mused. "Am I jealous? I love it. I am happy that so very many women see the same fine qualities in Liberace that I do and love him for them."

The Liberace camp was incensed over the articles and used them in an attempt to convince Lee that Joanne Rio was merely using him as a means to promote her own negligible career. Meanwhile, the sobbing letters of disbelief continued to flood the fan mail office.

Show-wise Eddie Rio, who had worked with many homosexuals during his performing career and as union chief, from the beginning had his doubts about Liberace as a match for his daughter. "Joanne, darling," he told her, "your mother and I are very fond of Lee, but I don't know what kind of a husband he would be."

"He'll be a wonderful husband," she argued. "He's so kind and thoughtful."

"Yes, but he's not very—well, manly."

"Oh, Daddy, he's just a mama's boy; everybody knows that. He'll change."

Still, Eddie Rio nursed a father's concern. His fears were confirmed when he received a telephone call from a longtime friend in show business. He told Eddie of an incident involving Liberace that had the makings of a scandal but had been hushed up.

Eddie decided the engagement had to be terminated or Joanne would suffer great emotional damage later on. He told her what he had learned. She was at first unbelieving, then inconsolable. When Liberace next came to the Rio house, Eddie invited him for a walk.

With an arm around Liberace's shoulder, Eddie began: "Lee, this may be the most painful thing I ever had to do. You see, I was hoping you and Joanne could have a happy life together. Now I realize it couldn't be." He related the news he had heard. Lee didn't flinch, but his eyes were glistening.

"Lee, you're a wonderful person, and I know you're going to have a magnificent career," Eddie continued. "But you can't marry my daughter. I want to have grandchildren, Lee. I want her to have a family of her own. The marriage wouldn't work, and you know in our church there is no divorce. I'm sorry, Lee. I'm really sorry." As they walked back to the house, Lee was crying softly.

Liberace departed on a concert tour, and en route he gave interviews declaring he was upset by the *Mirror* articles. "When I get married; *I* want to be the aggressor," he said.

It sounded like a rift, and I telephoned Joanne. "The romance is over," she confirmed. "I don't think it's right for either of us."

Liberace admitted they were no longer dating. "I have no further comment to make," he said.

Joanne had the last word. She maintained that the articles had been read and approved by Liberace and his manager (Seymour Heller said they had merely been read to him over the phone). "His manager ought to be able to advise him on whether such publicity would be favorable," she continued. "I don't like to be made out a liar."

Millions of American women breathed more easily. But a few weeks later, just before Christmas 1953, came the alarming news that Liberace had suffered a slight heart strain. "He started breathing heavily when he played," reported George Liberace. His physician ordered Liberace to rest until February and placed him on a rigid protein diet.

Mom felt compelled to deny reports that her son was heartsick over the broken romance: "He has been giving so many concerts, working and traveling so much without a vacation. It has nothing to do with Joanne Rio."

The Joanne Rio–Liberace affair had a bitter aftermath two decades later.

Joanne's career never caught fire, and her most notable work was doubling for Elizabeth Taylor in several films. She retired and married a fashion designer, David Barr. She helped him build the company into a thriving enterprise. A daughter, Bridget, was born to them in 1960.

In 1973, *Liberace: An Autobiography* was published by G. P. Putnam's Sons. In a final chapter Liberace took up the matter of why he had never married. Partly, he said, it was because of the divorces in his family: his parents; Angelina; George, four times. Also, every time he considered marriage, something happened to warn him that it wouldn't work.

That brought him to Joanne Rio.

"Everyone thought ours was one of those matches made in heaven because we met in a church," Liberace wrote. "There was a lot of sideline cheering from both our families trying to push things too fast."

Publicity is what killed the romance, he said. A "very ambitious" reporter convinced her to go along with the series "My Dates with Liberace," which contained "many intimate details, confidences and personal confessions that two people share when they're in love (or think they are)." The articles dogged him as he traveled the country, causing embarrassment, "but what finally hosed me down and cooled me off was the discovery that Joanne had been paid a tidy sum by the newspaper syndicate to let them publish details of our romance."

Now it was Joanne's turn to be incensed. She filed suit against Liberace, Putnam, the *National Enquirer* (which had excerpted the book) and others for $1.5 million in damages. She alleged that he had portrayed her as "an untrustworthy person who could not be trusted with the intimate details of a relationship and/or as an opportunist who would exploit any personal relationship." Also that he implied that she "had been intimate with him and accordingly was unchaste."

In a deposition on December 30, 1974, Joanne Rio Barr said she had dated Liberace for three months, despite her bylined statement, "We had known each other for five years and had been dating steadily but quietly for six months when suddenly our romance became front-page news." Explained Joanne: "That's what Mr. Liberace wanted me to say."

From her testimony, it appeared that everything was planned. When news of the romance broke, Seymour Heller told her "that I should let Mr. Liberace do most of the answering and if I was questioned at all, I was to be as vague as I could be and make denials that it was a hot and heavy romance or that we had any definite plans to get married." At first she rejected the idea of a three-part newspaper series about the romance, but Lee said "he didn't think it would hurt anything and he thought it would be nice." Lee suggested she could write about their dates—"where we went, what we did, what we liked."

After reading the excerpt of Liberace's book in the *Enquirer*, Mrs. Barr said, "I became very hysterical and I just kept saying over and over again, 'Why was he degrading me to justify why he never got married? Why was he lying about me?' "

She added that after Liberace's book was published, friends asked her such questions as: "Was he homosexual? Did you go to bed with him?" Her reply: "I dated him, but I never went to bed with him."

Liberace himself was also called for a deposition in the case. He declared that *Los Angeles Mirror* columnist Paul Coates had told him that Joanne received "a tidy sum" for the three articles. They had upset him because they were "silly like a puppy-love, school-girl kind of thing, not a grown-up, adult thing."

His conclusion: "As far as I am concerned, Joanne Rio does not exist because this is something that happened twenty years ago. We all agreed it was like a ghost coming out of the past to haunt me. I see nothing in that book that was damaging or derogatory to Miss Rio. As I remember it, she was a very pretty girl, a very nice girl. I liked her very much. I wanted to marry her, and that's exactly what I said in my book. The reason I didn't marry her was because of these goddamn articles and her father screaming at me and calling me all kinds of names. I suddenly realized I had found out in the nick of time that all was not going to be sunshine and roses."

Liberace and his advisers certainly didn't want to have the old romance, with all of its implications, sifted over in a courtroom. The suit was settled for a "substantial amount."

Joanne Rio Barr died in 1985 of a rare liver ailment.

Chapter 7

LIBERACE REALIZES HIS AMBITION TO STAR IN A MOVIE, AND THE RESULTS ARE NOT WHAT HE HAD WISHED

With Joanne Rio removed as a threat to Liberace and his devotion to Mom, his fans breathed more easily. Now he could give all his time to her and to bringing pleasure to the millions, without the distraction of a domestic alliance. Liberace's popularity, which had momentarily faltered, regained its forward thrust, and his syndicated show remained the most widely distributed program in the United States. Despite his enforced rest, the "Liberace" show still reached a waiting audience every week, thanks to a backlog of productions.

I paid another call to the Liberace house in early January 1955, and he greeted me at the door in robe and slippers. We sat down in the black-and-white living room, where the oversize Baldwin grand piano now had a twin.

"I never would have found out I was ill, except for an insurance physical I had," he said. "Every once in a while, the office takes out another annuity for me, and I have to go in for a checkup. The doctor told me I would have to cut down all activity and get a complete rest. I came back from the last tour quite heavy. You know how it is on the road, you eat a lot of heavy stuff. The doctor told me that globules of fat were clogging my arteries, cutting off the flow of oxygen to my blood. That's why I had been feeling so bad. When I did the TV show, I'd get to the point at four o'clock in the afternoon when I didn't have the strength to continue. I had to ask Duke Goldstone to shoot around me for half an hour while I got some rest."

Lee said the doctor had put him on a diet of steaks and salads, and he had lost seventeen pounds, with three to go. For a change, he looked younger than his years, which were thirty-five, and not so cherubic. He still was required to rest until February, when he would ease back into the television shows. Meanwhile he played piano a half-hour daily with his arranger, made candelabra lamps for friends, planned a projection room, and tried to cope with the bushels of Christmas and get-well cards.

"In April, I'm going to open the new Riviera Hotel in Las Vegas," he said excitedly. "Do you know what they're paying me? Fifty thousand dollars a week! Can you believe that? Nobody ever got paid that much in Las Vegas."

Liberace related how the deal came about. He was dining with Seymour Heller and his wife, Billie, in a Los Angeles restaurant, and Seymour excused himself to speak to friends in the next booth. He returned to explain that they were the owners of the Riviera Hotel, which would soon be opening in Las Vegas. "They want you to be the first act at the hotel," the manager said.

"Seymour, I'm very happy at the Last Frontier," Lee answered. "They treat me nice. They gave me my first break in Vegas when nobody wanted me. I've been there twenty-five times, and they've raised my salary to twenty-five thousand. I like it there."

"Yes, but it would be a great honor to open the hotel, Lee," Seymour argued. "It's gonna be the tallest hotel in Vegas—nine stories. They're calling it 'New High in the Sky.' "

"Seymour, what could I tell Maxine Lewis and all those wonderful people at the Frontier? I've got an idea. Tell the Riviera people I want fifty thousand. They'll never pay it."

Seymour returned to the other table and came back to say, "They accept."

Before I left the Liberace house, he showed me some of the Christmas presents from fans: a large statue of a naked Mercury, an antique silver candelabra, an ancient clock. "These are from people I don't even know!" he said. "Isn't it wonderful!"

Liberace figured he needed something spectacular for his record-breaking salary at the Riviera (the previous highs had been $35,000 per week for Judy Garland and Marlene Dietrich). When he walked on-stage on opening night, he was wearing a white silk lamé tuxedo that he had commissioned from Christian Dior. He returned for the second half of the show in a jacket that drew gasps from the audience. It was a black tuxedo jacket studded with tiny sequins—1,328,000 of them, his press agent informed reporters. Most of the reviewers wrote as much about his wardrobe as the performance, confirming Liberace's belief that he had come across something highly exploitable.

The next milestone in his career was what he had forever dreamed of—his own movie.

A Warner Bros. executive who later denied it managed to persuade the studio boss, Jack Warner, to travel to San Francisco to witness the hottest thing in show business. Warner flew northward, surrounded by his most important aides, including son-in-law William Orr, to witness a performance of Liberace at the cavernous Cow Palace. Tipped off about the important guests in the audience, Liberace performed magnificently, drawing on every crowd-pleasing trick in his repertoire.

"You got it, kid," Warner told him afterward. "If you can do on the screen what you did on that stage, we're both going to have a gold mine."

Not all of Liberace's associates shared Warner's enthusiasm. Lee's television director, Duke Goldstone, thought it was a chancy and possibly ruinous endeavor. He persuaded Lee to consult with his uncle, Phil Goldstone, an industry sage who had weathered decades of change in Hollywood.

"You're the hottest personality in the country right now," Phil Goldstone expounded. "I've seen others like you—Red Grange and Babe Ruth—who tried to transfer their fame to movies. It didn't work."

"But they were athletes," Liberace protested. "I'm an entertainer."

"Right, and there's no one better. But you're not an actor."

Liberace's Magic of Believing would not allow himself to accept such negativism. But one other member of the Liberace team was concerned enough about the venture to consult Phil Goldstone: John Jacobs.

"I can see that your client will not be dissuaded from making a movie," said Goldstone. "Then you should take out some insurance against disaster."

"How can we do that?" Jacobs asked.

"Go to Jack Warner and tell him Liberace has been working for peanuts on his television show with a percentage of the profits—but he hasn't seen any. Tell him instead of giving you a big piece of the net, you want three hundred thousand up front against a smaller cut."

Jacobs followed his advice. After lengthy negotiations between Jacobs and the Warner Bros. lawyers, a contract was concluded for Liberace to star in a movie, with options for more. Warner assigned his most prestigious producer, Henry Blanke, to prepare the project. The German-born Blanke had been with the studio for twenty years, producing such films as *The Petrified Forest, The Life of Emile Zola, The Adventures of Robin Hood, The Maltese Falcon,* and *The Treasure of the Sierra Madre.*

Warner Bros., like all studios in the 1950s, was in an economic slump and had been exploring its vaults for old movies that could be refurbished. Blanke reached back and found *The Man Who Played God,* a tearjerker that had starred George Arliss in a 1922 silent version and a 1932 talkie. Based on a Jules Eckert Goodman play, the story concerned Montgomery Royale, a concert pianist until his hearing is ruined by an anarchist's bomb. The beautiful young woman he loves is willing to spend her life with him, but he sacrifices her to the arms of another man. The pianist spends his day studying strangers in the park with binoculars and lip-reading, then does good deeds for those in trouble. Into his life comes another young woman—in the 1932 version, Bette Davis, chosen for the role by Arliss himself—and she and his good deeds contribute to a happy ending.

Perfect, thought Blanke: concert pianist, deafness, good deeds, love interest, happy ending. Just what was needed to please Liberace's greatest fans, middle-aged women. And, it was hoped, they would bring the rest of their families as well.

Blanke assigned a studio contract writer, Irving Wallace, to prepare a script. Wallace had been a foreign correspondent and magazine writer before turning to fiction and movie scripts. He lunched with Liberace at the piano-pool house.

"What I'd like to see in the script," suggested Liberace, "is more emphasis on the romance with the two women. I'd like that."

The script was written and approved by Warner and Blanke, and production was scheduled to begin in May 1955. The director was Gordon Douglas, a tough-talking film veteran who had started with Laurel and Hardy features and had ground out *The Devil with Hitler, Zombies on Broadway, Dick Tracy vs. Cueball,* and *First Yank in Tokyo.* At Warner Bros. he had earned a reputation for delivering workmanlike movies on-budget and on-schedule with such stars as Errol Flynn, Alan Ladd, Frank Sinatra, and James Cagney.

The blunt director and his new star formed a surprising rapport. Douglas realized that Liberace would require extra rehearsal time because of his newness to acting. But little rehearsal was required for the piano sequences, of which there were many. Despite the modest budget of $1.1 million, the supporting cast was good: Dorothy Malone and Joanne Dru for the love interest, plus William Demarest, Alex Nicol, Lori Nelson, Lurene Tuttle, and young Richard Eyer.

Sincerely Yours, as it was called, was a co-production of Liberace's International Artists, Limited, and Warner Bros. Liberace moved in his own team: John Jacobs and Seymour Heller received credit as associate producers, George Liberace as music adviser, and Gordon Robinson as music arranger. Liberace collaborated with Paul Francis Webster to write a title song.

The plot was unabashed corn. As the distinguished pianist Anthony Warrin, Liberace finds himself with encroaching deafness. He asks his socialite fiancée, Dorothy Malone, to give him time alone "to think things out." His secretary, Joanne Dru, who secretly adores him, encourages him to learn how to read lips, and he uses his new knowledge to spy on people from his apartment overlooking Central Park. He brings happiness to a crippled boy, Richard Eyer, who wants to play football, and a mother, Lurene Tuttle, whose daughter is ashamed of her.

The ending is neatly managed. Malone finds love with another man. Liberace realizes Dru is the one he should marry, and he undergoes dangerous surgery to restore his hearing. The finale comes at Carnegie Hall, where he is once again playing in concert. Watching him are all the figures in his life: the socialite and her new husband, the loving secretary, the cured boy, the happy mother. He plays everything from Tchaikovsky's First Piano Concerto to the Notre Dame Victory March, and the mother leads one and all in a chorus of "When Irish Eyes Are Smiling." The blessedly happy Liberace does an off-to-Buffalo to get offstage.

When I talked with Liberace on the set of *Sincerely Yours,* he was as exuberant as I had ever seen him. He had asked Irving Wallace to provide love scenes, and the script called for several kisses with his co-stars. "I did a kiss with Dorothy Malone, and we had to hold it while the camera panned over to Joanne Dru and William Demarest," he said boyishly. "The camera panned back to Dorothy and me, still kissing." He added that Miss Dru had been undergoing massage for an out-of-joint bone in her neck, "and when I grabbed her and kissed her, I heard a strange noise—you can hear it on the sound track. Her neck snapped back into joint."

He continued: "I have a close-up that may be the biggest in history. It's the scene where I realize I am going deaf. Nothing but my eye and ear on the screen!"

The Liberace presence was visible at the Warner Bros. studios. Parked outside the stage was the long white limousine, the one with leather seats that looked like piano keys. Wrapped in a red silk dressing gown, Lee was entertaining his sister, Angie, in his oversize dressing room. "It was Judy Garland's," he said proudly. "It was painted pink, but I had it done over in my favorite colors." Black, white and shades of gray, just like the Sherman Oaks house.

Gordon Douglas, usually a sardonic, somewhat cynical man, had praise for his pianist star. "His performance is remarkable," said the director. "He did a crying scene the other day that will knock people off their seats."

Jack Warner was equally enthusiastic with his staff. "We got a winner here, boys," he insisted. He was so confident that he invited Samuel Goldwyn to the first preview.

"Jack, that's a beautiful picture," Goldwyn enthused. "If you want to sell it, I'll pay you three million dollars."

"No chance," replied Warner. "This is gonna be one of the biggest grossers Warner Bros. ever had. This guy is better than Jolson."

The sagacity of the film pioneers seemed to be confirmed by the trade reviews. The *Hollywood Reporter* trumpeted: "*Sincerely Yours* Headed for Bonanza at Box Office." The review by Jack Moffitt began:

"This picture will probably make a grand piano full of money for Warner Bros. It is corny in the same sense that *The Jolson Story* was corny. It's filled with the corn that is the box-office staff of life."

The reviewer declared that Liberace gave "a remarkably good performance," holding down "that old smile that on TV sometimes makes him seem to be matching ivory with the piano." In the deafness scenes, Moffit said, "to my utter amazement, I found him making me gulpy."

The trade reviewers agreed that *Sincerely Yours* seemed deftly calculated to satisfy the Liberace fans. Thirty-one piano numbers, encompassing every kind of music, had been included. Howard Shoup designed brocaded tail coats and sequined tuxedos for Liberace to wear in concert; director Douglas was careful to have him play emotional scenes in sports clothes. For the mothers who loved Liberace, the Lurene Tuttle role offered enough to satisfy their maternal instincts.

The Los Angeles reviewers were coolly complimentary. Philip K. Scheuer in the *Times* remarked of Liberace: "I was prepared to blush for him, but almost never had to." Liberace "appears to have mastered the rudiments of acting; i.e. when you say that, don't smile."

Ruth Waterbury in the *Examiner* commented that the film "is so overboard with sentiment, with everybody in it being just gooder than gold, that somebody like Jack the Ripper would have seemed like a living doll just coming into it. Nevertheless, the genuine warmth of Liberace's personality radiates from it, and his really superb showmanship frequently rocks you. . . ."

The Hollywood premiere was held at the Pantages Theater on November 22, 1955, with Liberace himself and Art Linkletter greeting all the arriving celebrities on television. Crowds lined up at the theaters the following day, many of them mature women who rarely attended movies anymore. They filled the seats the following day as well. Then they stopped coming.

The Warner Bros. film sellers were puzzled. Jack Warner was alarmed. Liberace was stunned. All his sunny optimism had been crushed by a plummeting box office. But he quickly recovered, and he offered explanations why *Sincerely Yours* wasn't drawing customers: "I think first-run admissions are too high. How many families can afford a dollar and a quarter each at the box office? . . . the initial ads made the picture look like a blown-up version of my TV show. . . . My movie has even been compared to *Going My Way, Magnificent Obsession,* and *The Jolson Story.* It's been said that it is worthy of some Academy consideration."

One cynical columnist didn't think so. He cracked: "You know what Liberace's looking for with those binoculars in *Sincerely Yours?* The audience."

Nonetheless, Liberace maintained that Jack Warner was already planning a second vehicle for him, perhaps the life of Franz Schubert.

Wise old Billy Wilkerson, who operated *Hollywood Reporter,* contemplated in his Tradeviews column why fans rushed to Liberace concerts and ran away from his movie. His conclusion: "There is good foundation for thinking that customers won't pay to see a star they can get for nothing on TV."

Because of its $1.1-million cost, *Sincerely Yours* lost no money for Warner Bros. As Liberace had predicted, the film played better in Europe, especially in countries where they could understand the music but not the dialogue.

The London critics were inhospitable to the wavy-haired piano player from America. "He gave me the mental burps," said the *Daily Herald's* man. "He has a voice like a dormouse with adenoids." The *Daily Sketch* commented on Liberace's "two basic expressions—one of ineffable nobility, the other of tear-dripping joy."

Except for a brief portrayal of a casket salesman in Tony Richardson's 1965 *The Loved One* and a guest appearance in an MGM B musical, *When the Boys Meet the Girls* the same year, Liberace's film career was over.

"Nobody loves me but the people," Liberace often commented in reply to criticism, and he returned to the people as an elixir for the hurt caused by *Sincerely Yours.* A concert tour repolished his self-esteem. Unlike motion pictures, where he was subject to the control of other talents, he was alone and in complete command on a concert stage. He could handle any eventuality.

In San Diego, Liberace was fifteen minutes into a concert, only to sense the crowd becoming restless. Clapping in unison broke out in the balcony, and he realized what had happened: the sound system had failed. When it was repaired, he asked the audience: "Shall I start all over again?" The delighted audience roared approval, and from then on, he could do no wrong.

In Cleveland, he went through his customary routine of asking for requests. A heckler in the balcony yelled, "Take a slow boat to China!" Liberace was momentarily taken aback, then he sat down to the piano and improvised an intricate arrangement of "Slow Boat to China," interweaving the Frank Loesser melody with Chinese overtones. He finished with a smile in the direction of the heckler, and the crowd applauded in appreciation.

In the summer of 1955, Liberace decided to take his family and close associates on a grand tour of Europe. The climax of the trip would be Rome, where Lee had planned to give Mom the thrill of her lifetime: meeting the Pope. The Catholic archbishop in Los Angeles had provided a letter requesting a private audience.

When the party arrived in Rome, the Vatican said that because of the failing health of Pius XII, private audiences had been eliminated. But the Liberaces were welcomed to join the mass audience to be held at St. Peter's. So Lee, Mom, George, and their party, along with eight thousand others, received the benediction of the Pope from afar.

The time arrived to leave Rome, and all the Liberace luggage was stacked in the lobby of the Excelsior Hotel. A letter bearing the papal seal arrived for Liberace. It contained an invitation for a private audience with Pius XII at his summer residence at Castel Gondolfo. "To hell with the reservations," Lee declared. "You don't turn down the Pope!"

The Liberace party was granted twenty-two minutes with the Pope, and toward the end, Lee said, "We are thrilled to have this chance to meet you, Your Holiness. I'm curious as to why we were granted the opportunity."

As Liberace later told the story: "The Pope said that his private monsignor secretary happened to have been in the audience of my TV show the time we asked the nun to kneel while I played 'Ave Maria.' And the secretary told the Pope: 'Ya gotta meet this guy.'"

The "Liberace" television show died in 1956 after 117 performances. The cause of death: greed.

The series had been one of the most profitable ventures in the brief history of television. Produced for $10,000, it had circulated more widely than any other program in television. It was a money machine for Guild Films, and producing more programs seemed a needless expense. "We've got maximum saturation anyway," reasoned Reub Kaufman. "We'll get another star and do the same thing we did with Liberace." His candidate: Florian Zabach, a handsome violinist who combined pop and classic in the Liberace manner.

Duke Goldstone agreed to direct the new series, but he was dubious about its changes. "Florian is a great musician, but he has no soul," he argued. "Liberace is not a great musician but he *has* soul. That's the difference in the two artists." His analysis proved correct. "The Florian Zabach Show" had a brief run.

"The show has reached its fulfillment," Liberace remarked, nodding once more toward the bank. He had been paid 20 percent of the profits on the first run, his percentage ranging up to 80 on the fifth run. His income on the series amounted to $7 million in the first two years.

He was full of plans for the future. He was returning to the Riviera in Las Vegas with his biggest show ever. He called it "Liberace Takes a Bridey," a reference to the best-selling book of the day, *The Search for Bridey Murphy.* The reincarnation theme would be explored, with Bela Lugosi as a hypnotist reverting Liberace to earlier lives. "I sing, dance, do comedy, ballet, have ten changes and work in everything from tails to tights," he announced. He planned to take the show to Broadway for four weeks, appear with George in *The Great Waltz* in Dallas, then play concerts in England for the first time.

"My career is just beginning," he vowed.

Liberace continued making news. After appearing on "The Ed Sullivan Show" to promote *Sincerely Yours,* he complained about lack of rehearsal time and the lack of ample plugs for the movie by the television host. Sullivan responded with a burst of Irish temper.

"It's absolutely enraging," said Sullivan. "What's biting this guy is the flop of his picture. How he can blame it on us, I haven't the slightest conception. We have always been good friends, and I paid him a good salary." He detailed his efforts in persuading Risë Stevens to sing "Cement Mixer (Put-ti Put-ti)" with Liberace, hiring George Liberace and other musicians, sending a Baldwin piano to Liberace's Ambassador Hotel suite for practice while he was ill. Liberace was afforded so much rehearsal, said Sullivan, that another guest on the show, Phil Silvers, asked: "What do I have to do to get rehearsal time—play the piano?"

Sullivan concluded: "Liberace won't be on our show again."

A different kind of confrontation occurred in Las Vegas. One night during Liberace's engagement at the Riviera, Elvis Presley appeared in the audience. Liberace sent a message that he would be happy to meet with the new musical sensation in his dressing room.

The Riviera press agent hurriedly notified reporters and photographers, and they were present to record the meeting of the two musical idols. "Elvis, why don't you and Lee change jackets?" suggested the press agent. Elvis donned the gold-sequined tuxedo jacket, and Liberace put on Elvis's sports jacket. The cameras clicked.

The press agent had borrowed a guitar from a member of the band, and he handed it to Liberace, saying, "How about another switch? You play guitar, and Elvis can play piano." The photographers shot furiously as Liberace and Elvis conducted a jam session for twenty minutes, playing "Hound Dog" and "I'll Be Seeing You," and other songs associated with each of them.

Liberace provided the moral for reporters: "Elvis and I may be characters—me with my gold jackets and him with his sideburns—but we can afford to be."

Chapter 8

*AN INNOCENT ABROAD; OR, WHY AREN'T THE
BRITISH POLITE ANYMORE?*

The European trip of early autumn 1956, planned with the greatest care, was designed to enhance Liberace's international reputation and to create publicity to shore up his popularity back home. The eventuality proved anew that Liberace and his handlers, at this stage in his career, were unable to maintain control of happenings.

During the planning stage, a press agent was dispatched from Hollywood to London to work out details of the trip in conjunction with British counterparts. The auguries seemed favorable, since Liberace had become something of a fad, especially with mature women but also with teenage girls, because of his television show, *Sincerely Yours,* and his record albums.

The Liberace troupe, which included Mom, George, and Seymour Heller, sailed on the *Queen Mary* from New York in early September 1956. On the second day of the voyage, Liberace was walking around the deck when he encountered a slim figure with a bored, instantly recognizable face.

"Liberace, I believe," said Noel Coward.

Amazed to be recognized by such an eminence, Liberace wondered if he would next be skewered by the famed Coward wit. The mandarinlike smile gave no hint.

"I've seen your act," Coward continued, adding another pause to allow Liberace to wonder what was coming next. After a long beat, the conclusion: "You do what you do—*very* well."

The Liberace party arrived in Southhampton on September 25, 1956, and was greeted by members of the press and a crowd of cheering fans. The press and some of the fans climbed aboard a train called the Liberace Special, which had been chartered for $2,000. Liberace walked through the cars on the journey to London, chatting amiably with everyone.

The arrival at Waterloo Station was more than the advance men had bargained for. The crowd, a curious mixture of motherly types and girls in short skirts and bobby socks, surged forward to gain a view of Liberace. He remained cool, observing, "I understand you've had a rather unpleasant summer. Perhaps we can bring a little sunshine to England."

The crowd shouted approval. "Isn't he lovely?" shrieked a girl who was clutching a bouquet of fake flowers. There was a dissenting vote in the crowd. A handful of men were booing. They held signs proclaiming, "We Hate Liberace—Charlie Kunz Forever!" Kunz was a fiftyish pianist who had been playing jazz for English audiences since the 1920s.

The Waterloo station foreman told a reporter that the Liberace reception was akin to that accorded royalty. The difference was that British Railways did not provide a red carpet. Instead, Liberace walked on a carpet of paper rose petals.

Fifty police struggled vainly to control the crowd, and several formed a flying wedge to escort Liberace and his party to a pair of Daimlers, the car favored by the royal family. Chauffeurs and footmen bowed as Liberace approached. The Daimlers departed amid great cheers.

Liberace received a different kind of reception at his first press conference. A few of the reporters tried to be objective, but the others questioned him as if he were the latest serial murderer.

"Do you have a normal sex life?" a reporter demanded.

"Yes," Liberace responded blandly. "Do you?"

The reporters bore in on their quarry, hoping to trap him in absurdities. Liberace never lost his equilibrium, but that didn't stop the reporters from twisting his words to fit their purposes.

More hostility at the Royal Festival Hall. Pickets appeared outside with signs reading: "It's Alive!"; "Down with Liberace"; "Britain Will Rise Again."

The pickets were scarcely noticed by the four thousand who poured into the venerable concert hall at admission prices ranging up to 42 shillings, or $5.80. (By comparison, the incomparable Dame Myra Hess would play Beethoven the following Sunday at a top price of 15 shillings, or $2.10.) The hall manager said ticket demand for Liberace could have filled the place three times over.

When Liberace came onstage in his gold jacket, the audience reacted in a manner seldom seen in Britain, and certainly not in the Royal Festival Hall. Screams and yells as he waved hello. Shrieks and shouts at every sly remark. Thunderous cheers at the end of every selection.

Each time Liberace wore a new jacket, he inquired: "Do you wanna come up and feel it?" Girls vaulted over seats and raced down the aisles for the opportunity.

"I'm glad you like my jacket," he cracked with a line that became standard in his act: "You ought to—you paid for it."

Liberace admitted that his press notices had been less than complimentary, but he didn't want to name any of his critics—"it would just make them famous." Besides, "I love everybody." Loud, persistent cheers.

The press reaction to Liberace's performance was far different. The more polite notices assailed his "smirk and smarm act" and suggested that he should be "stoned with marshmallows." The *Times,* which rarely took notice of such populist happenings, published a review that stated:

> *The golden boy of a myriad households . . . can sing quite agreeably and can amuse with his tap dancing. He can also play the piano quite unmusically and often in deplorable taste. . . . His resourcefulness extends to variations on the conventional theme of evening dress. [His black and gold suit] looks more becoming in real life than it did on television when it appeared to be spun out of frogspawn.*

The apex of invective was produced by the notorious Cassandra (William Connor) of the racy tabloid the *Daily Mirror,* circulation 4.5 million. He wrote:

> *He is the summit of sex—the pinnacle of masculine, feminine, and neuter. Everything that he, she, and it can ever want.*
>
> *I spoke to sad but kindly men on this newspaper who have met every celebrity coming from America for the past 30 years. They say that this deadly, winking, sniggering, snuggling, chromium-plated, scent-impregnated, luminous, quivering, giggling, fruit-flavored, mincing, ice-covered heap of mother love has had the biggest reception and impact on London since Charlie Chaplin arrived at the same station, Waterloo, on September 12, 1921.*

This appalling man—and I use the word appalling in no other than its true sense of terrifying—has hit this country in a way that is as violent as Churchill receiving the cheers on V-E Day.

He reeks with emetic language that can only make grown men long for a quiet corner, an aspidistra, a handkerchief, and the old heave-ho. Without doubt, he is the biggest sentimental vomit of all time. Slobbering over his mother, winking at his brother, and counting the cash at every second, this superb piece of calculating candy-floss has an answer for every situation.

Cassandra then cited examples of Liberace's comments on religion, mother love, world peace, and money and added:

Nobody since Aimee Semple McPherson has purveyed a bigger, richer and more varied slag heap of lilac-covered hokum. Nobody anywhere made so much money out of high-speed piano play with ghost of Chopin gibbering at every note.

There must be something wrong with us that our teenagers longing for sex and our middle-aged matrons fed up with sex alike should fall for such a sugary mountain of jingling claptrap wrapped up in such a preposterous clown.

By the time he reached Paris for a sightseeing tour, Liberace had grown incensed over the British attacks, particularly Cassandra's. He was concerned about Mom, who had brooded over the articles so much that she had made herself ill. She had remained in London under a doctor's care.

Reporters and photographers greeted Liberace as he arrived at the Paris airport. He poured out his anger against the "degenerate attacks" in London that had implied he was an "unmanly man."

"If my mother's health doesn't improve, I'm certainly going to do something about it," Liberace warned, adding that he had already consulted his Hollywood attorney, John Jacobs, on the matter.

"I just don't understand how they can write things like that," he continued. "Just look at the number of women fans I have. They can't be all wrong. . . . People should write news that's fit to print, things they would want their children to read. . . . I guess everyone has to expect a number of nonbelievers, and I suppose that's why they shot Lincoln."

As he ended the press conference, Liberace suffered another indignity. A wasp flew into the room and stung him on the right thumb. Liberace insisted on being taken to the airport dispensary. "My thumb doesn't move!" he told the doctor in a panic. The doctor assured him it would.

Liberace continued his plaint about the London press in an interview with a young columnist for the *Herald-Tribune*, Art Buchwald.

"I must admit I was shocked by the vulgarity and underlying degenerate tone of 25 percent of the British newspaper stories," Liberace said. "My mother, a sweet, simple person, was exposed to those articles and has needed medical attention ever since. Mom, who had arrived in England with such a light heart, told me: 'I should have stayed at home. Then they wouldn't have said all these terrible things about you.' "

Buchwald observed that Philip Wylie, the inventor of "Momism," had also attacked Liberace.

"Am I bitter?" Liberace said. "I am never bitter about things that are written about me. But I must admit that I do become bitter when my love for my mother is described as any kind of ism, whether it's Communism, Fascism, or Momism."

Liberace's morale was boosted by his Sunday Night at the Palladium performance, in which all of his crowd-pleasing skills worked to perfection. As the Liberace party left the theater, more than a thousand fans swept over them. George disappeared in a tide of humanity. Women screamed, others fainted, hysteria everywhere. Bobbies rushed in on foot, some on horseback, to control the mob. Liberace enjoyed himself immensely.

But in Manchester it was a different story. Pickets appeared outside the theater with such signs as "Send the Fairy Back to the States" and "We Want He-Men, Not Momma's Boys." In Sheffield, Teddy Boys, the new breed of ruffian rebels, stood in the back of the auditorium and shouted: "Queer, go home!" and "We don't want Yankee fairies!" Liberace was shaken. He had faced all kinds of hecklers in his saloon-playing days, but nothing like this. He had to summon all of his powers as an entertainer to make it through the performance.

The Cassandra article had inspired a flood of Liberace jokes in the London cabarets and some were printed in the gossip columns. A song that appeared in a stage revue and was repeated on television contained the lyric:

> *My fan mail is really tremendous,*
> *It's growing so fast my head whirls;*
> *I get more and more,*
> *They propose by the score—*
> *And at least one or two are from girls.*

Something had to be done, he realized. The demonstrations would increase, and they would spread back to the United States, making it impossible for him to continue entertaining. He telephoned John Jacobs in Hollywood: "Let's sue the bastard."

On October 22, 1956, the British High Court issued a writ on behalf of Liberace against the *Daily Mirror* and William Connor on a charge of libel.

"It was just too much for any man to stomach," Liberace told reporters. "If I didn't have the contract dates in the immediate future and my appearances didn't depend on my hands, I would knock Cassandra's teeth down his throat. And I ain't kidding."

Mom called them "hillbillies."

That was her euphemism for the young men who hung around the Sherman Oaks house, sometimes in large numbers. They sat around the swimming pool in their bikinis, of which Mom did not approve. They drank her son's liquor. They stayed until late at night, playing loud music and laughing hysterically at their own jokes. Often Lee joined them. When he was on the road, they came and made themselves at home. Sometimes Mom called John Jacobs to complain, and he summoned the police to roust them.

"I don't like those hillbillies," Mom complained. "I wish you could get rid of them."

"Oh, Mom, they're harmless," Lee answered. "They amuse me, and they relax me. It's the only time I can just be myself."

That much was true. Now in his mid-thirties, Lee for the first time in his life was able to fraternize openly with other homosexuals. He had never dared before. Exposure would destroy his career. Now he was rich enough to take chances, and the sense of danger appealed to him.

His managers and publicists had attempted to counteract the recurring slurs against Liberace's masculinity. From the outset, Gabbe, Lutz and Heller eliminated from his biography references to the star's love of sewing and other domestic pursuits. Efforts were made to encourage him to take up horseback riding, to no avail. After the Joanne Rio fiasco, Liberace had a purported romance with Frances Goodrich, a pretty young heiress to a California citrus fortune. He maintained that the romance ended when her family wanted him to give up the piano and manage their orange ranches.

Next came Sonja Henie. They met at a Ciro's party, and Lee invited her to the wedding of his sister, Angie, who was taking a second husband. Sonja not only came, she sent a pair of ice sculptures to the reception, one of her skating, the other of Lee at a piano. Lee visited her huge Bel-Air house, where they sipped champagne and watched her old movies, much like William Holden and Gloria Swanson in *Sunset Boulevard*. Their dating was duly noted by the gossip columnists, but their careers kept them apart. The "romance" faded, and Sonja later married her third husband, a Norwegian multimillionaire.

In England and everywhere he went, Liberace repeatedly stressed in public that he was not a homosexual. Sometimes he became demonstrative about it. After a concert in his hometown of Milwaukee, he was approached backstage by an effeminate man. "We're so proud that you are one of us," the stranger gushed. Liberace's eyes hardened. He shoved the man away from him and exclaimed, "I am not a homosexual!"

Yet evidence continued to mount, and the biggest blow came from a disreputable rag called *Confidential*.

Nothing had scared Hollywood so much in years. Not since the nation's moralists poured their wrath down onto the wicked city of the 1920s had the movie industry's leaders been in such panic. All this because of a monthly magazine with lurid headlines printed on cheap newsprint and ads for men's potency pills and mail-order diamond rings.

Confidential was the brainchild of Robert Harrison, a small-time New York publisher who understood the public's thirst for the inside dope about Hollywood celebrities—the *real* inside. *Confidential* seemed to have sprung up overnight into a full-sized monster. It appeared in groceries and on newsstands everywhere with catchy headlines about the stars and their sexual/alcoholic/narcotic misadventures. The reaction of the public was: "There must be truth in those stories or the magazine would be run out of business."

In most cases, there was a degree of truth, enough to discourage litigation. As *Confidential* boomed—its five-million circulation was the largest of any monthly—it could afford to take chances on lawsuits. It could also support a small army of reporters and private detectives and pay large fees for scandalous information. Hospital nurses, hookers, discharged servants, out-of-work publicists turned informers for *Confidential.* So did legitimate reporters, who risked loss of their jobs to accept a big check for stories they couldn't print. One gossip columnist was said to have been trapped in a homosexual liaison; in return for *Confidential*'s suppression of the story, he passed along tidbits to the magazine.

"Everyone in Hollywood reads *Confidential,* " the sardonic Humphrey Bogart remarked. "They all deny it. They say the cook brought it into the house."

Most people in the film community were not as amused as Bogart. Careers were being hurt by the allegations, and the studio bosses feared another national backlash, such as the one in the 1920s.

The July 1957 issue of *Confidential* offered such cover lines as: "Anthony Quinn—Caught with a Gal in a Powder Room!"; "When Nancy Kelly Learned Her Love Scenes in a Car"; "Eartha Kitt and the Man Who Sat There—All Night!" The biggest display was given to a grinning photograph of Liberace under which was printed: "Exclusive! Why Liberace's Theme Song Should Be 'Mad about the Boy'!"

The story was written in *Confidential*'s titillating style, stretching what seemed to be minor events into episodes worthy of a Henry Fielding novel. Here is the story, according to the author, who called himself Horton Streete:

A handsome young press agent was dispatched from New York to Akron, Ohio, to hype a Fourth of July extravaganza that would feature stock car races, fireworks, and—Liberace. Ticket sales had been languishing, and the press agent organized an airport extravaganza to greet Liberace on his July 3 arrival.

All went well, the story continued, until the press agent was alone with Liberace in his suite at the Sheraton-Mayflower Hotel. "Whatever you want I'm your boy," said the young man. After they had a drink together, he found Liberace sitting on his lap! A wrestling match ensued.

"Once during the scuffle, the press agent let out a yelp of pain, and no wonder. . . . For Luscious Libby, it was strictly no-holds-barred. Finally with a combination of wristlock and flying mare, the publicity man wrenched loose from his host's embrace and fled from the suite, leaving Liberace sprawled on the floor."

End of story? Not yet. Because of litigation concerning the show, the press agent later had to fly to California to obtain Liberace's signature. Liberace insisted on taking the emissary to dinner at Trader Vic's and later made advances in his car, the one with the piano-key upholstery.

Liberace wouldn't sign the releases, and the press agent followed him to Dallas, where the star was appearing in *The Great Waltz*. The Akron incident was replayed in the Dallas suite: "The floor show reached its climax when Dimples, by sheer weight, pinned his victim to the mat and mewed in his face: 'Gee, you're cute when you're mad.' " The match ended when the press agent's friend, instructed beforehand, burst into the suite like "the U.S. Cavalry riding to the rescue in the nick of time." The press agent's lesson: "hit the road when a client tries to turn public relations into private relations."

All the Liberace advisers agreed that the scurrilous article, coming in the wake of the Cassandra attack, had to be answered—immediately. John Jacobs filed suit against *Confidential*, Robert Harrison, Horton Streete, a publishing house and distributor, a research company, plus Doe corporations and individuals, for $25 million in libel damages because of the article "Why Liberace's Theme Song Should Be 'Mad about the Boy.'"

The complaint termed the article "malicious, false, libelous, defamatory, degrading, and unprivileged" and claimed it had subjected Liberace and his family to "public scandal, embarrassment, disgrace, contempt, and ridicule." Press reports of the suit did not disclose the nature of the article, since editors considered it unsuitable for family newspapers; besides, repeating a libel might itself be grounds for a damage suit.

Liberace told his troubles with *Confidential* to a Los Angeles County grand jury investigating charges of criminal libel against the magazine. Also testifying was Maureen O'Hara, whose Irish temper had been inflamed by a *Confidential* article alleging she had a romp with a Mexican boyfriend in the back seats of Grauman's Chinese theater. She had also sued the magazine for libel.

The grand jury indicted *Confidential*, Harrison, and others on grounds of criminal libel. This was the result of pressure by studio bosses on California politicians to rid the state's most celebrated industry of an evil that threatened to destroy it. For two long months I reported the trial as one Hollywood figure after another took the witness stand to testify how *Confidential*'s outrageous lies had caused them immense grief. The trial ended in a fourteen-day jury deadlock, but the issue was resolved when Harrison agreed to stop delving into movie stars' private lives in *Confidential*.

Liberace persisted in his libel suit and proved that he was not in Dallas at the time the alleged incident took place. *Confidential* finally settled by paying him $40,000. Liberace said that after his legal costs were paid he would donate the remainder to charity.

The specter of the Cassandra case hung over Liberace's head for almost three years, requiring all the teachings of Claude M. Bristol to prevent it from depressing his spirit. When the time of the libel trial finally arrived in June 1959, Liberace had psyched himself into believing that his suit amounted to a crusade against the malicious wrongdoing of the irresponsible press. Also, he was convinced, his vindication would silence the horrid innuendos that followed him everywhere.

His entrance on opening day of the trial was as shrewdly calculated as any of his stage appearances. He arrived at the Queen's Bench Division Court in London alone and unattended, wearing a conservatively tailored blue suit, white shirt, and plain tie. The court, presided over by Justice Sir Cyril Salmon, was jammed with reporters of the British and American press, middle-aged women fans of Liberace, and other spectators. Many had waited three hours for seats inside the courtroom. The judge's wife, Lady Salmon, watched attentively from a position in the distinguished visitors' section.

Representing the plaintiff was a veteran of the London courts, Gilbert Beyfus. He began by observing that Cassandra—the Trojan princess whose warnings of misfortune were disbelieved—was a curious and somewhat somber nom de plume for William Connor, albeit an appropriate one.

Beyfus traced the life and career of Liberace, beginning with his birth to a French horn player and a former concert pianist (*sic*). He outlined the family's hard Depression times and told of the boy's devotion to his mother, who had nursed him through life-threatening pneumonia and had saved his poisoned finger from amputation. Although his father, disillusioned by the failure of his own musical career, wanted Walter to become an undertaker, the boy persisted with his piano studies. The long years of patient work paid off and by 1951 he was earning $50,000 a year. Then came television and the fateful engagement at the Hollywood Bowl when he wore the white tails. The fancy wardrobe followed.

"Before we jeer at the American public for enjoying this added glamour," cautioned Beyfus, "remember that less than 150 years ago in the Regency period men dressed up and one of the greatest arts was that of tying a necktie.

"In these days of somewhat drab and dreary male clothing, remember the guards at Buckingham Palace, the horse guards in Whitehall, the Beefeaters at the Tower, the uniforms of the Privy Councillors, Knights of the Garter, and Peers of the Realm. Look at the hunt ball, when tough hunting men prance around in pink coats with silk lapels of different colors. Some add dignity, some add glamour.

"Look at me, My Lord and my learned friends, dressed in accordance with old traditions. We do not dress like this in ordinary daily life, nor does Liberace."

Beyfus went on to recount Liberace's arrival in England, the pickets with signs like "We Hate Liberace—Charlie Kunz Forever" (much laughter in the courtroom), then he read the screed by Cassandra. He concluded by saying that he did not intend to paint William Connor as a buffoon. No, he saw Connor as "a literary assassin who dips his pen in vitriol, hired by this sensational newspaper to murder reputations and hand out sensational articles on which its circulation is built."

"I call Mr. Liberace to the stand." The courtroom stirred with anticipation as the stern-faced Liberace made his way to the witness box. Under his counsel's prompting, he recounted the meeting with Paderewski, the introduction of the candelabra, the gaudy clothes.

When other entertainers copied his garb, he testified, "that was flattering but it meant that, being considered a top man, I had to dress better than the others that were copying me. One was a young man named Elvis Presley who was coming up at the time."

He added that when he returned to Las Vegas with his gold lamé jacket, he was told: "That's old stuff. You wore it last year. You've got to get something new." So he devised a black tail-suit with diamond-studded buttons worth $10,000.

Q. When you came to England in 1956, had you reached the summit of your career in the United States?

A. It is presumed by many that I had.

Q. How did the Cassandra article affect you?

A. I was deeply shocked, and my only thought at the time was that it would certainly have to be kept from my mother. I felt this so strongly because my mother has a hypertensive heart condition. Further, I know she is extremely proud of her children, perhaps a bit more proud of me. . . . It was brought to her attention by someone. She immediately became very ill and was attended by a physician. It was decided by everyone concerned with her welfare that she leave the country.

Q. Are you a homosexual?

A. No, sir.

The defense counsel, Gerald Gardiner, rose to protest: "There is no suggestion and never has been anything of the kind." Beyfus replied: "The defense is that the comment is fair." He continued with the witness.

Q. Have you ever indulged in homosexual practices?

A. No, sir, never in my life. I am against the practice because it offends convention and it offends society.

Salvatore Liberace and Frances Zuchowski at the time of their wedding.

Wladziu and teddy bear at the age of three.

George, Angelina and Wladziu line up for a portrait.

Walter with a fellow graduate from West Milwaukee High in 1937.

Posing with brother George, on leave from the Seabees.

Liberace brothers during a happy time: Lee, Rudy, George.

Publicity photo, 1947

Liberace poses in his famed piano-shaped pool.

Hand in hand, "fiancée" Joanne Rio and Liberace attend a Helen Hayes play opening at the Huntington Hartford Theater.
(AP—Wide World Photos)

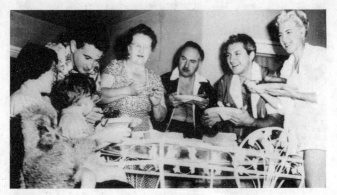

Family gathering, 1954: Mrs. Rudy Liberace with Rudy, Jr., Rudy, Mom, George, Lee, and Mrs. George Liberace. (AP—Wide World Photos)

Opening at the Riviera with Elvis, November 1956
(Las Vegas News Bureau)

The clinch with Dorothy Malone
(Warner Bros.)

*Liberace arrives in conservative attire
for the start of his libel trial in
London.* (AP—Wide World Photos)

*With newlyweds Nancy
and Ronald Reagan and
Bob Cobb, owner of the
Brown Derby restaurant.*
(The James Agency)

*Nose to nose with Jimmy
Durante* (NBC)

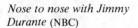

On tour with one of his custom pianos (The James Agency)

Playing the piano car (Las Vegas News Bureau)

Flying at the opening of the Las Vegas Hilton (Las Vegas News Bureau)

At the Las Vegas Hilton, 1981 (Las Vegas News Bureau)

The Las Vegas house master bedroom with "Sistine" ceiling (The James Agency)

The customized etched mirror tiled piano (The James Agency)

Before the fall: Liberace and Scott Thorson dine in a Boston restaurant in 1981. (AP—Wide World Photo)

Liberace told of the shouts of "queer" and "fairy" at his English concerts following the Cassandra article and how they upset him as well as the audiences.

Q. Was there anything sexy about your performances at all?

A. I am not aware of it if it exists. I am almost positive that I could hardly refer to myself as a sexy performer. I have tried in all my performances to inject a note of sincerity and wholesomeness. I am fully aware of the fact that my appeal on television and personal appearances is aimed directly at the family audience.

Q. Do you ever tell what we know as dirty stories?

A. I have never been known to tell any so-called dirty stories. I have told of experiences that happened to me that might have been termed double-meaning in referring to some of my sponsors. Among them was a very famous paper company who among their products make toilet tissue. I mentioned them among my sponsors and the audience found it very funny. But the audience in no way found it offensive.

The defense counsel, Gerald Gardiner, took over on cross-examination. In response to his questions, Liberace testified that he earned $1 million from television and concerts, and had other income from records, piano instruction courses, and real estate; had more than two hundred fan clubs in the United States; received between six thousand and ten thousand fan letters a week, and twenty-seven thousand Valentines. Also an average of twelve marriage proposals each week.

Q. Including one from a lady who offered to put down $200,000?

A. Yes.

Gardiner bore in on the fact that an American publicity agent had come to England to prepare for the Liberace appearances.

Q. Is it true that you told him or his organization that you would be showered with bouquets when you landed at Southampton, and you wanted to have the pier swept immediately so the other passengers would not have to step over them?

A. No.

Q. So you never had the pier swept at all?

A. No.

Liberace admitted that at Southampton, women were screaming, sobbing, fainting, throwing themselves forward to kiss the window of his train compartment, and people lined the track en route to London to catch a glimpse of him. At Waterloo Station mounted police were required to handle the crowd. Liberace commented that he had been a controversial figure ever since he started on television. Music critics had attacked his playing, whereas he had received generally good reviews before television.

Q. I quote from an article in the *Daily Sketch* that says "even bankers behave like bobbysoxers" at your concerts. You wouldn't suggest that meant you are homosexual?

A. No, sir.

Q. Are the words "nausea" and "emetic" common in criticisms of you?

A. I would not say so.

Q. There have been articles in which these words appear?

A. If you say so, I don't doubt your word.

Q. Is Beethoven's "Moonlight Sonata" a work which takes a concert pianist twenty minutes to play?

A. Approximately seventeen minutes.

Q. On television do you play it in four minutes flat?

A. I play an excerpt of the "Moonlight Sonata" and it lasts about four minutes.

Q. Is Tchaikovsky's Piano Concerto Number One a piece in 153 pages of music?

A. Yes, sir.

Q. When you play it, you usually play the first twelve pages, the last eleven, and four bars in the middle that aren't there at all?

A. That is true, sir.

Gardiner mentioned the concert pianist Semprini, and Liberace admitted never having heard of him. When Gardiner compared Semprini's playing to Liberace's, the witness remarked, "Evidently he doesn't do it so successfully." The defense attorney seized upon this.

Q. That is a very pertinent answer. He doesn't have a fan club or bring his mother onstage, like you.

A. I can't make a comparison since I haven't seen his performance.

Under questioning, Liberace agreed that his wardrobe included sixty suits and eighty pairs of shoes. He did not recall that *Time* magazine had referred to him as "the musical momist." He admitted that a booklet, "The Liberace Story," published for the English tour, had several misquotations and added that he had never met the author.

Q. But you signed a foreword saying it was authentic in every detail?

A. That was done by my secretary.

Q. That is a deliberate imitation of your signature?

A. Yes, she does it very well. [laughter]

Q. Why does this booklet and other publicity say you were born in 1920 when you were in fact born in 1919?

A. We find it desirable to make the birth date a round figure. I borrowed the idea from Jack Benny.

Liberace conceded that it was generally part of his performance to kiss his mother. George kissed her, too. Asked about his philosophy, Liberace cited *The Magic of Believing* and told how he had written an introduction for an edition of the book. He quoted from it: "To experience *happiness,* one must express happiness. To find *love,* one must give love, etc."

Gardiner tried to make points with the English jury of ten men and two women by quoting from Liberace's interview with Edward R. Murrow on the CBS television program "Person to Person" on January 6, 1956. Liberace had commented about Princess Margaret: "I would like to meet her very much, because I think we have a lot in common. We have the same tastes in theater and music, and besides, she's pretty and she's single."

Liberace responded: "I was not referring to the Princess as a marriage prospect, I assure you, and if any such interpretation was given, I apologized for it since. I was referring to her solely on the premise that she had been known to, and been widely publicized as, having accepted the performances of Americans who have come over here to appear—Danny Kaye, Johnny Ray, and many others. Since it appeared to be a foregone conclusion that I only appealed to matronly women, it would have been very lovely and wonderful to be accepted in my performance by the lovely young Princess. There is no connection between my views on marriage and Princess Margaret."

The first day of the trial was over, and Liberace was clearly the victor. He had remained cool under hostile questioning, and he gave the appearance of being down-to-earth and not ostentatious.

The Liberace-Cassandra trial was mother's milk to the London dailies. The *Daily Telegraph* devoted six and a half columns to the testimony, and even the *Times* gave it three full columns.

Gardiner resumed his cross-examination of Liberace on the second day. The counsel quoted from London reviews of Liberace performances. *Evening News:* Liberace "delighted his fans and sickened the critics." *Daily Herald:* Liberace's "leers and dimples make me heave." *Evening News:* Liberace's smile "had a mildly emetic affect on me."

Liberace's comment: "This emetic language is new to me. No American critic has referred to me in such words. There sure seems to be an incidence of weak stomachs among critics here in England."

Gardiner brought up an interview that *Daily Mirror* movie critic Donald Zec had written about Liberace from California. Liberace claimed certain inaccuracies in the interview: "He said I got up and did a little springy walk around the piano. That would be an impossibility. I would have to go through a wall to walk around my pianos, because they are against the wall." He also denied that during the interview he had imitated a girl raising her skirt.

"I am grateful to Mr. Zec," said Liberace, "for the fact that at no time in his interview did he use the expressions 'he, she, or it' or 'masculine, feminine, or neuter' or 'fruit-flavored.' These are all expressions which in America are termed homosexual."

Gardiner seemed frustrated in his failure to destroy Liberace's aplomb, but he kept trying.

> **Q.** In the booklet "The Liberace Story" you are quoted as saying you had turned down marriage proposals because you are still looking for a girl "just like Mom." Is that correct?
>
> **A.** That's right.
>
> **Q.** The booklet says you are "the hottest personality ever to melt the TV airways." Won't you agree that you have sex appeal?
>
> **A.** No. I consider sex appeal as something possessed by Marilyn Monroe and Brigitte Bardot. I certainly do not put myself in their class. [laughter]

Q. Do you used scent or scented lotion?

A. I use after-shaving lotions and underarm deodorants.

Q. And they are scented?

A. Yes.

Q. When you come into a room at a press conference, does a noticeable odor come with you?

A. I would not say it is an odor. I would say it is a scent of good grooming, that I smell clean and fresh. I always smell clean and fresh. I have noticed the smell of the press many times. [laughter]

More seriously, Liberace declared from the witness stand that the Cassandra article had "cost me many years of my professional career by implying that I am a homosexual. . . . It has caused untold agonies and embarrassment and has made me the subject of ridicule."

Liberace's two days of testimony ended with a distinct tone of triumph. He was exuberant that night at a concert in suburban Finsbury Park, where he abandoned his drab courtroom garb for his usual onstage glitz. He stayed onstage an extra half-hour and exulted to the audience: "I've had such a marvelous time out here that I'm ashamed to take the money." He added with a wink, "But I will."

Liberace's lawyers called character witnesses to the stand—entertainers the jurors would recognize and respect. Comedienne Cicely Courtneidge declared that the Liberace performances she had seen were "pure as driven snow." Were they sexy performances? "Oh, no I couldn't say that at all."

Helen Cordet, a French-born entertainer who had been a childhood friend of Prince Philip, declared: "I have seen several of his television shows and a concert he gave at the Royal Festival Hall. There was nothing sexy or suggestive in his performances."

Entertainer Robert Monkhouse agreed: "There is nothing suggestive [in the Liberace shows], nothing improper, and nothing to stimulate the sexual appetite."

Annuncio Paolo Montovani, the mood-music maestro who had accompanied Liberace on part of the 1956 British tour, testified that Liberace was "an excellent pianist, a first-class entertainer, and a most charming person. . . . There are few who do as well as he does."

The window dressing out of the way, reporters readied themselves for the major event—testimony by Cassandra himself. William Neil Connor, a fifty-year-old battle-hardened veteran of the North African and Fleet Street wars, testified calmly and dispassionately.

Q. What did you mean when you wrote that Liberace "is the summit of sex—the pinnacle of masculine, feminine, and neuter. Everything that he, she, or it could want"?

A. I was referring to the comprehensive nature of Liberace's technique.

Q. What was your reaction to Liberace's performance?

A. I was nauseated.

Q. Why?

A. Because of the flamboyant nature of his appearance, the actual spectacle of the man, and then because of the cloying, sickening nature of what he was singing and trying to put across.

Q. Did you at any time have any intention of imputing homosexuality to Liberace?

A. None at all.

Q. You compared Liberace to Aimee Semple McPherson. Would you explain why?

A. Aimee Semple McPherson was a Los Angeles evangelist who promoted her movement with a million-dollar temple, a private radio station, and supporters dressed up like angels. Part of her technique, I suggest, has been followed by Mr. Liberace: to exploit firstly, what he gets out of it; secondly, religion; thirdly, love, affection, and friendship. I think he is prostituting those things. That was the opinion I held when I wrote the article. That is the opinion I hold now.

Connor, who termed himself an agnostic, declared, "When Mr. Liberace constantly refers to God in his performances, for which he gets money, I am revolted."

The defense lawyer asked the witness to explain some of the hyperbolic phrases he employed in his article. Connor's comments:

" 'Deadly'—He overwhelms one, he attacks the senses.

" 'Winking, sniggering, giggling and snuggling'—I had read a number of reports which contained these adjectives, and I had observed him doing these very things on television.

" 'Chromium-plated'—That, to my mind, means a bright, light-reflecting surface. In his performances he seemed to have these light-reflecting surfaces such as a completely white suit of tails, a candelabra, an enormous ring on his finger.

" 'Scent-impregnated'—The question of his scent had been mentioned in previous reports in the *Daily Mirror, Daily Express,* and *Evening Standard.*

" 'Fruit-flavored'—That was part of the impression of confectionery which Mr. Liberace conveyed to me. Over-sweetened, over-flavored, over-luscious, and just sickening."

On his second day of testimony, Connor-Cassandra remained unrepentant. Liberace's attorney, Gilbert Beyfus, was unable to shake the witness.

Q. The article in question was written, was it not, to express your detestation of Liberace?

A. Dislike. I did not detest Mr. Liberace. In his personal capacity he is entirely unknown to me, but I strongly dislike what he does on the stage, in the concert hall, and on television.

Q. Was it not intended to hold him up to hatred, contempt, and ridicule?

A. I don't know whether it was. I wrote what I thought about it. . . . I do not think any person reading the article, and believing it to be true, would consider Liberace to be a hateful person.

Q. You don't think he would be a contemptible figure in the eyes of the reader?

A. I don't know about that. I think he would be an unworthy figure. I thought the article would reduce him to his correct proportions—as a contemptible clown.

The audience, especially the women, gasped in disbelief, and a few hisses were heard. Connor continued airily, condemning an English television show in which Liberace played "Ave Maria" while a woman dressed as a nun "began to writhe in front of the figure of the Madonna."

Beyfus dwelled on Connor's use of the word "it" in his review.

Q. Was the word "it" thrown into the phrase for confusion?

A. No.

Q. It doesn't mean to suggest that the poodle sits up and the cat purrs and the budgerigar goes "tweet, tweet" when the TV is turned on and Mr. Liberace's face appears?

A. No. "It" is part of the continuity of the theme of the totalitarian appeal of Liberace which transcends anything any entertainer has done. He goes into a place like Madison Square Garden where there are 60,000 people [*sic*], and then, armed with nothing except a piano, a candelabra and possibly his mother, attracts a whole community, defying all the critics and getting everybody of every age and every sex. . . . There was no sexual implication or suggestion that he was a homosexual.

Q. You knew that the word "fruit" was slang in the United States for "homosexual"?

A. I did not. I am well acquainted with many hostile words, including those imputing homosexuality. But I did not know that "fruit" was one of them.

Beyfus next attempted to categorize the *Mirror* and its sister publication the *Sunday Pictorial* as "completely reckless" in their attempts to gain circulation. He cited a reprint of a cartoon from an American magazine in which Queen Elizabeth cautioned her small son Charles: "Stand still, Charlie! Stop fidgeting! Hold your head up! People are watching!" To which Prince Philip replied: "I say! Leave the boy alone, Liz! Stop nagging him!" This was a commentary on a real-life incident at a polo match when the Queen was overheard saying: "Charles! Sit down!"

Q. Is this not a most revolting attack upon Her Majesty the Queen?

A. I would not have published it had I been the editor of the *Sunday Pictorial.* It was ill-advised and unwise.

Connor's testimony ended, and the entertainer Jimmy Thompson took the stand. He had imitated Liberace in a revue and on television in the ditty about receiving marriage proposals by the score "and at least one or two are from girls."

"That's about as offensive as anything could be," thundered Beyfus, and Thompson replied weakly: "It was intended to reflect on the persons who make the proposals and not the persons who receive them."

Thompson was pressed for other lyrics, and he quoted: "When Mom and I wear our mink coats, oh, my, to tell us apart takes a vet." Thompson admitted, "I realize now that was offensive."

A week of the headline-making trial ended, and Justice Salmon advised the jury not to watch the television show Liberace was appearing on that Sunday. "It might convey the wrong impression in your mind," he said.

As the trial approached the end, a confident Liberace switched from Savile Row attire to something more characteristic: a bronze shantung suit, gold-buckled crocodile shoes, and piano-shaped diamond and onyx cufflinks. In its desperation, the defense brought in Peter Stephens, chief of the *Mirror*'s Paris bureau, to testify that Liberace's perfume overpowered the antiseptic used for his wasp sting.

Q. Did you ask Mr. Liberace what he was wearing?

A. Yes. He said it was American toilet water.

Q. Was there any further discussion of perfume?

A. Yes, Mr. Liberace told me he had heard they had very good perfume in Paris, and he intended to buy some.

On cross-examination, Stephens admitted that most men who visit Paris buy perfume for their wives.

Q. But you immediately assumed the worst and thought he was going to buy perfume for himself?

A. That was the impression I got.

The jury deliberated three hours and twenty-four minutes before returning to the courtroom. One of the women jurors winked at Liberace and mouthed the words "It's all right." The message was perceived by the women spectators, and a cheerful murmur spread through the courtroom.

William Neil Connor and the *Daily Mirror* were found guilty of libel for implying that Liberace was homosexual. The *Mirror* was cleared of a second charge stemming from a television listing of church sermons followed by one for a Liberace concert with the comment: "Never has the sacred been so well marshalled alongside the profane."

Women spectators squealed their approval of the libel conviction. Liberace was awarded £8,000 ($22,400) in damages, and the defendants were ordered to pay court costs of £14,000 ($39,200).

"I am delighted that my reputation has been vindicated," Liberace told reporters. He made his way through the largely feminine crowd amid shouts of "Jolly good!" and "Well done!" Back at the Savoy Hotel, he immediately telephoned Mom in California to tell her the good news.

Chapter 9

*UNDER A SHOWER OF SLINGS AND ARROWS,
LIBERACE STRIVES TO REBUILD A CAREER IN
DANGER OF EXTINCTION*

The late 1950s brought bad times for Liberace. The *Confidential* and Cassandra cases would have been enough to destroy a more fragile career. But Liberace was also suffering other personal and professional crises that threatened to crack his seemingly impenetrable armor of positivism.

One July evening in 1957, Angie drove her mother to the Liberace house in Sherman Oaks and waved good-bye. Mom tidied up around the house and accumulated trash for the garage incinerator. As she entered the garage, she saw two men in business suits, their faces hidden by black hoods with slits cut for eyes, their shoes covered with black stockings. Horrified, she turned and tried to reenter the house, losing her shoes as she ran. The intruders grabbed her on the service porch. One kicked her in the back, and she dropped to the floor.

"Kick her again," one of them said. "Then we'll have something to laugh about later." They pummeled her again and again. Just before losing consciousness, she heard a car engine starting.

Mom, who was sixty-eight, wakened forty minutes later. She struggled to her feet and reached a telephone. Realizing that Lee and George were performing that night, she called George's wife, Jane.

Lee arrived home to find police officers, reporters, and photographers swarming around the place. He was horrified to hear what had happened, but relieved that Mom was in good condition at a nearby hospital, though having suffered bruises, contusions, and a broken rib.

Liberace issued a statement: "Speaking for myself and members of our family, it is shocking that anyone could attack our mother in such a cruel, inhuman way. But rest assured, we intend to investigate this matter thoroughly. Every precaution will be taken from this moment on to protect our homes, our lives, and our American rights that entitle us to peace and security."

Police investigators could find no evidence of burglary. "It looks like a sadistic act of revenge," said a detective. "Do you have any enemies?"

"Me? Of course not!" Liberace replied. Or did he? Was someone angry because of the *Confidential* case or the Las Vegas hotel switch, someone who might want to hurt him the worst way possible: through his mother? He never found out. The case was never solved.

Even before the tragedy, Liberace had grown disenchanted with the piano-pool house. The most famous residence in the San Fernando Valley, it became a target for vandals who threw beer cans through the windows and hurled debris over the wall and into the pool. Liberace had made the mistake of remarking in an interview that fans were always welcome to say hello to him. They came by day and night, whole families arriving on his doorstep or simply appearing with their cameras beside the swimming pool.

There were other vexations associated with the Sherman Oaks house, mainly family. George and Angie were always wanting something from him. But the major problem was Rudy.

Liberace reflected in later years:

"I think I've developed a kind of strength in dealing with adversity. People sense that I can handle a problem. Like when my kid brother was living. He was an alcoholic, a strange alcoholic who used to drink on weekends. He was so good-looking—he looked like Errol Flynn— and so sweet and lovable. But when he'd get drunk, he was mean as a bastard. He'd call you names, throw the latest suit you'd bought for him on the floor and stomp on it. Mean, mean, mean. And everyone would come to me and say, 'You handle it, we can't.' "

Lee, who was thirteen years older, had always been like a father to Rudy. After his brother returned from infantry service in Korea, Lee arranged for Rudy to work as a film editor on "Liberace." When the series ended, Lee used his influence to secure Rudy a job in the editing department at Warner Bros.

During the week, Rudy ably performed his editing chores at the studio and was a good husband and father. But on the weekend he became drunk and mean. Often his wife telephoned Lee, who drove to Rudy's house in Granada Hills, on the other side of the valley. Lee tried to reason with his brother, who became more abusive until he finally passed out.

One night a Granada Hills resident heard someone pounding on his front door with a rubber hose. "I know you've got my wife in there!" a voice screamed. The police arrived and arrested Rudolph Liberace, twenty-four, on suspicion of burglary. He answered the description of a suspect who had been seen near the site of recent burglaries.

Lee bailed his brother out of the Van Nuys jail and told reporters that Rudy had been drinking and became desperate when he couldn't locate his wife.

"He'd taken a couple of drinks when he shouldn't have," Lee explained. "He has a stomach ailment that he got in Korea, and it becomes poisonous when he takes a drink. He's a wonderful brother, and I love him very much. It's just unfortunate that he is named Liberace. Otherwise I don't think anything would be made of this incident."

Charges of burglary and disturbing the peace were dropped, and Rudy returned to his weekend binges.

Liberace needed escape from the constant pressures from his family and fans and from the incessant decision-making concerning his career. He found that escape in Palm Springs.

Duke Goldstone had introduced Lee to Palm Springs in the summer of 1953. Duke had directed the television show of Horace Heidt, the band leader whose enterprises included the Lone Palm Hotel. Like all Palm Springs hotels, the Lone Palm closed down for the torrid summer months. Heidt gave the hotel keys to Goldstone, who invited Liberace to accompany him and his wife for a week in the desert heat.

It was love at first sight. Lee was entranced by the informal, almost frontier atmosphere, the eye-filling vistas of slate-blue peaks, the pure, unpolluted air. He even enjoyed the 110-degree heat. "I've got to buy a house down here," he announced. And he did. Soon he owned four.

Palm Springs provided more for Lee than relaxation from the pressures of his family and career.

One hundred miles from the scrutiny of columnists and photographers, Lee could indulge himself in the gay life. Mom was seldom there to frown her disapproval of the "hillbillies" who were Lee's guests. After buying his own luxury house, Lee purchased less ostentatious quarters for his visitors. No one commented on the comings and goings at the Liberace house, nor his appearances in restaurants with blond young men. Palm Springs had long observed with tolerant eyes the peccadillos of Hollywood celebrities who enjoyed unwinding and sometimes misbehaving in the desert.

Only George could challenge Lee on his behavior. Over the years George had never criticized Lee for his homosexuality; after all, George himself was vulnerable for his womanizing. But now Lee was endangering the act.

"Goddammit, Lee," George finally said, "how can you keep saying in public and in courtrooms that you're not a homosexual and then you hang out in the Springs with a bunch of faggots? You're gonna get nailed someday."

Lee would not accept such talk from his brother or anyone else. He declared that George was no longer a part of the act. He could find employment elsewhere.

The official story was that George wanted to spread his own wings professionally and he was organizing his own orchestra. Few people knew that the brothers weren't talking to each other, and it might have remained secret—except for Mom.

Rumors of a feud between the two brothers circulated for months, but both denied them. Then Mom went public.

"I refuse to attend Lee's shows ever since George left him," she declared in October 1958. "I can't watch him on television, either. It would break my heart. I love both my boys. They have been wonderful to me. But I cannot watch either of them until they are back together again. Always since little boys, they were so happy together."

Mom admitted she was home alone most of the time in the big Sherman Oaks house, which was guarded around-the-clock in the wake of the attack on her. The piano pool was never used, since she didn't swim.

"Lee lives in Palm Springs most of the time," Mom said, "surrounded by a gang of what I call hillbillies and freeloaders. One of these days, Lee will wind up broke—and these characters won't even buy him a sandwich if he's starving. Lee is too trusting. He doesn't know who his true friends are." She declined to identify the "hillbillies and freeloaders," but admitted that they were the principal cause of the rift with George.

"We are simple people from Wisconsin," Mom continued. "You can only live in one house at a time. Lee has four houses in Palm Springs—and you can only rent houses there for a few months of the year. You call that an investment? Give me the old bankbook. That's what counts. When you are hungry, you can't take a hunk of wood out of an empty house and buy bread with it."

Pizza also entered into the family feud. On a television talk show, a woman in the audience inquired: "Where's George?" Lee responded with a calypso song from his nightclub act that said George was now in the frozen pizza business. George had lent his name to a pizza enterprise.

In Dallas, where he was playing a hotel engagement, George issued a statement: "Everybody knows that I'm no longer with my brother Lee. But let it not be said that I make my living selling frozen pizza pies. Music is my life and so it shall always be."

George also told reporters: "Naturally my mother is upset by the fact that we split. I definitely have no argument with my brother, only his yes-men."

Lee tried to smooth things over from Palm Springs: "George left me of his own volition. I wish him all the success in the world and I'm happy he is doing so well. I'm sorry about the pizza pies, but I thought George was still in that business. By the way, I ate some, and they were very good."

Six months later, George and Lee staged a public reunion at the Beverly Hilton Hotel, where George was appearing with his orchestra. Lee came onto the bandstand and played a couple of numbers for the dancers. "The candelabra isn't the best," Lee said to George with a smile. "I'll see that you get a better one."

Mom had a cold and couldn't attend the reunion. But the brothers appeared later at the Sherman Oaks house to receive kisses from Mom for press photographers.

"Our professional split was amicable except in Mom's eyes," George insisted. "She felt that since I was the older brother, I should stay with the act. But Lee is no longer 'a little brother.' "

"Mom doesn't criticize my real estate ventures anymore," Lee said. "She thought I was plunging in too deep. But that was only because envious people misled her because I was the most successful person in the family."

To all outward appearances, the Liberace feud was over. But many years would pass before the two brothers would be friends once more.

In the wake of the personal upheavals came disturbing signs that the Liberace touch at the box office was no longer golden. In 1957 he was booked into New York's fabled Palace Theater, where Judy Garland had made her spectacular comeback. Liberace was scheduled for a four-week run, but ticket sales were so slow that he closed on Friday night of the second week.

In early 1959 Liberace embarked on what was to be a triumphant tour of Australia. After a successful opening in Sydney, he was served with an injunction forbidding him from performing a medley of songs from *My Fair Lady*. The copyright owner, Chappell & Co., held exclusive rights to performance of the score, which had not been released outside the United States. Liberace was threatened with six months in jail if he played even a few bars of "I Could Have Danced All Night."

"Impossible!" Liberace said in a pique. "The *My Fair Lady* medley is a big part of the show. This whole thing is Communistic or Communistic-inspired. Cancel the tour!"

When his decision was announced to a matinee audience, a thousand people, most of them women, booed and shouted epithets. Police were summoned to maintain order as the enraged Australians lined up for refunds of their $4.50 tickets.

The Australian newspapers featured the Liberace debacle in headlines, and wire services transmitted the story to the United States. Alarmed by the bad publicity, Liberace agreed to reinstate the tour, and it required all his skill to convert hostile audiences to his side.

He arrived for a performance and discovered police officers throughout the backstage area. "What's going on here?" he demanded. No one wanted to tell him, but finally he learned that his life had been threatened. He was undisturbed. "What happens when I go out in the spotlight? I'm a perfect target," he reasoned. "You guys can go out and sit in the audience. You'll do more good out there."

The judge who had issued the injunction said Liberace had behaved like "a petulant child" and ordered him to pay $450 for the copyright infringement. Liberace apologized for his accusations of a Communist plot, adding: "My only thought is that I felt it was unfair not to be able to perform here music I have performed many times in my own country." But his lawyer in Hollywood, John Jacobs, set him straight on the facts, he said, "and I have made an issue of something which should not be the concern of an entertainer."

Obviously the Liberace career was faltering, and the opportunistic John Jacobs perceived the chance to enhance his position beyond that of company lawyer.

"You're paying those guys too much," Jacobs told Liberace, referring to his managers, Seymour Heller and Sam Lutz. "What do they do for their 10 percent? M.C.A. gets your bookings. Heller and Lutz are deadweight. I can do what they do, for a lot less money."

"I don't know," said Liberace. "Seymour and Sam have been awfully loyal to me."

"Sure they have, and they have been paid royally for it. Lee, the money isn't rolling in the way it used to. At least let me negotiate for a lower percentage of the take."

Liberace reluctantly agreed. Jacobs proposed to Heller and Lutz a reduction of their commission from 10 to 7½ percent. The partners flatly refused. Their association with Liberace was terminated, as John Jacobs had planned. Gabbe, Lutz and Heller then sued Liberace, Jacobs, and their company, International Artists, for $2.3 million, charging concealment of funds on which the agency deserved a commission.

The first new project of the Jacobs regime was another television series. Don Fedderson had sold the ABC network on the notion of starring Liberace in a daily musical-variety show during the daytime. It made perfect logic: Liberace's biggest following was America's women, who could take time off from their household chores to watch their hero.

"But we can't give 'em Liberace in white tails and sequins," said a network executive. "He's coming into their living rooms and kitchens in the daytime, for God's sake."

And so it was determined that Liberace would wear customary suits and sports coats. He even had his hair trimmed so he resembled a Wall Street broker. In place of George, Gordon Robinson was the musical conductor. Liberace was surrounded by people who would be attractive to viewers: an announcer, Steve Dunne, for Liberace to chat with; a young recording star, Marilyn Lovell, and a baritone, Dick Roman; a bongo player, Darias. The music would range from Chopin to the current rage "Purple People Eater."

The Liberace half-hour show, produced live from New York five days a week, pleased no one. Liberace fans were disappointed by his new image. Other housewives remained with their soap operas. After six months, the show had failed to attract an acceptable rating and was canceled.

The failure of the ABC daytime show inspired a chorus of doomsayers in Lindy's and the Brown Derby. Liberace was washed up, finished, yesterday's news. Las Vegas was no longer booking him. He couldn't buy a guest shot on TV variety shows. His concert dates were in backwater towns. Even the Liberace jokes weren't funny anymore.

Liberace returned to his gospel, *The Magic of Believing*. He steeped himself in the Bristol doctrine, and he preached it to those he thought needed it, especially newcomers to show business. One of them was Phyllis Diller.

He saw her first at the Bon Soir in New York, a small club that became the proving ground for many future stars. Lee was impressed with her rowdy, self-effacing comedy, and he met with her after the show.

"You're great," Lee said. "You knock me out. I just wish you would play more piano in your act. You're damn good."

After more conversation, he remarked, "You know, there's no limit to what you can do in show business, as long as you believe in yourself. I want to recommend something that can really help you. It's a book called *The Magic of Believing.*"

"Are you kidding? Are you kidding?" she exclaimed. "Let me tell you a story. A few years ago I was working as a copywriter at Kahn's, a big department store in Oakland. One day when I was waiting for a buyer to okay a full page of prices, I reached up and pulled down a book from her little office. It happened to be *The Magic of Believing*. I opened it somewhere in the middle and started reading it. I said, 'Oh, my God, this book is talking to me!' I borrowed it and took it up to my little cubicle. When I started reading it, I realized that I wanted to underline it. I called the book department, and they said they had it. But they also said that the store owner had given copies to every buyer, hoping they would apply the principles the way he had without knowing it. I bought my own book, underlined it, carried everywhere I went for two years, read it over and over until the theory was firmly in my mind. That's when I decided I could do comedy. Without Claude Bristol there would be no Phyllis Diller."

Realization of their mutual savior made them immediate friends, and the closeness remained to the end of Liberace's life.

The Liberace philosophy dictated that in times of trouble, act boldly. Such thinking led to the new house, grander by far than the one with the piano-shaped pool.

Liberace was bored with the Sherman Oaks house, and Mom hated it. Tourists and vandals made living there a misery, and the twenty-four-hour guards were a heavy expense. Besides, he cracked, "Every time I wanted to take a swim, the pool was out of tune." He started looking for a new place, something that could house his "happy-happies"—the artifacts, knickknacks, and gimcracks he had collected around the world.

As soon as he had acquired wealth, Liberace became a world-class shopper. In every city on his concert tours, he inquired for the location of antique shops, curio stores, junk shops, galleries. His trips abroad inevitably resulted in a stream of packages and crates en route to California. If he heard of an antique shop in Edinburgh that specialized in vintage crystal, he would make a pilgrimage there. His inspiration for the new house came when he was in England and visited the Duke of Bedford at Woburn Abbey. Liberace was overwhelmed by the burnished elegance of the French decor. "That I gotta have," he told himself. He returned to London and embarked on a shopping spree for French furniture.

Back in California, Liberace hunted through the hills of Hollywood, Beverly Hills, and Bel-Air for a suitable repository for his collection. He found it on Harold Way above the Sunset Strip, a few blocks from Ciro's. One of fourteen estates in a 1920s development called Hacienda Acres, it had been owned by Rudy Vallee and Ann Harding, but had been vacant for several years. The paint was peeling, plaster was falling off the ceilings, but Liberace saw in its twenty-eight rooms a vision of his French palace. He bought the place and started a massive renovation.

By Bastille Day 1961 he had moved in, and he invited members of the press to view its splendor.

"There are none of the old gimmicks in this place," he assured a visitor, "except my piano-shaped bed and an ancient gramophone that I converted into a hi-fi."

The front door looked like solid gold; it was gold-leafed and covered with coatings of plastic. The fifty-foot living room had gold wallpaper and thick off-white carpeting trimmed in gold. Designed by Liberace, the carpet had been woven in Japan. Crystal chandeliers everywhere; he had discovered them, blackened and broken, in the depths of antique shops and had them restored to gleaming beauty. Two chairs, worn and cracked from years on movie sets, had been repainted and reupholstered with tapestry Liberace had bought in Spain. The living room was dominated by a $20,000 gold-leafed French baby grand piano, topped, of course, with a gold candelabra.

On to the Organ Room—all the rooms had names so the servants would know where to go. The organ had been built into the living room by the original owners, but Liberace felt it looked too much like something out of *The Phantom of the Opera*. He had it moved to an adjoining room, restored mechanically, reupholstered, and gilded. "I don't really play it too well," he admitted, "but I'm working on it."

There were two formal dining rooms, glistening with gold and crystal, and even the kitchen had chandeliers. Downstairs was a huge game room that included enough body-building equipment for a professional gym. Liberace admitted he hadn't used the equipment much, but he planned to. The outside area looked like a huge putting green with its plastic carpeting. Hidden heaters would warm the outdoors to a comfortable temperature on cold California nights. The pool was oblong. "The piano pool was a gimmick," he said. "It was fun, but I wouldn't do it at this house. It's not French."

The master bedroom had the piano bed, but also French Victorian antiques and cabinets fashioned by André Boulle in the early eighteenth century. The Roman tub was done in white and gold, with golden Italian torches above it. Everywhere in the house were Liberace treasures: a dinner service that had belonged to Tom Mix; mad King Ludwig's candelabra with a huge piece of opaline glass; an onyx table made from sections of a German altar.

The entire house, which he valued at $250,000 including $140,000 in furnishings, was pure Liberace, and he was unabashed in his admiration of it. To those who cried kitsch he turned a deaf ear. As he once explained: "I love the fake. As long as it looks real, I'll go for it."

More than anything, Liberace loved Christmas.

"Don't book me in December," he instructed Gabbe, Lutz and Heller when he first signed with them. "I don't want anything to interfere with my Christmas."

He devoted each December to the full-time occupation of shopping for presents, decorating his house, and giving Christmas parties. The house-decorating tradition began in Sherman Oaks. Since he had been named honorary mayor of the Los Angeles suburb, he felt a duty to add a festive touch to his neighborhood. His touch included a life-size crèche, a mechanical Santa Claus and reindeer, trees festooned with thousands of lights. The voice of Liberace crooned carols over a loudspeaker and often he announced greetings to passersby. They came by the thousands every night, cars inching by on Valley Vista Boulevard while traffic police struggled vainly to keep them moving.

Every room inside the house was decorated lavishly, and each year Liberace tried to top the previous Christmas in displays. One year he was shopping in Nieman-Marcus when he spotted a magnificent Christmas tree hanging with hundreds of miniature toys. "I want it," he announced. "I'm sorry, Mr. Liberace, that's a store decoration; it's not for sale," said the manager. "Okay, then make me another one just like it," Liberace ordered. The tree was reproduced and shipped to his house.

When Liberace moved to the Hollywood Hills, he eliminated the outdoor decorations to discourage the traffic. But the displays inside the house became even more lavish. In 1962 he decided to have a feather Christmas. He bought all kinds of fluffy chicken feathers, dyed blue, pink, red, all colors, and attached them to a tree, one by one. A six-man crew helped him decorate each room with $25,000 worth of ornaments he had collected on a recent world tour that took him from Japan to Czechoslovakia.

The major focus was the living room, which contained six trees flocked in different colors and a Nativity scene that he had bought from a Houston museum for $1,120. "Two Texas women spent five hundred hours making the main figures," he said.

"I have a party every single night. One night is just for the family, one is for business associates, one is for producers and directors, one is for show business friends, one for friends not in the business, and so on. I'll have a thousand people here before the holidays are over."

And no one left empty-handed. Liberace had gifts for all, and the parties for his family and business associates were incredibly lavish. The gift-opening continued for three hours, and Liberace enjoyed every moment. "Save the wrappings!" Mom always said, and by the end of the evening she had accumulated a pile of folded paper several feet tall.

"Seymour, this is Lee."

The telephone call was a difficult one to make, because Liberace would be admitting that he had followed bad advice. What's more, he would have to concede that he had abandoned someone who had been totally loyal to him and a dominant force in building the Liberace career.

"Seymour, I need you back with me. Things haven't been going well."

"Yes, I've heard," Heller answered.

"I'd like you to talk with John Jacobs about working out a new deal."

"Jacobs? He's the guy who fired me in the first place."

"I know, and I realize now I was wrong to let him talk me into it. Please talk to him, Seymour, so you and I can be a team again."

As Heller had anticipated, the gruff old lawyer was opposed to having his power over Liberace diluted. He offered a contract that was unacceptable to Heller. Liberace intervened and made the deal himself.

Seymour Heller and Sam Lutz had continued as partners until 1961. Then they dissolved their company, and Lutz devoted most of his attention to Lawrence Welk. Now Heller could direct the majority of his efforts to restoring and sustaining the career of Liberace.

Heller helped convince the Las Vegas operators to book Liberace again. He chose concert and nightclub dates with care and arranged for heavy promotion to assure attendance. He advised his client to limit his television appearances, thus reducing overexposure and inducing people to buy tickets to see him.

Heller's strategy succeeded, and once again Liberace was one of the biggest money-making stars in show business.

Chapter 10

*LIBERACE LENDS A HELPING HAND TO A GIRL
FROM BROOKLYN; HE ALMOST DIES IN
PITTSBURGH, LITERALLY*

She had stringy hair, thrift-shop
clothes, a nose that wouldn't quit—and she sang like a choir of angels,
in unison.

When Liberace first saw Barbra Streisand at the Bon Soir in New
York, he was overwhelmed, though not by her appearance. "She'd be
terrific in my show," he remarked. Seymour Heller was doubtful. He
argued that the Liberace show was always heavy with glamour, and
his supporting star was usually a stunning, operatic-voiced singer like
Jean Fenn. Streisand was devoid of glamour.

Liberace wasn't convinced. He had heard how Streisand had

stopped the show as Miss Marmelstein in *I Can Get It for You Wholesale* on Broadway. She had also made a couple of albums for Columbia that were creating a stir. To his surprise, he and Streisand were booked on the same "Ed Sullivan Show"—Lee and Ed had patched up their feud. Lee noted at rehearsal how everyone in the theater paused at what they were doing to listen to Streisand sing. He heard them praise her singing, though there were comments like, "Too bad about that beak."

After hearing Barbra once more at Basin Street East, Lee announced he wanted to feature her on his concert tour. Impossible, his people insisted; she would flop miserably in Middle America.

"Okay," he conceded. "But I'm going to take her to Las Vegas no matter what you say. At least the crowd there will be hip enough to appreciate her."

Barbra wasn't sure she wanted to sing for the gamblers, but Seymour Heller made an offer that convinced her: $7,500 a week, several times what she had earned before.

Liberace was returning to the Riviera Hotel for the first time in five years, and he wanted to assure himself a triumph. He prepared a program of all his surefire numbers and commissioned a magnificent wardrobe. Opening night on August 4, 1963, was nearly a fiasco, due to Barbra Streisand.

She sang in her brilliant style, but the crowd didn't dig her Brooklyn wisecracks and found her anti-glamour appearance jarring amid the glitter and beauty of the Las Vegas Strip. The applause was barely polite, and when Liberace came on he could sense a cold house. It required all of his repertoire of shtick to restore the audience's favor.

When the same thing happened at the second show, Liberace called a conference in his suite. "Here's what we're gonna do," he declared. "I'll open the show with a fast number, and then I'll introduce Barbra as my discovery. Big hit in New York and all that. Then she'll come on and they gotta like her because she has my seal of approval. Okay?"

The device evoked a better audience reaction on the second night, and the Riviera bosses quieted their talk about firing Streisand. But it was too late to stop the reviews. The reviewer for the *Hollywood Reporter,* which was read by all the movie people, observed: "Singer Barbra Streisand was a sharp contrast to the star. Her makeup made her look like something that just climbed off a broom, but when she sang, it was like the wailing of a banshee bouncing up and down on marionette strings. It wasn't until she does three or four songs that her voice is noticed as being very pleasant. Her outrageous grooming almost nullifies her talent."

"Maybe you should make your wardrobe a little snazzier," Lee suggested.

"Like yours?" Barbra replied defiantly.

"Well, I wouldn't go that far. But a little class wouldn't hurt."

Liberace kept telling his Riviera employers: "You'd better sign this girl up for future dates. She's gonna be a big, big star." They were unconvinced until one Saturday night when Liberace presented a third show. The casinos sometimes staged a third performance on Saturday nights, affording performers in the other shows to see new acts. Facing a largely professional audience, Barbra belted her numbers in electrifying style, and the applause was thunderous. The Riviera hastily signed her to a long-run contract, beginning at $20,000 a week.

Two important figures flew from Hollywood to see Streisand perform—Ray Stark and Jule Styne. In her suite, Styne played songs he had written for a Broadway show about Fanny Brice, which Stark would produce. After two weeks at the Riviera, Barbra opened at the Coconut Grove in Los Angeles to a cheering crowd of celebrities. That night Ray Stark made an agreement for Barbra Streisand to star in *Funny Girl.*

Two weeks later, Barbra returned to Nevada to appear with Liberace at Harrah's Lake Tahoe. When Bill Harrah saw her perform in rehearsal, he exclaimed, "My God, I can't have her in my show! She'll scare the customers out of the room." Liberace assured him Barbra would be well received, particularly when he introduced her as his discovery.

During the engagement, Elliott Gould flew in from London, where he had closed in a revival of *On the Town,* and he and Barbra drove to Carson City and were married. Harrah's provided a big house for the honeymooners, and Barbra turned domestic and announced she was giving a birthday party for the stage manager. What's more, she was going to bake the birthday cake herself.

They turned out to be individual cakes for all the party guests. Barbra watched expectantly as they blew out the candles and started to eat. "Do you like it?" she asked.

"Well," Liberace said slowly, "the frosting is a bit tough."

"Oh," said Barbra, "I ran out of a sugar so I used flour instead."

November 22, 1963, the day every American remembers.

Liberace was scheduled to open his show that night at a popular nightclub, the Holiday, in the Pittsburgh suburb of North Hills. As he always did before a performance, Liberace checked over his wardrobe in his hotel room that morning. He noticed some of the cuffs and collars were dirty. Since his dresser had gone on errands, Liberace walked through a snowstorm to a nearby hardware store and bought a gallon can of cleaning fluid.

Back in the hotel room, Liberace was patiently dabbing cleaning fluid on his costumes when his New York manager, Dick Gabbe, appeared at the door, looking pale and shaken. "Something terrible has happened, Lee," he said. "Someone shot President Kennedy in Dallas. He's dead."

Lee was staggered. "The show," he said. "How could I make anyone happy tonight? Surely they'll cancel."

"I'll go ask them. If they don't cancel, I'm afraid you'll have to do the show, Lee. If you don't, it's a breach of contract."

Gabbe departed to confer with the owners of the Holiday. The terrible news had made Lee feel sick at heart, and he lay down on the bed. Soon he was asleep.

He was awakened by Dick Gabbe knocking on the door. "They say they want a show," he reported.

"Oh, God!" Lee exclaimed.

"I'm sorry, Lee, you gotta do it. They could sue us if you don't."

They turned on television and watched the tragic events in Dallas. "What's that strange smell?" Gabbe asked. Lee explained about using the solvent, and the manager kidded him about trying to save money by cleaning his own costumes.

Heartsick and feeling slightly nauseous, Lee took another rest and fell asleep immediately. When he awoke, it was late afternoon. That was strange, he thought; he rarely took afternoon naps. Perhaps it was the excess sleep that made him feel logy and under-par. Or it might have been his ear infection troubling him again. He had no time to think about it. He was scheduled to leave for the club.

Never had Liberace felt less like giving a performance. In truth, he had *never* approached any show without psyching himself into believing that he was going out to give the customers an experience they would long remember. Part of the process was a ritual that members of his troupe came to recognize. Moments before he was announced, he stood alone in the wings and gave a silent prayer for strength to give the people an hour or two of entertainment to relieve them of their cares. On the night of November 22, 1963, Lee prayed for extra strength.

The audience was small, and, like the performers, stunned by what they had seen on television that day. Lee forced a smile and began playing the rousing first number.

By the time he finished he could scarcely see the piano keys. His head was reeling, and he feared he would throw up on the stage. He hurried into the wings, and the program was hastily rearranged to fill in for his absence. Lee retched again and again, wiped his face with a wet towel and said, "I think I can go back now."

But it was no use. Before he could complete the next number, he was overcome with nausea. He apologized to the audience and staggered into the wings. An ambulance rushed him back to Pittsburgh and St. Francis's Hospital. The problem, doctors decided, was his kidneys. Uremic poisoning, caused by carbon tetrachloride. Lee was placed in intensive care and attached to an artificial kidney machine. His personal physician, Dr. Frank Taylor, was summoned from California. Because of the Kennedy assassination, the news of Liberace's collapse received no coverage in the press.

Lee's condition was grim. His kidneys were not responding to treatment. He could tell from the doctor's faces that the outlook was poor for his survival. Finally Dr. Taylor told him it would be wise to settle his affairs.

First of all, his relations with God. Despite his boyhood training, Lee had not attended Mass regularly, nor had he taken the church sacraments. He called for the hospital chaplain, who administered the last rites of the Catholic Church. Next Lee called his accountant and asked, "How much am I worth? Figure it up and let me know." The answer: $750,000.

Lee then set about disposing of as much of his wealth as he could. Christmas was approaching—just the time for it. He bought Angie a house, his mother a full-length mink coat and jewels, and sports cars, diamond rings, motorcycles, gold jewelry, fur coats for the twenty-eight members of his staff. He wanted all of them to have and enjoy those things before he died.

Liberace liked to tell another story about his near-death. He said that late one night when his strength seemed to be draining, a nun he had never seen before appeared in his hospital room. She said to him: "Pray to St. Anthony. He has worked many miracles." She touched his arm and disappeared. He took her advice and prayed to St. Anthony.

In the morning he described his visitor to the other sisters. They could think of no one on the hospital staff who fit her description. "She was wearing a white habit," he said.

The nuns looked at him blankly. "But we have no sisters with white habits at St. Francis," one of them said.

A day later, Dr. Taylor said to Lee: "I don't know what you're doing, but whatever it is, it's working. Your condition has improved enormously. You're going to make it."

After he stopped weeping, Lee telephoned California and ordered $25,000 in Christmas decorations for the Harold Way house. This was going to be his greatest Christmas ever.

Liberace's attitude toward his work was never the same afterward. He demanded more time for his houses, his antiques, his restoration work, his dogs. Often this exasperated Seymour Heller.

Lee was on vacation in Palm Springs when Heller called him with the message: "I know you're vacationing, Lee, but I've just received the most fabulous offer you've ever had."

After listening to the proposal, Lee replied, "It sounds wonderful, Seymour, but I can't take it."

"For God's sake, why not?"

"Because my orchids are in bloom. I've been waiting all year for this."

The young man from a Texas hamlet found it incredible to be attending a birthday party for Liberace's valet and chauffeur. Jamie James had been invited by a friend to accompany him to Liberace's storied mansion above the Sunset Strip. For a newcomer to California it was an amazing experience. James had watched the "Liberace" show as a boy in Texas, trying to determine why his mother was so excited about it. Now he was going to Liberace's house!

The party room was downstairs in what had been Liberace's gym— so many guests had hurt themselves on the punching bag and other equipment that the insurance company demanded their removal. Now the principal features in the room were the host's first and dearest piano, the glass-topped Bluthner grand, as well as a bejeweled honky-tonk piano used for nightclub appearances. Shy among the unfamiliar faces, James found a place behind the grand piano where he could observe without being conspicuous.

"Hi, I'm Liberace, what's your name?"

James turned and saw his smiling host in front of him. Answering Liberace's questions, he explained that he was a free-lance art director new in Los Angeles. "We're always needing art work for my shows," Liberace said. "Why don't you go see my lawyer, John Jacobs, and take some of your samples? Maybe we'll have some work for you."

The conversation continued, and James felt emboldened to say, "Don't you feel a little embarrassed?" "About what?" Liberace asked. "You're drinking champagne out of a silver goblet, and everyone else has glass," James said. Liberace disappeared and returned with a silver goblet that he presented to James.

Liberace liked the outspoken young Texan, and he noted the rapport between him and Gladys, Liberace's cook and general factotum. Gladys Luckie had been a caterer for Hollywood celebrities, and Liberace hired her to arrange a large dinner party. She stayed for thirty years and became Liberace's "black mother." Because she was also from Texas, Gladys made immediate friends with Jamie James.

John Jacobs approved of the sample work, and James was hired to contribute designs for Liberace tours. After the Hollywood Bowl appearance was scheduled, James was asked to propose a publicity campaign. Although he had no expertise in publicity, Jacobs submitted his proposals. They so impressed Seymour Heller and Liberace that he was hired to work with the company's publicist. Soon James had the job by himself.

One of James's first assignments was to accompany Liberace to New York, where he was opening at the Royal Box of the Americana Hotel. Liberace was delighted with his young friend's awe of New York, and they went for a walking tour on the first day. "Have you ever seen Radio City Music Hall?" Liberace asked. No, James replied. They sat in the balcony and watched Deborah Kerr and Hayley Mills in *The Chalk Garden* on the tremendous screen, then saw the stage extravaganza featuring the Rockettes. "Wouldn't it be great if you could play your show here?" James suggested. "I've thought about it," Liberace admitted.

On Broadway they arrived at the Winter Garden, where Barbra Streisand and Sydney Chaplin were starring in *Funny Lady*. "Want to see the show?" Liberace asked. "Sure—but tickets are impossible to get," said James. "Don't worry, I'll handle this." He returned from the box office with two single seats in the orchestra section.

Streisand had been alerted that Liberace was in the matinee audience, and during one of her musical numbers she interpolated "I'll Be Seeing You." A woman sitting next to Jamie James turned to her companion and whispered: "I didn't know Fanny Brice sang that song."

Liberace was invited backstage, and Barbra greeted him affectionately. "Gee, you must really like this show—you've been here four times!" she said.

Lee studied her stylish orange dressing gown and said, "I'm glad to see that you're dressing with some class, Barbra."

"Oh, this," she said. "I wore it in the show but they cut the scene, so they let me keep it."

Later that night a message came to the Liberace suite at the

Americana: "There's a woman down here who says she's Barbra Streisand and she wants to see the show. But she's a blonde." It was Barbra Streisand in a blond wig, appearing incognito to watch her onetime mentor perform.

In 1964 Liberace was still rebuilding a career that had been declared in rigor mortis by show-business wise men. The Americana Hotel engagement was typical. Although he had played to capacity in Madison Square Garden ten years earlier, he could not fill the Royal Box every night. Instead of changing his act and adding rock 'n' roll numbers to appeal to a younger audience, he continued his diet of standard melodies and condensed classics. The *Variety* critic noted, somewhat condescendingly:

> *He takes his audience along on a ride that is beset with familiar and pleasant landmarks. He trods no new musical paths, neither does he disturb the swaying pattern that he establishes early in the turn. . . . Indeed, he gives the impression of a handsome, graying man rambling along the keys in the living room. Kinda makes you want to hold hands with mother while he ambles through such delights as a Chopin medley, a brace of Gershwin, and a series of old pops.*

And the costumes. They became even more garish, and he never failed to draw belly laughs with: "Pardon me while I slip into something more spectacular." The next outfit inevitably evoked gasps and his aside: "I don't wear these clothes to go unnoticed." In case any of his fans remained unsatisfied, he appeared in the lobby after the show to give autographs and pose for tourists' cameras.

Jamie James in his early years as publicist tried to suggest innovations in the Liberace image.

"Don't try to change me," Liberace cautioned. "I've spent years creating who I am, and I know that it works. Whenever somebody tries to change me, I get in trouble. Like when ABC cut my hair and put me in Brooks Brothers suits. That wasn't me, and I've been trying to recover from it ever since."

James had to agree that Liberace was his own best press agent. He was masterly in interviews, always giving the reporter more than expected. That sometimes meant embellishing the truth, but it was for a good cause, Liberace believed. Whenever he started veering into the land of fantasy during an interview, he always shot James a glance that indicated: "Yes, I am going a bit overboard, but it does make a good story, doesn't it?"

It was a basic tenet of the Liberace doctrine that he would never become involved in anything the least bit controversial. "Once you take a public stand on anything, you alienate a segment of your audience," he theorized.

And so he never supported any political candidate or issue. No one, not even his closest associates, could tell for sure whether Liberace was a Democrat or Republican, or neither. Although his Italian-Polish parenthood made it certain that he had been raised a Catholic, he never flaunted his religion in public as did some entertainers. He was even wary of being too closely associated with charities. "I don't want people looking at me and thinking of some disease," he reasoned. He conducted his personal charities in private.

He was seemingly indefatigable in granting interviews. In 1953, when Liberace was playing at the Ambassador East Hotel in Chicago, a nineteen-year-old from Portland, Oregon, named Dale Olson telephoned with a request for an interview, saying he wrote a teen-age column for weekly newspapers. Liberace arranged for the young reporter to attend a dinner show, then entertained him for two hours in his hotel suite, playing piano and chatting with George and Mom.

Ten years later, the same Dale Olson was a reporter for *Daily Variety,* and an interview with Liberace was suggested by Jamie

James. The only time available was during a trip to the Movieland Wax Museum, where Liberace was to be enshrined in wax. Olson conducted the interview in the gold-plated limousine en route to Orange County.

After the ceremonies, the officials announced a gala luncheon. "But I have a two o'clock deadline back in town," Olson said. "Gentlemen, I'm sorry, but we have to leave," Liberace announced.

On the way back to Los Angeles, Liberace said, "I'm starving." He directed the chauffeur to exit on the next freeway off ramp, and the limousine pulled into a McDonald's. Liberace ordered hamburgers with everything and milkshakes, to the astonishment of the other McDonald's patrons. After signing a few autographs, he continued on the drive.

In 1965, Liberace, who was forty-six, announced he was celebrating his twenty-fifth year in show business. He had actually started as an entertainer earlier than twenty-one, but twenty-five years was a convenient anniversary to elicit interviews from the press. Indeed, *Time,* the *New York Times,* the *Los Angeles Times,* and other publications were prompted to take fresh views of the faddish entertainer who refused to fade away like 3-D movies, hula hoops, and the twist.

The articles noted that he continued to be single and devoted to Mom, that he was earning $800,000 a year from concerts and television, and was still responding to his critics by crying all the way to the bank. Because of Elvis Presley and his imitators, Liberace complained mildly, "I really have to exaggerate to look different and to top them." His onstage outfits cost $10,000, and they tarnished so fast that he needed ten a year. He did, however, move his $8,000 diamond buttons from suit to suit.

His automobiles were not meant to be overlooked. The stretch Cadillac was equipped with television, stereo, a bar with silver goblets monogrammed with *L* in script, and two diamond-studded chandeliers. For going to the market he had a porcelein-white Rolls-Royce.

He drove down to the Scandia restaurant one day in 1965, and we talked about his twenty-fifth anniversary and his career. He was in excellent trim, having lost forty pounds. He wore a pearl-gray suit with an Eisenhower jacket, with heavy cufflinks of diamond-studded candelabras and a matching ring. He rubbed the ring fondly with his thumb as he reflected on the turnaround in his image:

"My image in the beginning, in the white-heat period, was mocked and mimicked. But as the years went on, people began to realize that I myself kidded the Liberace image. I make an act out of my image. As soon as people understand that I don't walk down Sunset Boulevard in a gold lamé cape and pants, they they come over to my side. They're always surprised to find out I'm a nice guy.

"Now I'm getting something new at my concerts: standing ovations. I think it's partly because I always ask for requests at the end of my show. Strange thing—it's always the men who stand up first. That's because their wives or girlfriends have dragged them to the show, and they want to express the turnaround in their thinking.

"The turning point in my career came after the white-heat period was over. My managers were still trying to put me into forty-thousand-seat arenas and field houses. The climax came when I was booked into a huge stadium in Akron on the Fourth of July. It rained, and I stayed over two days to fulfill the engagement. Well, the excitement of the Fourth had died, and we drew six thousand disgruntled people. The promoter paid me part of the fee, and when I got back here, the check bounced. That's when I told my people: "Stop booking me in big houses and try to develop the concerts. Once the word gets around that you drew six thousand people in a forty-thousand-seat place, you're dead.

"Now I can control my career, instead of having my career control me. I've been able to devote more time to other things, such as my interior decorating shop."

That was his new indulgence: Liberace Interiors and Objets d'Art.

The Harold Way house could absorb no more of the objects he had collected around the world, and they were piling up in warehouses. So why not share them with the public?

He opened the shop on La Cienega in the heart of Los Angeles's interior design belt, and he filled its seven rooms with treasures from his collection. Not only candelabras and piano-shaped oddities. He also offered a desk he maintained once belonged to Louis XV of France, available for $250,000; a curving twenty-foot sofa for $20,000; a French cabinet outfitted to house a stereo and television set, $5,000.

Liberace proudly pointed out to visitors the handsomely decorated men's room with its statuary and paintings of male nudes.

"I've been giving a lot of thought to bathrooms lately," he told a reporter. "For example, I'm designing a disappearing toilet. I see no reason why you should walk into a bathroom and immediately see a toilet. It's so unglamorous."

Many visitors were attracted to Liberace Interiors and Objets d'Art by the window display of a plaster figure of the owner in a sequined robe, sitting at a piano. Many others visited the place in hopes, often realized, of seeing and chatting with Liberace himself. But few bought objets d'art or availed themselves of decorating services. Nor could Liberace bear to part with well-loved pieces. He closed the shop and shipped its contents back to the warehouses.

Las Vegas was the perfect place for Liberace. There he could find an ever-replenished audience for his entertainment skills. Mr. Showmanship, he called himself, and the billing was earned. No casino star exerted more effort and expense to send customers away happy. The pit bosses welcomed him because, while he attracted many elderly patrons of the slot machines, he also brought in husbands who gambled heavily while their wives were watching Liberace's glittering performance.

Liberace never failed to give the customers their money's worth, whether he was making his entrance from a ten-foot cake in a red velvet cape or parading with a brass band in embroidered hot pants. Before anyone could deride his outrageousness he disarmed them with a remark: "Actually, I never wear clothes like this offstage—oh, no, I'd be picked up for sure!"

Before starting to play a serious composition, he rose and commented: "I like to get up from the piano once in a while—it straightens the shorts."

For those confused about his gender, he offered the story: "I met this fellow who asked me why I was always smiling. 'If you knew some of the stories that go around about you, you wouldn't be so happy,' the man said. And I said, 'What do you mean? I started them!'"

He left the customers with "I'll Be Seeing You" and a final analysis: "I'm no good—I've just got guts."

At the Riviera and later at the Hilton and Caesar's Palace, Liberace was treated like royalty, and he loved every minute of it. Always he was accorded the most magnificent quarters and any services he desired.

The best times for Liberace came after he had finished an engagement. At last he could relax from the discipline of two shows every night. On the evening after closing, he gathered in his luxury suite a few friends and members of his staff, usually all-male. First came cocktails. Liberace always had Dubonnet, sometimes laced with vodka or gin. His doctor had cautioned against too much liquor as well as heavy sauces with food, lest he acquire gout; the specter of his hands crippled with gout was enough to convince him.

The party departed in limousines for another casino on the Strip and a dinner performance of a star Liberace wanted to see. He and his guests were escorted to the best ringside table; all charges were on the house, of course. During the performance the star always introduced Mr. Showmanship to vigorous applause. The ritual would be repeated at a second show. After that came the gambling.

Liberace rarely played craps or blackjack. Most of the time he spent at the slot machines. He bought trays of coins for his guests and reacted gleefully when they hit jackpots. Liberace also fed quarters into the slots, chatting happily with the elderly women to whom the machines were a passion. During most of the long evening, he had a cigarette in his hand. But if a photographer approached, the cigarette always disappeared. Smoking did not fit the Liberace image.

The Nevada sun was beginning to rise when Liberace and his party returned to the hotel. Then he cooked a German breakfast for all, complete with potato pancakes. The end of the meal signaled that the party was over, and the guests made their fond farewells.

Brother Rudy was a problem that wouldn't go away.

Somehow Rudy managed to hold editing jobs at the studios, but his weekend binges remained out of control. All of the pleas of his wife, the lectures by Lee and George, the gentle scoldings by Mom were ineffectual. Rudy drank and drank, and his once-handsome face had become bloated and debauched.

Lee was giving a party one night at the Harold Way house when Rudy suddenly appeared, bleary-eyed and disheveled. He started shouting insults at his brother. Lee detested drunks; he had seen too many in Wisconsin bars. He hurried Rudy out of the room and escorted him upstairs to the Marie Antoinette room, which overlooked the pool. It had been exquisitely decorated all in red, with French furnishings including a spinet piano and a music box on which a Marie Antoinette doll danced.

Rudy collapsed on the bed, and Lee returned to his party. In the morning Lee discovered that Rudy had vomited all over the room.

Lee rarely displayed anger toward anyone, especially his own family. But Rudy had gone over the brink. "I've done everything I can for Rudy," Lee said. "I give up. I don't want to see him anymore— until he can help himself."

His mind was firm. When Lee felt betrayed or insulted by someone, he eliminated that person from his view. Lee continued sending money to Rudy's wife, his three sons and daughter, but he would neither see nor discuss his younger brother.

On April 30, 1957, the manager of a Culver City motel opened one of the rooms and found the body of Rudolph Liberace under a sheet in the bed, clad in T-shirt and shorts. Several liquor bottles were nearby and there was no evidence of foul play. Mom came to the motel to identify her baby boy.

At the funeral, Lee wept uncontrollably. "Why? Why?" he wailed. "He was such a beautiful boy. Why did he destroy himself?"

Chapter 11

MOSTLY A PORTRAIT OF LIBERACE AT THE
HALF-CENTURY MARK OF AN EVENTFUL CAREER

Liberace returned to England in
the spring of 1969 to appear in ten television programs to be broadcast on CBS as a summer replacement for "The Red Skelton Show."
It was Liberace's first television series since the ill-advised daytime
show on ABC in 1958–59.

By the late 1960s he realized that he needed to make television
appearances to maintain his visibility with the public and hence enhance his concert attendance. He plotted his return strategically,
making nine major guest appearances in one season with such stars
as Dean Martin, Jimmy Durante, and Red Skelton. This was a differ-

ent Liberace from what television viewers had seen before. The syndicated show had been almost devoid of humor; now he enjoyed making jokes about his image. His drab concert-hall clothes had been supplanted by the most outrageous of costumes, and they could be enjoyed in living color.

Red Skelton recognized Liberace's appeal, and his company packaged the summer show.

En route to England, Liberace made two appearances. One was in South Africa, where he was completely unknown. Attendance was so sparse that tickets had to be given away for the first four performances, then the word-of-mouth attracted crowds. In Monaco Liberace performed at a charity gala for Prince Rainier and Princess Grace and drew laudatory reviews from the French critics, most of whom had never seen him.

Liberace approached England with trepidation, knowing that reporters would dredge up the Cassandra affair. When the matter arose, he smiled, "Why don't we let sleeping dogs lie?" Reporters were delighted with the double entendre.

Arriving with thirty-five pieces of luggage, Liberace found a London far different from what he had seen ten years before. The Beatles and other pop groups had electrified Old Blighty. Carnaby Street clothes were everywhere, making Liberace seem almost conservative. He signaled his approval of the new style by letting his sideburns grow an inch longer.

The new "Liberace Show" was elegantly produced for $100,000—Liberace estimated the same show would cost $250,000 in America—with a full symphony orchestra and guest stars such as Lena Horne, Jack Benny, Shani Wallis, and Terry-Thomas. Far different, Liberace reflected, from his $10,000 syndicated show, for which a stagehand searched the alley for a cat to illustrate "Kitten on the Keys."

"It was time to do another series," Liberace commented to an American reporter in London, "to see if lightning could strike twice." It couldn't. "The Liberace Show" did not survive the summer.

"I'm at the halfway mark in my life," Liberace announced as he approached May 16, 1969, his fiftieth birthday. He explained: "In the next twenty-five years they will make new discoveries about longevity, and I think it will be possible to live to be one hundred. I take something now. I was put up to it by Marlene Dietrich. Funny—older people want to live longer, and the younger ones are trying to kill themselves with pot, and worse."

At fifty, Liberace was satisfied with his life. Perhaps he could not reestablish himself in television (he did have a romp as the villain Fingers in "Batman"), and there was no work for him in the movies. But those were minor frustrations. He found immense pride in the fact that he could make more money in Las Vegas—and in many other locations—than any other performer. That was his lifeblood: to *perform.* The adulation of an audience reached into his soul and nurtured him. No kick from cocaine could equal the high he felt at the end of a performance. His associates marveled at his elation. It was positively orgasmic.

His homosexuality remained hidden, necessarily so. But during the periods of leisure at the Harold Way house and in Palm Springs he could spend time with his "hillbillies" and perhaps form a temporary liaison with one of them. He could lavish gifts and delight in his lover's boyish gratitude. When it was time to return to work, the parting could be without guilt or acrimony.

Liberace was almost childlike in his gift-giving. He adored watching the faces of those to whom he gave outrageously lavish presents. He was not like Elvis Presley, who reportedly would hand over a ring to a fan on impulse. All of Liberace's gifts were well thought out, and given to people he felt deserved them. Never was a Liberace gift to be anticipated. Persons who thought they *deserved* beneficence from him would be sorely disappointed.

Christmas brought forth an outpouring of gifts, not only for relatives and staff but for longtime friends, business acquaintances, and members of the press. Each year Liberace planned a special gift: a silver calling-card tray, a porcelain mug bearing the person's name and birth sign, etc. One year he sent out miniature candelabras with candles. A columnist returned his gift with the comment: "If you can't send two, don't send any."

Liberace was incensed. "From now on, no more gifts; I'll send Christmas cards," he decreed. Since he was Liberace, the cards had to be the most elaborate imaginable. Each year Jamie James and his staff were required to produce designs that would meet Liberace's standards. Some were pop-up cards, others were studded with Austrian rhinestones—for VIPs, real diamonds. The cards cost between $3 and $4 apiece, and the mailing list included seven thousand names.

During all his years in Hollywood, Liberace never lost his thrill at meeting stars he had idolized in the movie palaces of Milwaukee. Mae West became a special friend. She had been a fan of his early television shows, and when friends asked what she wanted for her birthday, she replied. "Liberace." They informed Lee, who delightedly appeared at her doorstep wearing a large bow and announcing, "Miss West, I'm Liberace, your birthday present."

They often met over the years, and she shared her knowledge of showmanship. "You know how I got that sexy walk of mine?" she said. "I put a half-dollar between my buttocks and tried to hold it there." Liberace roared. "Maybe I should try that," he mused, "but I don't think I'd achieve the same result."

Mae West and Liberace created a hubbub among photographers and reporters when they arrived together for the opening of a puppet extravaganza in which both were caricatured. Asked what they planned after the show, Miss West replied: "Mr. Liberace invited me to come up and see his house. I'm gonna look at his gold organ."

Liberace was a master of publicity, and he could smile his way through endless interviews. But there were times when he balked. When he arrived for an interview on "The Today Show" early one New York morning, he gazed at a piano on the set and blanched. He turned to the ever-present Seymour Heller and muttered, "Seymour, I am *not* going to play that piano. I am not going to *touch* that piano." Playing a strange and possibly untuned piano on an early-morning talk show simply was not in keeping with the Liberace image.

Heller carried the message to the show's producer. The interviewer, Barbara Walters, came over, and Lee told her firmly, "Barbara, I just do not want to play that piano." She employed all her charm and persuasion to change his mind, but he would not budge: "Barbara, I will *not* play that piano." The interview was cool, and Walters made a point of remarking that her guest did not choose to play.

An engagement in Sacramento had an advance sale of $283,000, and the promoters convinced the Liberace management to bring him to Sacramento early for publicity to help sell the remaining $100,000 in tickets. Liberace was in a grumpy mood on the plane to Sacramento. When Jamie James showed him the press schedule, Lee complained, "What's this about a press luncheon when I arrive? I don't know anything about that." James said he thought Seymour had told him about it. "Nobody tells me anything," Liberace continued. "Well, I can't do it. This is a new theater for me, and it's in the round, and I need all the rehearsal time I can get." James pleaded that the press had already been notified, but Liberace remained firm.

James managed to get the message to members of the media, and only one of them was miffed. On the following day, Liberace gave interviews to every newspaper, radio, and television outlet in Sacramento and charmed them all. The last $100,000 in tickets vanished.

The Liberace charm was not something manufactured to win newspaper space. Unlike some stars who could exert their patented personalities on visitors and then turn derisive when they left, Liberace genuinely appreciated the attention of both reporters and fans, whom he considered the lifeblood of his career. He would never consider being rude to any of them. The only thing he disliked about publicity was posing for photographs in a gallery. He detested sitting motionless in smiling poses under the hot lights. The only time when he failed to fulfill a request by his publicist came when he canceled a date at a photo studio for a *TV Guide* cover. He maintained that he had been overworked and had a cold.

Liberace loved nothing better than showing off his treasures to visitors at the Harold Way house. He preferred small gatherings, since big parties inevitably produced a disorderly drunk, and he loathed guests who destroyed the gaiety of the evening. He realized that first-time visitors, especially women, were often intimidated by the surroundings and the host himself, and he sought to disarm them immediately.

"My dear, I've got to warn you about this carpet," he said to women guests. "You're going to catch your heels in it. So why don't you come over here, and I'll fit you out with some slippers so you'll be safe and comfortable." He led them to a closet where he kept gold stretchy slippers, and he fitted them like a Prince Charming. By that time the guests were totally in his thrall.

While Liberace was completely at ease when he entertained, he was a different person at someone else's party. Entering a large gathering, he eyed the crowd, wary of possible hostility. Always he gravitated to one of the smaller rooms and sat in a corner surrounded by intimates. New acquaintances were astonished to learn that Liberace, so totally in command on a stage, was basically a shy person. Liberace shy? they wondered. It was true. When he found himself outside his protective circle of professional associates, there were glimmers of Walter Liberace, the mama's boy who practiced piano while the other boys were playing baseball.

This split in his personality could be detected in his walk. When he strode onstage, he took full steps and came down on his heels like a man in total control. The stage was his dominion, and he paced it imperiously, the microphone as his scepter. But offstage he took shorter steps, almost a shuffle, boyish and shy.

Liberace was ever cognizant of how he had transformed his life through *The Magic of Believing,* and he urged those around him to follow his example. One of his favorite people was Robert Agerman, an Indianapolis dentist. Lee had discovered him early in the Liberace career, and he often planned tours so he could have his dental work done in Indianapolis. Others in his staff also consulted Dr. Agerman on the tours. During a session in Agerman's office, Lee asked him: "Bob, would you be embarrassed to drive to work in a Rolls-Royce?" "Of course," the dentist replied. "Well, you shouldn't be," Lee commented. "You should be daring."

After hiring Jamie James, Lee was irritated because the Texan sometimes wore jeans to the Harold Way house. "Jamie, let me make a suggestion," said Lee with a phrase James learned was always followed by a criticism. "I don't think it's a good idea to wear Levi's when you're working. You're a good-looking man. You should always dress up, not down, if you want to be a success in business."

Liberace lived for the present. Except when he had to recount his early adventures for interviewers, he never reminisced. He wouldn't look at old newspaper articles about himself—"Show me today's clippings," he insisted. The only clippings he saved were for his "Eat Crow" file. These were written by critics or interviewers who came to scoff and condemn Liberace and ended up praising him.

By the time he had reached his fiftieth year, Liberace was inured to bad reviews. Almost. A few critics, he believed, carried on an anti-Liberace vendetta. A particular enemy was Martin Bernheimer of the *Los Angeles Times.* Customarily a reviewer of serious music, he had written a slashing review of a Hollywood Bowl concert by Liberace. He repeated the attack when Liberace appeared in 1970 at the Ahmanson Theater in Los Angeles.

Bernheimer made a point of correcting Liberace's usage of "candelabra." Afterward Jamie James went through his publicity stories and changed the word to "candelabrum." When Liberace reviewed the copy, he inquired, "What is this?" James explained, "Bernheimer is right: 'candelabra' is plural." Liberace replied: "Fuck Martin Bernheimer. We'll call it a candelabra."

Liberace often remarked, though not to interviewers: "Liberace is no Rubinstein, and Rubinstein is no Liberace." He made no pretense of being a classical pianist, but he offered no excuses for reaching the masses with his truncated classics. One of his favorite stories allegedly took place at NBC in New York. Arthur Rubinstein arrived for a broadcast and walked to the artists' elevator. "You can't use that one; you gotta use the visitors' elevator," the guard said. "But I am Rubinstein," the virtuoso announced. The guard answered: "I don't care if you're Liberace; you gotta use that elevator over there!"

The fans, Liberace realized, were the barrier between him and the critics, and he did everything possible to nurture them. A staff of secretaries was employed to answer every piece of fan mail, even the pleas for money, to which he never acceded. Letters of special interest were underlined and shown to Liberace for a personal reply. Longtime fans became like part of the family, and Liberace would call them by name when he visited their home cities.

His memory amazed his associates. He seemed to recall everyone who ever interviewed him. In staff meetings he sometimes had a faraway look, drumming his fingers as if playing some long-ago melody. Months later he would be able to recount in detail exactly what was said. His musical memory was astounding. He could play hundreds of pieces, even concertos, without referring to sheet music. Friends believed his I.Q. was remarkably high even though he lacked intellectual depth. He knew nothing of literature, political thought, or philosophy. His only reading was newspapers and magazines.

While he enjoyed entertaining more than anything, Liberace was never bored during his layoff periods. The same energy he exhibited onstage was devoted to his houses, antiques, cars, cooking, and dogs.

"Some people collect stamps; I like to collect real estate," Liberace once said. "I am a firm believer in the good earth."

After the Sherman Oaks piano-pool mansion, he never built another house. Always he found a place that was either brand-new or dilapidated, then he transformed its barrenness or dilapidation into a Liberace confection.

The Cloisters had been a hotel villa in the heart of Palm Springs, a collection of quaint bungalows that had first been built in 1925, when the town was little more than a desert way station. The original owner had planned it as one grand hall, then added wings so it could serve as a guest ranch. Gradually other buildings were added until it became a thirty-two-room hotel. The years took their toll on The Cloisters, and it became a cheap hotel with a shady clientele. By the time Liberace saw it in the early 1970s, the hotel was scheduled to be leveled and the property used as a parking lot for the adjacent golf course, Catholic church, and Jewish temple.

One of the early owners pleaded with Liberace to buy The Cloisters and restore its onetime glory. Liberace was immediately receptive. Often he had passed the place and regarded its elegant decay with the thought: "What a charming place; it's just crying out for love."

The entire block was for sale at $250,000. Liberace's business manager argued: "Why do you need a whole block? I'll let you buy half of it." Liberace paid $87,000 for half of the parcel, which, with his improvements and the increased value of Palm Springs property, was worth $2.5 million by the 1980s.

He poured his creative energies and $600,000 into The Cloisters. The ceilings, floors, gallery, and tower remained the same; everything else—60 percent of the space—was changed. The original roof was removed, and each tile repaired and replaced. The outdoor snack bar was converted into a small chapel, with a stained-glass window from Rhode Island. The centerpiece of the chapel was a statue of St. Anthony, the saint who had saved Liberace's life in Pittsburgh. It was an old piece from Italy that was stripped of several coats of paint to reveal its original beauty.

While the Palm Springs house was being reconstructed, Liberace launched a buying spree for furnishings to augment what he had already collected in warehouses. In Pensacola, Florida, he came across a magnificent French desk on which the last czar of all the Russias, Nicholas II, signed an alliance with the French. The desk belonged to an elderly woman who operated a private museum. Liberace was so impressed with the desk he bought the entire contents of the museum.

After The Cloisters was finally restored in 1967, Liberace delighted in conducting guests on tours. They often arrived in one of the five antique cars Liberace kept in Palm Springs. As the visitors drove into the driveway, the glassed garage doors swung up to reveal an ornate ballroom with glittering chandeliers. The car glided over the hand-painted Italian tile floor and came to a halt. A butler greeted the guests with a tray of cold drinks.

The entry hall contained Liberace's collection of icons from Greece, Russia, and other countries. Also an ancient mirror with carved wooden gold-leafed frame that had belonged to a Spanish king. The two-storied dining room was the host's special pride, and he compared it to William Randolph Hearst's at San Simeon. Indeed, he patterned the furniture after Hearst's, including a massive table that could seat twenty-four. As in all Liberace dining rooms, the table was always set with gleaming silver and crystal. "See the initial K on the silverware?" Liberace pointed out. "The silver set once belonged to John F. Kennedy."

The master bedroom with its vaulted ceiling contained the Nicholas II desk and other rare French pieces. The bathroom was glassed with French Baccarat, the chandelier over the sunken marble Jacuzzi tub once hung in a church. Always distressed by the sight of a naked toilet, Liberace disguised the one in his master bathroom as a throne, literally.

The rooms went on and on, ten guest bedrooms in all, including one containing the bed of Liberace's namesake, Rudolph Valentino. There was a basement bar resembling a 1920s speakeasy, complete with coffee cups to drink liquor from. A conservatory was highlighted by a large fountain surrounded by antique French baking racks laden with huge plants.

Visitors often admired the fireplaces, which glowed and crackled "just like an old-fashioned fire." Liberace confessed: "The fire is gas, the logs are cement, and the ashes are asbestos. The wood smell comes from a product I sprinkle over the logs, and it makes the fire crackle, too."

The flowers on the piano, visitors noted, were made of silk. "I used to have plastic flowers," said Liberace. "But I found that plastic flowers are inclined to turn brittle and fall apart. They also have an unpleasant smell."

Automobiles became another passion for Liberace, though not for the reasons other men loved cars. He never even drove a car until he was thirty, when he bought an Oldsmobile 88 convertible. Automobiles to him were another means of restoring "the glamour that was Hollywood."

His first ornate car was the El Dorado Cadillac with piano-key leather upholstery, mink carpeting, and gold trim. When he opened the Las Vegas Hilton Hotel in 1972, he needed a suitable means of entering the huge theater. His choice: a black and white Rolls-Royce Phantom V Landau, a model that only Queen Elizabeth, John Lennon, and four others owned. For his closing number, a ragtime-Charleston routine, he arrived in a fully restored, tomato-red 1939 Ford Model A.

The collection grew: an ice-blue Mercedes Excalibur; a 1957 London taxicab painted in black and white houndstooth; a diamond-studded dune buggy, air-conditioned; a 1900 Oldsmobile surrey, top speed 25 m.p.h.; a Cadillac Seville stretch limousine; a gull-winged, metallic gold Bradley GT; a Jaguar XKE; a Lincoln Executive limousine in white leather and blue velvet; plus station wagons and trucks to carry the Liberace costumes and artifacts.

Pianos were everywhere—seven in the Harold Way house alone. Liberace would play only Chopin on the nineteenth-century instrument he maintained Frédéric Chopin once used. And he allowed himself only Gershwin on the piano George Gershwin was said to have composed on. Others in his collection included the bejeweled honky-tonk upright and the double-keyboard grand.

Of all his possessions, the dogs were dearest to Liberace's heart. "They are my children," he declared fervently.

In his later years he owned twenty-one dogs, eleven pure-bred and the rest mixtures, all spayed or neutered ("I don't want any grandchildren"). Sixteen of the pets resided in Las Vegas, five special favorites commuted between Palm Springs and Los Angeles.

The first dog was a toy poodle named Suzette that shared the Sherman Oaks house with Lee and Mom. Next he adopted a huge standard poodle named Jo-Jo that Mom decried as more horse than dog. When Lee sold the house, Suzette went to Mom and Jo-Jo to the housekeeper, Gladys Luckie.

For years Liberace had no dogs, and he missed them. Then some San Francisco friends showed him a pair of adorable newborn poodles. They also had a sickly puppy that was going to be destroyed. "I'll take that one," Lee declared, and he nursed the puppy to robust adulthood. He began adopting hardship cases: a blind dog whose sight was restored by surgery; a Shetland sheepdog with broken spirit from being caged for six months. Then he began indulging in rare breeds: Maltese, Lhasa apso, Shar-pei, West Highland terrier. The dogs truly became like children. Whenever Liberace was on the road, he carried framed photographs of his favorite dogs and placed them around his hotel suite the way businessmen display family snapshots. During rare times when he was home alone for dinner, the dogs sat on other chairs at the table, waiting for handouts from their loving master.

Liberace's cooking, he often said, began in his earliest years, when Mom was running the family store. Since she was always up front taking care of customers, he, Angie, and George had to learn how to cook. By watching their father, they became proficient at making Italian dishes. All learned to make use of what went unsold in the store. Bruised fruit and damaged vegetables were rescued and integrated into improvised recipes.

Angie often bragged about her younger brother's cooking to her home economics teacher. When Walter arrived at West Milwaukee High School, the teacher proposed that he help organize a cooking class for boys. It would be called the Chefs' Course to make it sound less feminine.

Walter canvassed his friends, but they scoffed, "That's too sissy." Walter argued, "But the best chefs in the world are all men." The boys remained unconvinced. The school required twenty-six students for the course to be accredited; teams of two would work at thirteen stoves and ovens. So far he had only one enrollee, himself.

In desperation, Walter approached the football team. He had a special link with the athletes, since he played piano for their dances to raise funds for sports equipment. "Either join the boys' cooking class or I won't play for your dances," he said. They joined.

The Chefs' Course proved a rousing success. The football players became enthusiastic cooks, making double recipes so there would be plenty to eat afterward. Besides cooking, the students learned the various cuts of beef, lamb, and pork, how to shop for the best quality and bargains, how to can and preserve food.

Liberace liked to recount the culmination of the course, the Fathers and Sons Banquet. Most of the fathers approached the affair fearing the worst. All were surprised. The boys were divided into teams, each pair with a responsibility: table settings, salads, rolls, entrées, desserts, etc. The result was a Lucullan feast. The Chefs' Course became one of the most popular courses at West Milwaukee High, and a B average was required to enter.

While he was studying with Florence Kelly at the Wisconsin College of Music, Liberace worked in a restaurant owned by family friends. He started as a busboy and dishwasher, became a waiter, and always was studying the chef's techniques. This early training made him proficient in cooking for large numbers, and in later years he confessed an inability to prepare meals for two or three.

During his early career, Liberace ate in enough diners and hash houses to make him treasure careful cooking. As soon as he was able to afford better accommodations, he requested cooking facilities in his hotel rooms, and he prepared gourmet meals for members of his company and other guests after the shows.

Liberace Cooks!, subtitled "Recipes from His Seven Dining Rooms," was published in 1970 by Doubleday. It was written by Carol Truax, author of the *Ladies' Home Journal Cookbook* and seven other recipe books, and a special friend of Liberace's. She had been entertainment director for the Broadmoor Theater in Colorado Springs during his career slump in the late 1950s, and she had hired him at $25,000 a week.

The book's recipes ranged from almond tarts to zuppa di pesce, each chapter devoted to dishes suitable for the seven eating places in the Harold Way house. Dinners were designed for the formal dining room (avocado stuffed with shrimp, Rock Cornish game hens with wild rice stuffing, green beans au gratin, celery Victor, parfait) and the television room (moussaka). Several of Mom's dishes were described, including her potato salad and her potato pancakes. *Liberace Cooks!* became a best-seller that remained in print for years.

As his cooking skills progressed, Liberace developed a technique of preparing dinners in advance so he could spend more time playing host instead of remaining in the kitchen. Most of his pasta dishes were partially cooked the day before "because they taste better the second day, anyway." Then at the dinner he could amaze his guests by hastily heating and serving the gourmet dishes. On one occasion the system proved disastrous.

Liberace had planned a special meal for close friends, precooking two large pans full of the lasagna that always drew raves from dinner guests. After his guests sat down to the table, he served them a dish of melon balls with a melon liqueur to bring out the flavor, then a salad of exotic greens with a piquant dressing. Liberace excused himself to add final touches to the lasagna. He slid the pans out of the oven, saw the tomato sauce bubbling satisfactorily, and sprinkled on a final layer of Parmesan cheese.

He watched in horror as patches of blue began to spread over the top of the lasagna like an evil mold in a science fiction movie. As he studied the phenomenon, he automatically sprinkled the second pan. Again the blue mutations. He looked at the can of cheese in his hand. It was Comet cleanser.

He lifted a pan to the sink, burning his hand as he did. Desperately he scraped the blue off the top of the lasagna, then he took a bite. The lasagna tasted like garlic-flavored chlorine. He scraped more off, to no avail. The cleanser had permeated both dishes.

Liberace hastily consulted the telephone book. "Is this Chicken Delight? I've got fourteen guests for dinner. Send over enough to feed them." He returned to his guests and smiled, "Want some more wine? Dinner will be ready in a few minutes."

Chapter 12

THE WORLD CATCHES UP WITH LIBERACE IN THE
1970S; HE LOSES DAD AND MOM

The 1970s were a decade of redemption for Liberace. America was undergoing convulsive changes in fashions, politics, music, films, personal relationships, and sexual attitudes. Suddenly Liberace did not seem so outrageous after all. His garish houses and cars and his regal costumes evoked awe and admiration instead of scorn. Even his ambiguous sexuality was now accepted as part of his anomalous persona.

Liberace himself added to the confusion when he appeared in San Francisco at a 1973 press conference that resulted in the headline: "I Am Not a Homosexual, Says Liberace."

He was quoted in an AP dispatch as saying just that, adding: "As I told a British court in 1959 when I won a twenty-thousand-dollar judgment against a London newspaper, my sexual feelings are the same as most people's. I'm against the practice of homosexuality because it offends convention and society.... The only reason I never got married is probably because I come from a family of divorce. My parents, first of all. It put me off from marriage. It was a deterrent. ... I'm so tired of people writing stories about me that are dishonest and cancerous with innuendo. The only reason they started is because I was the first in my field to dare to be a nonconformist, to wear the fancy clothes I do.... Now if I were to emerge on the scene, I would probably go unnoticed. A lot of people nowadays can wear sequins on their eyelids and nobody puts a sexual label on them."

He continued in a more dramatic and fanciful vein: "I could have given up many, many times, professionally and personally. Why, I've been pronounced dead three times. I've had the last rites of the Church. I've been the victim of an international kidnapping attempt. Oh, mind you, I wouldn't trade my life for that of anyone else. I'm a person who was put on earth simply to bring happiness and love to people. And I get that back in abundance. It's what makes me go on living and doing my thing."

At least that much was true: he wouldn't have traded his life for anyone else's. He envied no one.

The San Francisco article caused Liberace great embarrassment. His many gay friends considered it a step backward at a time when closets were opening all over America. When he was interviewed for the Karl Fleming and Anne Taylor Fleming book *The First Time* (in which he detailed his loss of virginity), he spoke about the press conference: "This son of a bitch says, 'Do you feel the same way about homosexuality that you did when you fought your trial in London?' I said, 'Whatever I said in the high courts of London, I meant, and if I said it then, I say it now.' So he took this one line out of twelve days of testimony and quoted it completely out of context without any explanation at all. For me to say something like that today would be stupid. It made me appear that I'm down on gay people. Shit, I resented it."

In the seventies, Liberace still managed to make news, not always the kind he enjoyed.

The Internal Revenue Service questioned whether Liberace's mink-lined jackets, gold-plated limousines, and palatial houses qualified as business deductions. He maintained that they did, since they contributed to the opulence that was his trademark. He paid $300 a month rent on the living quarters of the Harold Way house, which cost $50,000 a year to maintain. The house was owned by International Artists, Limited, of which he held 78 percent of the stock.

The IRS was unpersuaded, and a tax court ordered Liberace to pay $60,000 in back taxes.

When Liberace was promoting his cookbook in 1971, he engaged in an uncharacteristic brouhaha with a woman reporter. A Long Beach, California, food editor had been invited to the Harold Way home to partake of Liberace's beef Stroganoff. The tasting over, the woman wanted her photographer to shoot Liberace in the kitchen.

He shook his head. "Too messy," he said. He agreed to pose elsewhere—with his cookbook in hand. "Too commercial," she snapped.

"Then I think we should forget the photo," he decreed.

"Then I think we should forget the story," she countered, "because you're a better piano player than you are a cook. Your beef Stroganoff tastes more like canned beef stew." She was asked to leave, and the contretemps was duly reported in the press.

The Liberace jewels proved a natural target for thieves. Several times he reported expensive items missing from his hotel suites. The caretaker of the Harold Way House once scared away a burglar in the living room. In 1975, Liberace reported the theft of a $28,000 necklace that had recently been given to him after his engagement at Lake

Tahoe. It contained five miniature gold pianos studded with jewels and a Rolls-Royce with diamond headlights. The necklace had been stolen while he was staying overnight at the $100,000 Bel-Air home of his houseboy, Gregory Scortenu. What Liberace was doing there and how a houseboy could afford such a house were questions reporters did not raise.

Liberace never fretted over loss of his treasures. "Whenever I'm robbed, the jewelry eventually shows up," he explained. "The pieces are easily identified. Nobody but nobody has jewelry like mine."

Nevada became Liberace's legal residence, largely because the state had no income tax. He was spending more and more time there, averaging sixteen weeks in Las Vegas and five or six in Reno and Lake Tahoe. He loved the glittery excitement of the casinos. Wherever he went, he was treated like royalty. No entertainer was paid more than Liberace. Elvis Presley had received a bigger weekly salary, but his appearances had been sporadic.

Liberace was loyal to his employers. He remained eleven years with the Last Frontier, leaving only because the Riviera's $50,000-a-week offer was irresistible. After seventeen years at the Riviera, he ended his association in 1972 because the new Hilton promised him $300,000 a week.

The casinos cherished Liberace because he attracted the customers they needed to fill their gambling tables: high rollers, often brought to the show by their wives or mistresses, plus a wide cross section of Middle America to keep the slot machines and bingo games busy. The only complaint of the pit bosses was the length of Liberace's show.

Most entertainers were cautioned to limit their performances so the audience could flow back into the casino. Such warnings were unavailing with Liberace. He insisted on giving the patrons their money's worth, even if the craps tables languished. Stagehands always organized a pool on the length of Liberace's opening-night show. One night the running time was two hours and fifteen minutes, about an hour beyond what the bosses would have liked.

Liberace was devoted to those who helped him put on the show. A backstage electrician had a habit of getting drunk after the show and often he landed in jail. His one telephone call was made to Liberace, who told his attorney to supply bail. When the head carpenter announced his forthcoming marriage, Lee said, "I'll stage the wedding." He made it a spectacular production with himself as best man.

His dressing room was always open to members of his company, and he listened to their problems, giving them advice and money. Everyone received a handsome gift at the end of an engagement. The dressing room accommodated a stream of visitors—movie stars like Cary Grant and Sophia Loren, old friends from Milwaukee, ordinary fans. All received equal cordiality.

Liberace never declined an interview and never appeared upset, no matter how hostile the interviewer seemed. One evening a reporter from a small radio station appeared backstage with a tape recorder. Liberace received him in the dressing room. "I saw your first show," the reporter began. "I was amazed at how well you coordinated with the playback." Liberace explained calmly that his performances were always live, not pre-taped. The reporter persisted along the same line until an assistant remarked that Liberace had to rest before his next performance.

After many years of appearing in Las Vegas, Liberace found it was more restful to reside away from the noise and constant scrutiny of the hotels. For a few years he stayed at the Bali Hi motel, which was favored by other entertainers as a quiet, convenient location. As he began playing more weeks in Las Vegas, he decided to buy his own house.

When Liberace purchased a tract house in a development started by Wilbur Clark of the Desert Inn, his friends remarked, "But it's so small." "Don't worry," Liberace assured, "it'll grow." One house grew to three, and he connected them to create a villa as luxurious as any residence in Las Vegas.

The centerpiece was the scaled-down Sistine Chapel ceiling, with nymphs and prophets floating in a pale blue sky over Liberace's bed. The artist was Stefano Angelo Falk, called by Liberace a "reincarnated Michelangelo." Falk decorated other ceilings as well. In the master bathroom, cherubs danced on piano keys under the baton of Liberace. The bathroom was like a large, marbled garden, the Roman pool contained two golden swans.

Marble, glass, and mirrors everywhere. The Baldwin grand piano was covered with etched mirror mosaic. Polished marble columns led to the soundproofed rehearsal hall and Liberace's library and writing room. Huge mirrors were etched with Aubrey Beardsley drawings. Next to the pool was a small lagoon that offered a miniature version of the Dancing Waters, a feature of the Liberace show.

The artist, Falk, was recipient of a grant from Lee's latest enthusiasm, the Liberace Foundation for the Performing and Creative Arts. For years he had delighted in introducing undiscovered talent in his shows—he never failed to mention that he gave Barbra Streisand one of her first important breaks. The foundation provided funds for performers and artists to pursue their talents. Among them: an opera singer whose only experience had been performing on cruise ships; a twelve-year-old girl with a Judy Garland voice; a ten-year-old boy juggler; a seventy-four-year-old mime who imitated Charlie Chaplin in a 1920s Liberace production number.

Liberace: An Autobiography was published in 1973 by Putnam. It was written by Carroll Carroll, a well-known writer of radio variety shows, who received only credit "for his editorial assistance in the preparation of this manuscript." The book is chatty, digressive, and disorganized, as revealing in what it omits as in what it includes.

On the first page of the introduction, Liberace told how *The Magic of Believing* changed his life, teaching him "the true meaning of Franklin D. Roosevelt's immortal words: 'The only thing we have to fear is fear itself.' "

The autobiography disclosed nothing about the author's sex life beyond a mention of his teenage experiences in Wisconsin roadhouses: "Needless to say, before the joint I was playing in was hit by police, I had ceased to be a virgin and found out exactly the meaning of the word 'prostitute.' "

In the final chapter, Liberace discussed his romances with the girl next door in West Milwaukee, with Joanne Rio (for which she sued him), the heiress Frances Goodrich, and Sonja Henie. Admitting that as a longtime bachelor he might be considered a poor prospect as a husband, he added: "Should the right woman come along, one who clearly loves me enough to take a chance on me and I feel that deeply for her, I'm sure we both will know that 'this is it.' "

Curiously, Liberace devoted almost fifty of the book's 316 pages to twelve days in his life—the London trial that vindicated him against the *Daily Mirror's* insinuations of his homosexuality.

Sam Liberace had grown old. He and his second wife, Zona, had moved to San Francisco in 1961, and she had died in 1970. Sam's health deteriorated after her death, and each time Lee visited his father, he was shocked by the change. Sam had reached his mid-eighties, and his body had withered to a small replica of the vigorous father Lee once knew. When it appeared that Sam could no longer care for himself, George stepped in with a solution. George had finally abandoned his lifetime of traveling, and he had settled with his fifth wife, Dora, in Sacramento, where he played occasional dates and conducted a television program. He moved his father to a nursing home in Carmichael, near Sacramento. George and Dora could watch after him, and he would be close enough for Lee and Angie to visit.

"Lee, you must come up and see Dad," George urged his brother.

"I don't know if I can, George," said Lee. "The last time I saw him I was depressed for days."

"He's your father, Lee," George said. "You gotta visit him."

When Lee arrived at his father's room in the nursing home, he was shocked. He could scarcely recognize the tiny figure with the lifeless eyes. "Dad, it's Walter come to visit you," George said. The head rose slowly, and the eyes stared blankly at the visitor beside the bed.

"It's me—Walter," Lee said.

The old man shook his head and turned to George. "That's not Walter," he muttered.

"Of course it is," George insisted. "Look at those rings. Who else but Walter would wear those rings?"

The old man stared again. "That's not my son," he said. "I'd know who my son was, wouldn't I? That's not him."

Lee felt the tears flowing, and he fled from the room. On the drive back to the airport, he said, "George, you must promise me that you will never try to persuade me to visit him again. I don't want to remember him this way. It tears my heart out."

Salvatore Liberace died April 30, 1977, the victim of his years, which were ninety-two.

More houses. As he was converting his three Las Vegas houses into one, Liberace bought four more nearby. He traded one of his Palm Springs houses for a chalet at Lake Arrowhead. Then he became entranced with Malibu.

Liberace had never spent much time by the ocean, and when he began visiting the beaches above Santa Monica, he discovered great peace of mind. He loved walking alone on the beach and watching his dogs chase the shore birds. He bought a small condominium and decorated it with customary lavishness. After listening to friends' lectures about the brush fires, high waves, and mud slides that sometimes afflict Malibu, Liberace sold the condo back to the builder. As always in his real estate ventures, he made a handsome profit.

The lure of the sea prompted him to buy another condominium not far from his earlier place. He bought three lower apartments in a six-unit building. Two of his units were converted into one, and the third became a guest apartment.

One day in January 1978, Liberace drove from his Malibu place to the Harold Way mansion for an interview. It had been several years since I had seen Liberace, but he seemed little changed. The hair was more bouffant, and the gray had disappeared. The occasion for the interview was a CBS television special, "Leapin' Lizards, It's Liberace," his first major television appearance since the London summer series ten years before. He explained the lapse:

"I never like to tamper with success. I appear on an occasional talk show, just to let people know I'm around and alive; some people have no contact with show business except what they see on television. My main output is personal appearances. I play about thirty-two weeks a year—sixteen in Las Vegas, four in Lake Tahoe-Reno, the rest one-nighters and week-long concerts in summer theaters, tours to Australia, South Africa, England—I'll be going back to the London Palladium this spring. I realize I must do some television, but too much can hurt the box office for personal appearances."

He talked about his houses, which now numbered ten. The extra Las Vegas houses, he explained, were used by stars like Debbie Reynolds and Ann-Margret, who preferred private homes when they were appearing in the casinos.

"My accountant wants me to get rid of the Lake Arrowhead house, and I suppose I will," said Liberace. "He pointed out that I spent four nights there last year, and he said, 'You know how much that cost you? Forty thousand dollars a night.' "

Liberace gazed around the living room, crammed with opulence.

"I guess this place will have to go, too," he sighed. "Mom lives most of the year in her own Palm Springs house, and I like to stay at Malibu when I'm in town. I tried to turn this place into a museum. In one month we had seventeen thousand reservations. But the neighbors complained. Not because of the tours; we ran three limousines up from Sunset Boulevard and parked them off the street. Trouble was, too many people drove up here to look the place over and see if they were going to get their ten dollars' worth."

Liberace sold the house, furnished, the following year. He found a new passion, an office building on Beverly Boulevard. The penthouse apartment hadn't been lived in for seventeen years, and it reminded Liberace of a scene from *Sunset Boulevard*. Layers of dust covered everything, and the swimming pool was opaque with trash and algae. "I'll take it," Liberace announced. "I can make something beautiful of it."

He transformed the penthouse into another wonderland of glass, mirrors, plush, and ferns, raising the roof to accommodate a shimmering chandelier hanging over the Plexiglas-topped, mirror-mosaic piano.

Thwarted in his attempt to make the Harold Way house into a museum, Liberace sought another way to share his treasures with the public. His thoughts turned to his homeland. Why not erect a Liberace Museum in the land where he was born, where his talent had been nurtured?

His fellow Milwaukeeans did not share his vision. When he announced a plan to convert a stately old Gothic mansion in the suburb of Wauwatosa into a museum celebrating his life and career, nearby residents and preservationists set up such a howl that he abandoned the notion.

If Los Angeles and Milwaukee declined a Liberace Museum, Las Vegas would not. After all, wasn't his name synonymous with the glitz and glamour that Las Vegas strove to promote, counteracting the town's sleazier side? Liberace searched for a suitable location and found a small shopping center a few minutes from the Strip. It afforded room for expansion, and the $2-million price seemed reasonable.

For a year Liberace poured his creative energies into the design of the museum, a one-story, 5,000-square-foot building in Spanish style. On Easter Sunday 1979 he stood at the door of the Liberace Museum to greet the first arrivals—the mayor of Las Vegas and other dignitaries and members of the media. Reporters noted that he wore a checkered jacket of pink, blue, and yellow, matching yellow shirt and slacks, a large gold cross around his neck, and six diamond-and-gold rings on his fingers.

"Welcome to the Liberace Museum," he announced proudly. "I don't usually wear diamonds in the afternoon, but this is a special occasion."

Liberace conducted the first wave of visitors through the displays, giving a brief history of the Chopin and Gershwin pianos. "I'm not playing them today—that costs extra," he grinned. Sitting at or standing beside the pianos were life-size mannequins of Liberace in his jeweled costumes.

"When I was in England I admired a painting of George V in his coronation robes," Liberace recounted, standing in front of another display. "I said to myself, 'This I gotta have.' I had my designer reproduce the robe in velvet and silk brocade, adding sixty thousand dollars' worth of chinchilla. I wore it at a command performance for the King's granddaughter, Queen Elizabeth. Nice, isn't it?"

He continued through the other costumes, the antique automobiles, the miniature pianos. "This is something very special to me," he commented, holding a highly polished French horn. "This was my father's. He played in Sousa's band, and he died at the age of ninety-two."

A pair of silver goblets. "These were a wedding gift to Rudolph

Valentino and Pola Negri. I was named after him, you know. Of course, the wedding never happened. He died."

After the VIP tour, the public was admitted. Some had been waiting in the desert sun for hours, and they gladly paid the $3.50 entrance fee, which benefited the Liberace Foundation for the Performing and Creative Arts. Liberace greeted each of them at the door and shook their hands, repeating, "Nice to see ya. Hi, glad you could come. How are ya?"

The Liberace Museum quickly became Nevada's third most popular tourist attraction, after gambling and Boulder Dam, drawing 120,000 visitors a year. The museum and the foundation provided an occasion for the reuniting of Lee and George after twenty years of separate careers and semi-estrangement. George was now sixty-eight and weary after a lifetime of smiling and bowing his violin. He was receptive when Lee suggested that he and Dora move from Sacramento to Las Vegas. George became curator of the museum and administrator of the foundation, and Dora conducted tours and handled public relations at the museum. The renewal of the brotherly bonds was a great comfort to Mom, now spending the remainder of her days in Las Vegas.

They thought she would die in 1978. She had a heart seizure at her Palm Springs house, and doctors said the prognosis was poor. Angie joined Lee at Eisenhower Hospital, and together they watched for hopeful signs of recovery. But Mom did not respond to treatment, and Angie began to despair.

"Lee, I think we have to talk about what will happen if Mom dies," Angie said. He stared at her coldly and walked away.

Later that evening, Angie said to her brother, "Lee, I know it's painful for both of us. But we've got to plan for the future. Now I've bought her a lovely black dress. . . ."

Lee glared at her with an anger she hadn't seen in him since they were children. "Angie, I hope you can wear that goddamned dress," he spat, "because she's going to outlive all of us!"

Mom recovered. She surprised everyone, except Lee, by shrugging off all her ailments. Lee realized that she was lonely in Palm Springs. She wanted to spend more time with her children, and all three were living much of the time in Las Vegas. She was thrilled when Lee said he would move her to a condominium in Las Vegas.

She thrived in Nevada. She never missed a chance to attend Lee's show, and Angie took her to see other performers as well. Mom even made friends with Gladys Luckie, Lee's longtime housekeeper who had been resented by Mom in earlier years. Now Mom and Gladys made regular forays into the casinos to play the slot machines hour after hour. After Mom broke her hip in a fall, she could no longer make her trips to the casinos. The Las Vegas Hilton sent several slot machines to Lee's house for her to play. When she hit a jackpot, she demanded that he pay her.

One day she said to Lee, "You know what would really make me happy? I would like to be able to walk again with my dear sister and with my brothers." All of them were dead. Mom died in her sleep on November 25, 1980, at the age of eighty-nine.

Chapter 13

"THE WAY YOU COUNTERACT NEGATIVE IS WITH POSITIVE"

Liberace was a show business loner. He was universally liked by his acquaintances in the entertainment world, but none knew him intimately. He greeted them cordially in his dressing room after performances, and he paid calls on other performers in Las Vegas. Occasionally he would cook dinner for favorites like Debbie Reynolds, Michael Jackson, and Isabel Sanford. But, like Rock Hudson and other homosexual stars, Liberace's private life remained secluded, and his privacy was respected.

Since he was not identified with any charities or show world clubs, Liberace was not the subject of the tributes that are endemic with any star who had remained in the spotlight for decades. The exception came on November 21, 1980, when he was presented with an achievement award by the Pacific Pioneer Broadcasters, a group of radio and television oldtimers who gathered at the Sportsmen's Lodge in Studio City periodically to reminisce about their glory days and honor one of their own.

Like all such affairs, the Liberace luncheon was part roast, part tribute. The best roasting was done by Pat Buttram, the cowboy humorist: "When I first saw Liberace, he couldn't afford all these coats covered with rhinestones and diamonds. In those days he wore five thousand lightning bugs in heat. . . . He and I did a pilot for a series once, it was a western called 'Trial of the Lonesome Pie-ana.' He played the roughest, toughest hombre that ever rode sidesaddle. The Indians had a name for him: Gitcheegooma Katchytomma. Which means 'White Brother with Too Many Teeth Who's Fulla Crap.' . . . Liberace's first name is Wladziu. His mother liked the name when she saw it on a doctor's eye chart."

Duke Goldstone reminisced about his days directing the Guild Films series. Seymour Heller paid tribute to "the most wonderful man in the world." Lurene Tuttle remembered playing the mother in *Sincerely Yours*, and Vivian Blaine talked of when she and Walter Buster Keys worked in the Jay Mills Orchestra forty years before.

George Liberace, mute in all the television shows with Lee, made an attempt at standup comedy: "My brother is the world's greatest showman, most gifted pianist, best-dressed entertainer. That's not just my opinion. It's his, too. . . . Yes, my brother Liberace is truly a legend in his own mind. . . . Everyone asks about Lee's love life. Well, of all the girls that he loved and lost, every one calls Lee their 'little cave man.' One kiss and he caves in. . . ."

It was a long monologue, accompanied by projected slides, then George introduced "not just my kid brother, but my best friend." After receiving his Golden Ike award from Jim Jordan (Fibber

McGee), Liberace cracked, "I guess you know now why George never talked on our television show."

Lee seemed genuinely moved by the tributes. As he gazed around the room at old friends like Maxine Lewis, Vivian Blaine, and Duke Goldstone, he recounted the old familiar stories about Walter Buster Keys and getting the job at the Last Frontier and mistaking Howard Hughes for the electrician and the last rites in Pittsburgh. The stories had been so polished for interviewers over the years that they sounded like a nightclub routine, with all the punch lines in the right places. Then he came to the chambermaid-and-the-toilet number, which had become the most surefire monologue of his act, the climax evoking laughter at every line.

The incident took place in Louisville, where Liberace was appearing, along with Jean Fenn, a Metropolitan Opera soprano. She and the musical director, Gordon Robinson, asked if they could use Liberace's suite to rehearse a new aria. He admitted them at 11 A.M., and they began to practice "Un Bel Di" from *Madame Butterfly*.

Liberace: "So I started getting ready for the day, and like most people, my first stop was the bathroom. I was sitting down with nothing on, and all of a sudden the door opened, and it was the maid. I said, 'Would you excuse me, please?' trying to cover myself as best I could. And she said, 'I thought you were playing the piano.' . . .

"I said, 'As you can see, I'm not.' . . . She said, 'Well, who *is* playing?' . . . I said, 'Would you *excuse* me? We'll discuss it later.' . . . She wouldn't leave. I said, 'Dr. Gordon Robinson, my conductor, is playing,' and she said, 'Well, who's singing?'

"I said, 'It's Jean Fenn of the Metropolitan.' 'What's she singing?' . . . ' "Un Bel Di" from *Madame Butterfly.*' 'What does that mean?' . . . I said, ' "One Fine Day." ' She said, 'Yes, it is.' . . .

"She was absolutely oblivious to the fact that I was sitting on the throne. Finally I said, 'Would you please close the door and come back later?' She started to close the door, then she opened it and said, 'I understand you're a collector. What do you collect?' . . . 'We'll talk about it later!' . . . Finally I got rid of her.

"Well, I put on my robe and went into the living room and told them the story. Jean said, 'You can't expect me to sing that song with you; I'd break up.' I said, 'Okay, you can sing *La Boheme* instead.' They left, and sure enough, the maid returned.

"She was carrying a cloth bag, and she said, 'Would you like to see my collection?' . . . I said, 'I guess so,' and she took out a small matchbox. There on a little piece of cotton are a couple of hairs. I said, 'What is this?' She said, 'Those are the pubic hairs of Rudolph Valentino!' . . .

"I said, 'You don't mean it!' . . . She said, 'I have many others.' . . . She kept pulling these boxes out of her bag and she opened them up one at a time, and she said, 'Guess who?' . . . I said, 'They all look alike to me. How do you get these things?' She said, 'When I make up the bed. I look on the sheets and I know who they belong to. It's a very valuable collection.' . . . I said, 'I don't think I'd be interested.'

"She said, 'Let me show you one more.' She opened up the matchbox and I said, 'All right, whose is it?' She said 'YOURS!' "

When the laughter subsided, Liberace commented that he was often asked if he would retire. He recalled visiting Jack Benny after a performance at Lake Tahoe. Benny was lying down, and Lee apologized for the intrusion. "That's all right," said Benny, "I like people to visit me. I get bored when I'm not around people. The only thing I have to do is lie down and rest. . . . I don't think I'll ever retire as long as I can make people laugh."

Liberace added: "I feel the same way. I don't think I'll ever retire. I look forward to every day of my life as a day to conquer and to win new friends. I hope I have the health and the energy and the opportunity to do it for another thirty-five years, God willing."

After he had moved Mom to Las Vegas, Liberace decided to sell the Spanish hacienda where she had lived behind The Cloisters. The buyers were Vince Fronza and Ken Fosler, who operated a gift shop in Palm Springs. A few years younger than Lee, they became friends as well as neighbors. Lee enjoyed being able to talk to people who were not imbued with show business, and he had a special designation for Fronza and Fosler. "You know how I have a personal manager and a personal valet?" he told friends. "Vince and Ken are my personal neighbors."

When Liberace was in Palm Springs, he often dined with his two neighbors. Fosler was also a gourmet cook, and he and Lee spent hours together in The Cloisters' kitchen preparing feasts. When Fosler and Fronza decided to build a garage, Lee said, "Make it larger so I can get two of my cars in. Then I won't have to go out on the street to get to my car." A doorway was cut through the back wall of The Cloisters, and Fronza dubbed it "the hole in the wall." Whenever Lee came to visit, he telephoned to say, "I'm coming through the hole in the wall."

He came often, though never when he saw a visitor's car in front of the house. He was shy about encountering strangers. After Mom died, Lee seemed to find solace in the house. One Christmas he asked if he and Angie could come to visit. After conversation over cocktails, Lee asked, "Would you mind if Angie and I went to Mom's bedroom?" They remained behind the closed door for several minutes, and they returned red-eyed from weeping.

One night Liberace came to his neighbors' house for dinner with Ruby Keeler and Ernie Flatt, the director. As they were dining, the music sheets suddenly fell from a stand next to a Liberace piano. As the startled guests looked around, Lee said, "Mom's here." He gazed upward. "Now, Mom, don't get excited. The boys are taking good care of your house. Everything's okay, Mom, you can relax."

During the day, Liberace enjoyed window-shopping down Palm Canyon Drive, the main street of Palm Springs. He strolled casually, often with Fronza and Fosler, devoting special attention to the jewelry stores. When he shopped in the stores, he knew many of the salespeople by name. He liked to buy his own groceries, and he startled shoppers by standing behind his cart in the checkout line.

Usually he wore a jumpsuit or casual slacks and shirt, with only a ring and wristwatch. He was recognized, of course, but the local residents respected his privacy, and the tourists often couldn't believe they were seeing Liberace. He explained his technique: "I'm a fast walker. By the time they realize it's me, I'm a block away."

He enjoyed sitting on the veranda of the Brussels café and watching the passing scene. He wasn't bothered there, but often tourists would wait for him to leave. "Would you like to take my picture?" he asked, and he posed patiently, always discarding his cigarette beforehand.

One day as he was strolling down Palm Canyon Drive, he overheard the conversation of two elderly women behind him: "It's him!" "No, it isn't." "I *know* it is." "Well, you're wrong." Liberace turned around and smiled. "It *is* him!" one of the women said.

"But you look much younger than you do on television," the other one remarked.

"You must have an old set," he replied.

In his later years as a performer, Liberace's costumes became as much a part of his act as his musicianship. His first designer had been Sy Devore, whose Vine Street shop tailored clothes for Bing Crosby, Bob Hope, George Burns, Martin and Lewis, and other stars. Liberace had consulted Devore on William Holden's recommendation, and Devore discarded Lee's wide-shouldered, formless suits for well-tailored styles. Devore created the white tails for the Hollywood Bowl concert and a gold lamé smoking jacket, gray silk suit, and black tuxedo with gold polka dots for *Sincerely Yours*.

After Devore's death, Ray Acuna became the Liberace designer. A native of Guadalajara, Acuna had created movie costumes for Douglas Fairbanks Jr., Tyrone Power, Gregory Peck, and Cary Grant, and his dramatic flair appealed to Liberace. He loved the costumes worn in historical and swashbuckling movies. When preparing for a tour, he sometimes invited Acuna to a screening of *Beau Brummell,* the 1954 movie with Stewart Granger and Elizabeth Taylor. "Make me one of *those,"* Liberace would say, pointing at a costume. Often he drew his own conception of a costume—he was a clever sketch artist.

He enjoyed taking costumes from another era and converting them to the twentieth century. The George V coronation robe was an example. A Louis XVI court portrait was reproduced in pink and white silk, encrusted with jewels.

Liberace liked to wear fabrics intended for other purposes: velours used for upholstery, brocades designed for wall hangings, oriental obi cloths. In a tailor shop in Rome he pointed at the window draperies and said, "I want a suit made out of that."

There was no stinting on ornamentation. The best sequins were made in Spain, where they were used for bullfighters' costumes, and Acuna ordered as many as the suppliers could provide. The rhinestones came from an Austrian manufacturer, and the beads and jewels were bought in Los Angeles. An elaborate costume required a month of work by the artisans in Acuna's workshop on the Sunset Strip.

Furs became an important part of the Liberace onstage wardrobe. In 1973 he made his entrance in a $35,000 blue shadow mink coat of one hundred Danish pelts. A black diamond mink cape lined with rhinestones weighed 135 pounds, enough to give one backstage helper a hernia.

In later years Liberace became a target of animal lovers. When he wore his baby seal coat to Bloomingdale's in New York, an indignant woman handed him a pamphlet describing how baby seals are clubbed to death for their pelts. "Gee, I didn't know they were killed that way," he said. "It makes me feel terrible." But he continued to wear the coat.

Liberace normally wore costumes for one year of touring, then saved them for overseas appearances or retired them to the museum. They required constant attention. The crystal beads became discolored under the stage lights and had to be replaced. Sequins came loose when he sat down at the piano. The costumes were hung on quarter-inch steel hangers, the heavier ones on hangers of one-inch steel. The weight of the costumes once pulled a hanging rack out of the wall, creating a disastrous mound of shattered glass.

When Ray Acuna retired in 1973, Liberace searched for another designer. One of those he considered was Michael Travis, who had created costumes for the Supremes, the Fifth Dimension, Dionne Warwick, Engelbert Humperdinck, Tony Orlando and Dawn, as well as the television series "Laugh-In." Travis's first assignment for Liberace was to create a chauffeur's uniform.

"I want a chauffeur's uniform for *me*," Liberace said. "I want to show off one of my new cars."

Travis designed a chauffeur costume so bejeweled and resplendent that Liberace was convinced he had found his new designer. Thenceforward they worked in close harmony, Travis exceeding the star's own extravagant ambitions for clothes that would astound and delight audiences. Bigger, flashier, more opulent. Each year brought Travis the challenge of topping himself. The coats and the capes made the statement, becoming larger and more stunning.

Each new batch of costumes required six months to prepare. Occasionally Liberace requested a special design, such as a Mexican costume when he was featuring the Ballet Folklórico of Mexico in his show. The only assignment Travis grumbled about was the hot pants. Liberace had once bought a pair of red, white, and blue leather hot pants for a Halloween party, and he wore them before a show to amuse the backstage crew. They insisted that he wear them onstage, and they created such a furor that he continued wearing hot pants in his shows. Travis hated hot pants.

Usually Travis submitted his own concepts. The tailoring and jewel work was done in Los Angeles, the furs were prepared in Las Vegas, and the fittings took place wherever Travis could catch up with Liberace.

Liberace always winked at the audience and himself, never failing to evoke a roar with "Well, look me over! I *did* wear it to be noticed." When he finished promenading, he drew another laugh by saying, "Take a last quick look. I'm taking it off. It's hotter'n hell!" He sometimes told interviewers that he dressed for the stage "just one step short of drag."

Travis disputed this: "The designs may be splashy, but they are masculine in every way. Nor are they circus costumes. Glittery and flashy, yes, but not circusy. The prime element is that they are fun. They give Liberace a chance to laugh at himself. And the audience laughs with him."

One night at the Las Vegas Hilton Liberace dashed offstage in his flowing cape and leaped into the air. To his astonishment, the aerodynamics actually flew him like Superman, not a couple of feet but three times that length. "Oh, my God, what a feeling!" he exclaimed. "I gotta do this in the act."

The answer was to hire Peter Foy of the English Flying Foys, who had propelled two generations of Peter Pans through the air from the beginning of the James M. Barrie play, most notably Mary Martin in the theater and television musical *Peter Pan*. But Foy was accustomed to flying one-hundred-twenty-pound actresses, not two-hundred-fifty-pounds of middle-aged pianist and his costume. In tests at the Las Vegas Hilton, Foy's efforts to convert Liberace to airborne grace were unavailing.

Seymour Heller placed a call to Debbie Reynolds, who was appearing at the Desert Inn. Debbie had some expertise, having flown in a stage musical and trained as an aerialist for the leading role in *Jumbo,* which was given to Doris Day. Debbie watched the attempts to elevate Liberace and advised raising the rigging because of his weight. She coached Lee to bend forward to balance his weight and create the illusion of flight. Soon he was able to soar like an immense, caped eagle.

Michael Travis devised an ostrich-feather cape for Liberace's first flight at the Hilton. It came at the end of the show, and the audience gasped, then cheered. Liberace landed and inquired, "Do you want more?" The response was thunderous, and he soared again.

The flying finale became standard in Liberace's casino appearances, and it usually was flawless. One night a substitute operated the rigging that carried Liberace across the stage. The first trip was perfect. When Liberace asked if the audience wanted more, the new man began running before Lee had been elevated. Liberace and ostrich cape were dragged bumpingly across the stage, and he tried to wave his arms and seem nonchalant.

Afterward, a surprisingly calm Liberace asked Peter Foy, "That wasn't supposed to happen, was it?" "No," Foy admitted. "And it won't happen again, will it?" Lee asked. "No, it won't," said Foy, and the matter was closed.

Liberace hated change. He liked having the same people around him year after year, and he enjoyed returning to the same theaters and arenas where he had appeared many times. He was sorry to leave the Las Vegas Hilton after ten years and thirty-four engagements, but in 1982 the hotel had changed to a different entertainment policy. Liberace was pleased to return to the Riviera, where he had broken the $50,000 salary mark.

Making sure that his return to the Riviera did not go unnoticed, he commissioned a $300,000, twenty-five-foot cape of white fox pelts. "They're *virgin* fox pelts," he told the audience, twinkling. "It took *forever* to find them."

"How do I know they're virgin?" he added. "It takes one to know one."

Liberace went on to star at the Sahara and the MGM Grand Hotel, always seeking to top his previous engagements with more outrageous glitz. He lent himself to any stunt the hotel press agents could concoct. Once he floated from his house to the front of the hotel in a hot-air balloon. For his birthday, he was lowered in a cherry-picker to a huge birthday cake. The press agents were amazed that he exhibited absolutely no fear on such occasions. He plunged into the stunts with enormous enthusiasm.

With the Liberace Museum thriving under the supervision of George and Dora, he plotted further development of Liberace Plaza. Foremost in his plan was a restaurant. After a lifetime of eating in everything from hamburger joints to five-star cafés, Liberace had firm notions of what a restaurant should be. A visit to Copenhagen's Tivoli Gardens remained in his memory as a prime example of how fine food could be enhanced by delightful surroundings.

The result was Liberace's own Tivoli Gardens, with old-world decor and cuisine. Each of the rooms in the 150-seat restaurant had its own theme: the Old English room, with royal-blue velvet and burnished furniture like a baronial hall; a French ballroom filled with Liberace's antiques; the Orchid Room, dedicated to Mom and decorated in shades of orchid; the piano bar in mirrored Art Deco.

Liberace delighted in entertaining fellow casino stars who visited the Tivoli Gardens. When Dolly Parton came to dinner, he gave her a tour of each room and his own quarters, pointing out the treasures he had collected. They spent hours together, and they dreamed up a movie that would costar themselves as President of the United States and First Lady. They couldn't decide which would be President, Dolly Parton or Liberace, but they did agree that in the movie they would redecorate the White House in their unique styles.

As they continued the fantasy, a restaurant patron approached their table. "Excuse me for interrupting, Dolly," he said, "but I had to tell you that I'm from Tennessee."

She smiled at him prettily and replied, "Who gives a shit?" The intruder was amused, and he walked away happily. Lee was amazed. "Oh, how I wish I could get away with that," he said.

Liberace had other plans for the plaza: expansion of the museum to house more of his treasures; a theater complex for screening films from his private collection, including his television specials; and a bank. "For years I've said I cried all the way to the bank," he said cheerily. "Now I can say I bought the bank."

Even though the nation was in a period of tight money and sluggish economy, Liberace was determined to fulfill his plan.

"The way you counteract negative is with positive," explained the disciple of Claude M. Bristol. "That has always worked in my career and in my personal life. I don't let anything drag me down. That includes people and recessions."

In early 1982, Liberace was facing the blackest period of his career. A festering scandal was certain to erupt, and just as his morale was at its lowest, something wonderful happened. Marty Pasetta, who had directed Lee in television specials, invited him to appear as a surprise guest on the Academy Awards show.

The audience at the Los Angeles Music Center was startled when the credits for *Sincerely Yours* appeared on the screen. The screen rose, revealing Liberace in sequined tails with embroidered green roses, sitting at his mirrored piano with candelabra glowing. After the applause, Liberace cracked, "I've done my part for motion pictures: I've stopped making them." The audience laughed, and he played the themes from the five nominated movie scores, then introduced the presenters: "Who better to give the scoring awards than the stars of *Body Heat,* Kathleen Turner and William Hurt?" The winner was Vangelis for the *Chariots of Fire* theme, which became a regular part of the Liberace repertoire.

The Oscar show bolstered the spirits of Liberace, who would soon face the ultimate test of his Magic of Believing.

Chapter 14

THE SCOTT THORSON AFFAIR

"Liberace Sued for Palimony by Chauffeur-Dancer, 23" Liberace read the headline as he walked from his hotel to the O'Keefe Center in Toronto, and he felt an onrush of terror. He had been expecting Scott's suit for months, and his attorney had called him with the news that afternoon. Only now, as he gazed at the blaring headline on the newsstand, did he realize that *everyone* knew about it. And he had a performance to give that night.

He stood in the wings of the immense, filled-to-capacity theater and wondered how the audience would respond. Would there be catcalls and shouts of "Go home, faggot!" as he had heard from the Teddy Boys twenty-five years before? Liberace had resolved to say nothing about the suit, even in a jesting manner. To do so would violate the Liberace code: never inject anything that would interfere with the audience's entertainment.

His pre-show prayer was longer than usual. He crossed himself and heard the words: "And here he is—Mr. Showmanship himself, LIBERACE!" He took a deep breath and strode onstage, smiling.

The sound swept over him like a tidal wave. The cheers and applause were so dense that he felt as if he could lose his balance. The musicians in the pit wondered if they had been struck by a seismic shock. The ovation continued for minutes, and Liberace stood stage-center basking in it, grateful tears in his eyes. "I'm gonna make it," he told himself.

The engagement in Toronto sold out, setting a new record at the O'Keefe Center, and Liberace had never known more receptive audiences. The same was true at an arena near Cleveland, and two following engagements in late 1982. The ovations were thunderous, and Liberace gave more of himself than ever before, confident that nothing could interfere with his lifelong mission of bringing happiness to the people.

For a dozen years, Liberace had taken on live-in lovers, usually blond, blue-eyed young men with strong physiques, easily found through his acquaintances in the gay milieu of West Hollywood and Las Vegas. They provided comfort and companionship during the long weeks on tour and enhanced Lee's periods of rest at the homes in Palm Springs and Malibu. Inevitably each liaison ended, usually because of Lee's boredom with his empty-headed lover. The parting was assuaged with gifts of jewelry and cash.

Sometimes the lover departed of his own accord, bored by life with the aging star. Lee would be devastated. A chauffeur recalled driving Liberace from Palm Springs after a bitter parting. Lee cried all the way to Los Angeles. Now in his sixties, he realized his diminishing capacity to attract young men. Both for them as well as his stage appearance, he embarked on severe diets, wore more youthful hairpieces to cover his baldness, underwent surgery to remove the lines in his face, and used more and more makeup.

The affair with Scott Thorson had begun almost five years before the headlines broke, with the fateful meeting in the dressing room at the Las Vegas Hilton. Liberace was in his customary state of sweaty exhilaration after the midnight show. His eyes fell on the blond young man among the after-show visitors, and he was intrigued. "Lee, this is Scott Thorson," someone said. "Pleased to meetcha," Liberace said with emphasis.

They all went out for a drink together: Liberace, his current lover, his show producer, Ray Arnett, Scott Thorson, and Bob Street, with whom Scott had driven to Las Vegas. During the conversation Arnett suggested, "Lee, I'm sure Bob and Scott would like to see your house; could I bring them by tomorrow?" Liberace readily agreed.

On the following afternoon Liberace came out of his bedroom to give the visitors a tour of the house. He paused lovingly over many of the objects and gave detailed reports on how he had found and restored them. He proudly displayed "my children"—his five dogs—and commented that they were having eye trouble.

"I work with animals, and I know of a new medication that will clear up their eyes," Scott volunteered.

"Oh, really?" Liberace said. "I'd love to have it. Let me give you my private telephone number."

Scott returned to Los Angeles the next day, and he called Liberace about the medicine. "Why don't you bring it up here?" Liberace suggested. Two weeks later Scott drove his Ford Capri to Las Vegas, and he attended Liberace's Friday-night show. They went to Liberace's house afterward and had sex together. Scott spent all day Saturday at the house, and on Sunday Liberace handed him $300 and said, "Fly back to L.A. and collect your belongings." Scott, who was eighteen years old, moved in.

Amazingly, Scott Thorson had never heard of his fifty-seven-year-old patron before coming to Las Vegas. Partly that may have been because Liberace rarely appeared on television, partly because of the jumbled life Scott had known.

Like Liberace, he was born in Wisconsin. His neighbors in La Crosse remembered him as a nice kid, pleasant to everyone and not at all effeminate. Unhappy with his stepfather, Scott wanted to leave home, and he worked at an amusement park to earn enough money to join his half-brother in California. When he was about thirteen, a friend recalled, Scott "left with everything he had in a cardboard box under his arm."

During the next few years he lived in northern California and then in Los Angeles, where he resided with a foster mother and later an aunt and uncle. In June 1977, he graduated from Walt Whitman High School in Los Angeles. He had a strong interest in animals and worked occasionally with a trainer who supplied animals for the movie studios. He was unemployed when a friend, Bob Street, suggested a weekend trip to Las Vegas. They had sex together, Scott said later, but they were not lovers. Street introduced Scott to Ray Arnett, who arranged for a ringside table at the Hilton and then introduced him to Liberace.

Scott and Liberace became inseparable. Lee showered his young friend with fur coats, jewelry, and cars and delighted in Scott's sense of wonderment at his newfound riches. During the opening of the

Liberace Museum, a reporter noticed that Scott wore almost as much gold and diamonds as Liberace. "I did not wear a lot of jewelry before I met Lee," Scott remarked. "But if you're with Lee, you gotta keep the image. And it's fun. It's become a company thing, a trademark for all his employees."

Liberace found other work for Scott to do. The show needed a stalwart, handsome young man to drive the Rolls-Royce onstage and off at Liberace's entrance. At six feet two inches, Scott was ideal for the role, and Lee ordered fancy chauffeur costumes for him to wear.

Lee made no attempt to hide his affection for his blond Adonis. Scott was often nearby during interviews, and Lee was photographed with him in restaurants and at parties. Scott became a constant adjunct to the Liberace social life, occasionally irritating Lee's friends.

Debbie Reynolds was genuinely fond of Lee, and they often visited when both were appearing in Las Vegas. Early one morning, after each had performed two shows, Debbie and Lee were relaxing over coffee at the Liberace mansion. Scott Thorson hovered over their conversation, adding his own comments.

Finally Debbie snapped, "Why do you keep interrupting? I came here to talk to Lee, not you. Why don't you go walk the dogs?"

When Scott departed huffily, Lee said, "Thank you, Debbie. I'm glad you said that. Scott is so young, he doesn't understand when he should just listen."

"Lee, you shouldn't have people around you who don't know how to behave," Debbie insisted.

"I know, I know," Lee replied sadly. "But you know how lonely it is on the road."

Lee never explained his relationship with Scott, and no one dared ask. Even in an era of gay liberation, some things could remain private. And Liberace would never do anything to alienate a segment of his audience, as he certainly would if he proclaimed his homosexuality.

It was the longest-lasting of Lee's relationships, but it was destined to end, like all the others. Not that he wanted it to end; he believed that he had found his lasting love. But after four years of closeness, Lee believed that Scott had developed a Jekyll-Hyde personality, and he blamed the change on liquor and drugs. When Scott's behavior became too erratic to tolerate, Lee decided to erase Scott Thorson from his life.

The process wasn't easy. Scott didn't want to leave the Beverly Boulevard penthouse he had shared with Liberace. Then one violent predawn morning in April 1982, he later claimed, several burly men awoke him in his bed, maced and beat him, expelled him from the penthouse, and had the locks changed so he could not reenter.

For six months, Liberace lived in constant fear of what Scott's next move would be. Then, on a chilly night in Toronto, he found out.

Scott Thorson's "palimony" suit against Liberace was eaten up by newspapers and television and devoured by the supermarket tabloids. The brief was full of delicious gossip, and the damages were Liberacean: $380 million. Thorson appeared at the Los Angeles County Courthouse looking every inch the Liberace protégé in a brocade dinner jacket with ruffled shirt. At last everyone's suspicions about Liberace's sexual preference were confirmed, or so it seemed.

These were Thorson's allegations. In early 1976, when he was seventeen and a half, he began dating Liberace and they soon developed an intimate sexual relationship. At the time Thorson was employed as a successful dancer, composer, and animal trainer and was enrolled in a special program in a California college with intentions of pursuing veterinary medicine.

During the summer of 1976, Thorson continued, he and Liberace entered into an oral agreement under which he would: (1) act as Liberace's full-time chauffeur, bodyguard, confidant, and secretary; (2) quit school; (3) perform only in Liberace shows; (4) render labor, skills, and personal services to Liberace and his enterprises; (5) participate in a homosexual relationship with Liberace; (6) cohabit in all of the Liberace residences.

In return, Thorson claimed, Liberace would: (1) give Thorson one-half equity in all his real estate and certain personal property; (2) support Thorson for the rest of his life in a manner and style consistent with Liberace's own lifestyle; (3) pay Thorson $7,000 per month; (4) pay Thorson between $20,000 and $30,000 to care for the pets; (5) cohabit with Thorson in all the Liberace residences; (6) participate in a homosexual relationship with Thorson; (7) adopt Thorson as his son. Thorson also maintained that he had been promised burial in the Liberace family plot at Forest Lawn Memorial Park in Glendale, California.

Thorson also filed a civil suit against Liberace and four men who rousted him out of the Beverly Boulevard penthouse in April.

The war of words began. Liberace's lawyer, Joel Strote, declared of the suit: "There's absolutely no truth in it . . . absolutely absurd, a publicity stunt." Liberace issued a statement: "[Thorson] is a disgruntled former employee who was fired in early 1982 because of the excessive use of alcohol and drugs and carrying of firearms, among other reasons. This is an outrageous, ambitious attempt to assassinate my character."

Liberace dreaded interviews because he knew the Scott Thorson business would come up. But he was in the middle of a nationwide tour, and he realized the need for publicity. As was his custom, Jamie James arranged five telephone interviews in a row with reporters from various cities. James cautioned them that Liberace did not want to discuss the lawsuit.

The first call was with a woman reporter in Atlanta. Liberace chatted about his new costumes for the tour, then he suddenly stopped. James noticed Lee's face turn from pink to white.

"I have said that he was a disgruntled employee, and that's what he was," Liberace said firmly. He listened again, and the brown eyes turned to a shade of black.

"If you continue with this shit, I'm going to hang up on you," he muttered. Pause. The color returned to his face, and he continued, "Yes, I'll be wearing the rings. . . ."

When Liberace complained after the interview, James told him the questions wouldn't go away, so he had better devise a strategy for fielding them. They agreed on three stages of replies depending on the reporter's persistence: (1) "I never discuss religion, politics, or legal matters"; (2) "I don't want to discuss this with you"; (3) "I thought you were from the [name of publication], not the *National Enquirer.*" Rarely was No. 3 necessary.

As the initial sensation of the palimony suit subsided, Liberace became more responsive. He commented: "[Thorson] was into heavy drugs. He threatened me: 'If you think the Billie Jean King [scandal] was something, wait till I get through with you.'"

To a Las Vegas editor Liberace declared: "I'm tired of being a target for people looking to capitalize on my money and good nature. I'm an easy mark for this kind of thing, and I'm not going to sit back and take it anymore. I'm tired of paying. It's a form of blackmail. I'm a nice guy, but I'm also a fighter, and from now on I'm going to fight back."

For a long time, he said, he had been unaware that Scott used drugs, "but finally I couldn't avoid facing it anymore. . . . I found out that he had false bottoms to hair spray, shaving cream, and deodorant cans and that he stashed drugs in the compartments. If that had been discovered going through customs or by the police, it would have been a reflection on me and my entire company. . . . Thorson had turned into a Jekyll and Hyde. He was lovable one moment and vicious and hateful the next. Frequently he would hallucinate that people were trying to kill him. On one occasion he was so paranoid that he called the police and had a huge police helicopter circle the house when he started imagining that someone was trying to kill him. . . . Later on I found that he had sent firearms through the airport concealed in his luggage. I shudder to think what would have happened had that been discovered."

The November 2, 1982, issue of the *National Enquirer* featured a smiling photograph of Lee and Scott on the front cover with the headline: "Liberace Bombshell—Boyfriend Tells All—World Exclusive." In a four-page spread accompanied by nine photos, Thorson told of meeting Liberace as a peachfuzz-faced kid of seventeen totally unaware "that men would get romantic with men." He related how Liberace seduced him, lavished gifts upon him, gave him the most important job in the organization, wanted to adopt him. They called each other "Libby" and "Boober," said Thorson. The end of their idyll began, he declared, when he caught Liberace with an eighteen-year-old boy. After that, fights and recrimination, ending in the unceremonious exit from the penthouse.

In a second *Enquirer* article, Thorson alleged that Liberace was almost totally bald, dressed like a slouch at home, and had undergone two major facelifts.

Later in 1982, the tabloid the *Globe* ran the headline "Wicked Past of Gay Suing Liberace." The article was purportedly based on an interview with Scott Thorson's half-brother, Wayne Johnson, who maintained that Scott was an experienced homosexual street-hustler before he met Liberace, had sex with a man at the age of eleven, and had once had sex with his foster father, since deceased.

Thorson filed an $18-million libel suit against the *Globe,* his half-brother, and the article's author. The suit also included Liberace, who, Thorson maintained, had paid Johnson to tell the story. Replied Liberace: "Just another attempt to use the media to grab headlines and cause me personal embarrassment. . . . Neither myself nor my staff members had anything to do with the article that appeared in the *Globe.*"

In October 1983, Liberace's lawyers had a chance to interrogate Scott Thorson in deposition. He corrected some of the statements in his complaint: he was actually eighteen and a half when he met

Liberace; he had never been employed as a dancer or composer, nor had he been enrolled at a California college. But the part about being an animal trainer was true, he said, explaining that he had worked on movie jobs for a trainer, Carl Miller.

Thorson had other revelations. Yes, he had used cocaine in "either '80 or '81," but never in the presence of Liberace. Nor had he seen Liberace use cocaine, but Liberace liked amyl nitrate, known in the gay community as "poppers." Scott had been drunk in Liberace's presence "maybe a couple of times."

Concerning his first sexual encounter with Liberace, Thorson said that "when he took me in his arms, it revolted me at first. I was unaccustomed to his full makeup." Thorson was asked if he was wearing makeup during the deposition. He replied: "Maybe. Probably am. Why? Why not?"

> **Q.** Was it your expectation that you would become a legally adopted son of Liberace?
>
> **A.** Yes.
>
> **Q.** And continue in a sexual relationship with him after the adoption?
>
> **A.** No.
>
> **Q.** Is that when you thought the sex would stop?
>
> **A.** Our relationship towards later on went from a sexual relationship to—he always thought of me more as a son. We had our sexual relationship in the beginning of our relationship . . . and he wanted me to think of him more as a father image.

Q. Are you telling me that the sexual relationship with Liberace stopped at a point in time?

A. It never stopped. It wasn't as often as it was at the beginning. . . .

Q. State what you consider in your own mind what you believed.

A. I considered at the time we were lovers. He stated often that I reminded him of his kid brother, Rudy. Another time he told me he always wanted children but couldn't have them. He thought—it is hard to explain.

In response to a question, Thorson gave this explanation of his services in the Liberace show:

"I started the car. I drove the car out onto the stage. I put it in park. I opened the door, I took about ten steps, I opened [the door for] Liberace, I threw my arm up, I shut the door. I folded my hands, he introduced me, I took my bow, then I saluted and then I got back. I took ten more steps, I opened the car door, I put the car in drive, I drove the Rolls-Royce offstage. Then I got into the Volkswagen Rolls-Royce, and I took his dresser or valet out there. The valet took his sixteen-foot fur coat into the back seat of the Rolls-Royce. I drove the little Volkswagen Rolls-Royce offstage."

A Liberace lawyer noted a little mark on Thorson's chin.

Q. How did you get it?

A. Liberace instructed his plastic surgeon to put that in there as a—he wanted me to have a cleft in my chin.

Q. Liberace didn't instruct any plastic surgeon to do that, did he?

A. I'm telling you that Liberace instructed Dr. ————— ———,
————— Boulevard, Beverly Hills, California, to put a cleft
in my chin along with an insert in my chin and along with
silicon injections to make my cheekbones more outstanding. Facial structure, bone structure come out more. . . .

Q. Was this all Liberace's idea?

A. Yes.

Q. Then you went along with it?

A. Yes.

Q. Are you happy you did it?

A. Yes, because I was making him happy.

Liberace managed to avoid being questioned, for a time. Thorson's
lawyers maintained that he had been served with the legal papers
while he was appearing at the Westbury Music Fair. A woman process server maintained that she had handed an envelope to a man who
was five feet ten inches tall, weighed 170 pounds, had brown hair, and
was wearing a brown business suit. It was Liberace, she was sure.

Not possible, said Liberace in a sworn statement. He recalled
hearing a woman shout his name at the stage door, but guards had
prevented her from approaching. Further—"I was wearing a black
coat with a black mink collar, a navy blazer with gray flannel trousers,
and a white shirt and navy tie. I neither wear nor own a brown
business suit."

The judge decided in his favor, reasoning, "That man wouldn't be
caught dead in a brown business suit." Process servers finally caught
up with Liberace in the parking lot of the MGM Grand Hotel in Las
Vegas.

When Liberace finally gave his deposition, he declared he had hired Thorson as onstage chauffeur and later promoted him to driver, road manager, and "buffer between me and my fans." No mention of any sexual arrangement. He continued:

"Sometime in 1981, I learned that Mr. Thorson was using cocaine. His behavior grew irrational, and I became concerned about his health and well-being. I urged him not to use any drugs and attempted to discourage him from using cocaine. In March 1982, Mr. Thorson telephoned me and threatened to kill me. At that time I became concerned for my own safety and concluded that I should attempt to persuade Mr. Thorson to seek medical treatment so that he could overcome his drug problem."

On the night of March 25, 1982, Thorson was at the Beverly Boulevard penthouse, where, he declared, he had "made love with Liberace regularly."

"I was outraged because I believed at that moment Liberace was in Palm Springs having sex with his two male house guests from France," Thorson said. "The thought of this outraged me because I loved Liberace, and I considered this type of conduct a violation of our trust."

In his deposition, Liberace said Thorson was very disturbed by the fact that he was entertaining house guests from France: "He shouted all kinds of obscenities at me. . . . I refuse to rename those obscenities. Let's just say that they were obscenities of the dirtiest kind you can imagine. . . . He threatened to kill me."

On the next day Thorson was evicted from the penthouse.

The Liberace forces placed their hopes on the *Marvin vs. Marvin* case. The first of the celebrated palimony suits, it had been a dispute between Michelle Triola Marvin and actor Lee Marvin over monies she claimed for having lived with him in an unmarried state. She lost. In its review of the case, the California Supreme Court held that "the courts should enforce express agreements between nonmarital partners except to the extent that the contract is explicitly founded on consideration of meretricious sexual services." Such contracts were deemed void because they were considered contracts for prostitution.

Superior Court Judge Ricardo A. Torres, on March 1, 1984, dismissed the palimony claims by Thorson, declaring that his alleged agreement with Liberace amounted to a contract for prostitution and such contracts are illegal and unenforceable. Thorson's lawyers vowed to continue pressing the other charges.

Elated over his victory, Liberace told a *Newsweek* reporter: ". . . I could have stopped the whole thing before it started by paying off. . . . But that would have been blackmail. And blackmail never ends. So I decided to stick it out and take the embarrassment and insults." Thorson's attorneys filed a libel suit against *Newsweek* and Liberace for $36.2 million.

The Scott Thorson affair continued with claims and counterclaims, suits and countersuits, until it finally ended with a whimper in December 1986. A confidential agreement was reached whereby Thorson would drop his remaining charges for a payment of $95,000. In an April 1982 agreement, before the palimony suit, Thorson had already received $75,000, plus one Doberman and one English sheepdog, a 1977 White Auburn, and a 1960 gold Rolls-Royce.

And so it was over. Having lived with the ordeal for five years, Liberace felt no elation. Nor was he chastened. He had already found a new young man on whom to bestow his affection and riches—Cary James, age nineteen. He was a fresh-faced Floridian who had been a member of the Young Americans, the troupe of singers and dancers who had appeared with the Liberace show in the Nevada casinos and on tour. Like Scott Thorson, Cary had a youthful exuberance that delighted and refreshed Liberace. Happily, Cary lacked the erratic qualities that had brought a crashing end to the Scott Thorson affair.

Chapter 15

A NEW AND LIBERATED LIBERACE RIDES OUT THE STORM AND MEETS ONE OF HIS GREATEST CHALLENGES

The Scott Thorson affair emboldened Liberace to speak more frankly to his audiences and to the press. Not that he ever recanted his Cassandra testimony. He admitted that his act bordered on drag, but added that he would never appear onstage like his good friend Danny LaRue, a female impersonator.

"I have a general family audience appeal," he explained, "and I don't want to develop only a gay following. It's going to take many, many years for [the family] audience to accept people who are totally gay or come out on Johnny Carson. I've seen careers hurt by that kind of thing—look at Billie Jean King. But with a name like Liberace, which stands for freedom, I'm for anything that has the letters L-I-B in it, and that includes Gay Lib."

He even admitted that he enjoyed watching porno movies on his video cassette player. His first porno film experience was with *Inside Jennifer Welles*, which concerned a young woman who accommodated seventy-two men in one night—"and she actually does it! Then she gives a Chinese dinner for all the men, and while they're having dinner, she takes on the Chinese waiters for an encore." When his "very respectable" friends learned he had dirty movies, they insisted on seeing them, he said, and they marveled, "Oh, look at the size of that!" and "Look at what he's doing to her!"

In his conversation for the book *The First Time*, Liberace was startlingly candid.

"Some people say that fucking saps your creative energy," he commented, "but I don't believe that. I think it's a very healthy thing. A healthy sex life keeps you young and vital. And it should be frequent. I don't mean three times a day. But frequent. Some of these sports managers tell their players no sex before the night of a game. That's a lot of bullshit. It's healthy to get your rocks off in a passionate way. Well, a lot of people have hangups sexually. I feel sorry for them."

In his act, especially in Las Vegas, where anything went, Liberace became spicier. "If I went streaking," he cracked, "Burt Reynolds would be jealous. I've got the diamonds, he's got the jewels."

Liberace maintained the standard routine of inviting members of the audience to touch an elaborate costume. He encouraged fans to touch the diamond buttons, especially the lower ones. "Right about here is where I get the message," he joked, pointing. "Now do the other one—I don't want to get frustrated."

Despite all the titillation, Liberace always clammed up whenever interviewers tried to inquire about his own sex life. "I don't think entertainers should publicly air their sexual or political tastes," he insisted. "What they do in the privacy of their own home or bed is nobody's business."

Liberace had not played New York in twenty years. Too many times he had been savaged by critics who reviled his bastardization of the classics. "Fuck 'em," he declared, and he took his show to New Jersey, Long Island, and Connecticut, where he was certain of a warm reception from suburbanites.

But one long-ago ambition nagged him—Radio City Music Hall. Ever since he first came to New York in 1941 and had thrilled to the dramatics of Greer Garson and Ingrid Bergman on the giant screen and marveled at the pageants on the mammoth stage, he had dreamed of appearing there.

The Music Hall wanted him. After abandoning its movie policy, the theater had enjoyed success with concerts by rock stars as well as mainstream performers like Frank Sinatra and Tony Bennett. Scott Sanders, executive producer for concerts, began wooing Liberace in 1980. A man in his mid-twenties, Sanders was more attuned to hard rock than schmaltz, but he was convinced that a star of Liberace's magnitude and showmanship could fill the Music Hall.

"New York needs Liberace," Sanders preached, but Seymour Heller wasn't buying. Sanders delivered his arguments while Heller ate a corned beef sandwich in an early-morning Las Vegas coffee shop. Heller countered them all. The critics would kill Liberace. His show was too "Las Vegas." The Music Hall was too big. A flop in the Big Apple would be disastrous.

Sanders continued his campaign for three years, but he failed to persuade Heller or Roger Vorce, Liberace's New York-based booking agent. In 1983 Sanders talked with Liberace during an Atlantic City engagement. Lee was intrigued. "You know, it might be worth a shot," he mused.

That summer he appeared at a tent theater in Cohasset, Massachusetts, and Sanders came with members of the Music Hall production staff. They outlined how the Liberace show could be fitted into the vast theater. "Easter is the hottest time of the year for the Music Hall," said Sanders. "You could be our Easter Bunny."

"Yeah," said Liberace, eyes gleaming. "Let's go for it!"

Sanders proposed that Liberace appear with the Hall's time-honored "Glory of Easter" pageant. Liberace realized that the show would then be over-length. "Either you can have the Resurrection or you can have Liberace," he declared. "But you can't have both." Sanders chose Liberace.

The campaign began. Liberace agreed to visit New York in December for advance publicity, which was handled by the firm of Solters, Roskin and Friedman. The account executive, Denise Collier, began calling the media. Not interested, sniffed the *New York Times*. Young reporters replied, "Liberace? Are you kidding? He's my grandmother's favorite."

Others were more receptive. Paul Shaeffer, producer of "Late Night with David Letterman," was eager to have Liberace on the show. Collier was reluctant, fearing that her client might fall victim to Letterman's acerbic wit. But Shaeffer persisted, and the booking was made. When Liberace appeared, he sat down at the piano and played a medley of Christmas songs with such poignancy that even the stagehands were in tears.

His appearance was so successful that he was asked back again and again. On his second show, the other guest was Bob Dylan, and everyone wondered how the rock deity would react to being paired with Liberace. Said Dylan: "I want my picture taken with you." Said Liberace: "That's great! Can I have your autograph?"

Liberace himself was reluctant about appearing on "Saturday Night

Live," which had satirized him viciously. But he agreed, and he proved to be a hit. His publicity efforts generated sales of forty thousand tickets even before the announcement ad in the *New York Times*. That meant six and a half of the ten scheduled shows had already been sold out. The Music Hall pleaded for more performances, and four were added.

As Easter approached, the campaign intensified. Posters appeared in Macy's windows and throughout Greenwich Village. Liberace gave cooking demonstrations in Macy's Cellar and on the Letterman show. He appeared on the Phil Donahue show and other television talk shows. Even the *Times* covered his reception at the Baldwin Piano and Organ Company's showroom on Seventh Avenue.

Liberace arrived in a white classic Rolls-Royce and was greeted by two red-plumed Rockettes carrying lighted silver candelabras, a band playing "There's No Business Like Show Business," and attendants tossing confetti over the white carpet that stretched to the doorway. Inside were two hundred music business executives and artists sipping champagne and milling among the pianos and organs. Liberace reached into a box and pulled out the name of a Brooklyn woman, the winner in a drawing.

"Hello, Mrs. Wilensky, this is Liberace," he said into the telephone. "You have just won a computerized piano."

"I think I'm going to faint," said the voice on the other end.

Liberace discussed his Music Hall show with reporters, describing it as "the culmination of forty years in show business" and "fantasy at its highest." Among the fantastic elements: three cars; five pianos; ten Liberace costumes valued at $1 million; a full line of Rockettes; a deep-sea extravaganza; the Dancing Waters. With his Music Hall engagement becoming a reality, he said only one ambition remained: "To be a sex symbol at eighty, like Cary Grant."

For critics who came to scoff, the Music Hall show gave them plenty to write about. The performance was pure Liberace, unabashed and unrepentant. As the huge theater faded into darkness, a voice announced: "Ladies and gentlemen, welcome to the Las Vegas home of Liberace!"

Against the five-story curtain was projected a movie scene of gates opening, then the curtain lifted and a screen descended as a sound track intoned Tchaikovsky's First Piano Concerto. Liberace was seen awakening in his bedroom. He took a monogrammed robe from a butler and went to a baroque piano to play a few bars to match the Tchaikovsky. The camera observed the Sistine Chapel ceiling above him and the cherubs dancing on piano keys on the ceiling of the bathroom, where Liberace luxuriated amid a cloud of bubbles in his marble tub. The tour of the house continued, extending to the swimming pool with the painted keyboard. Then he entered a white Rolls-Royce and drove off as the movie faded.

The screen rose and the same white Rolls glided onstage. Liberace stepped out, wearing the white fox cape longer than a wedding cape. "Well, look me over!" he commanded. "I don't dress like this to go unnoticed." He introduced his "chauffeur and friend," who removed the cape, which was borne off by a smaller white Rolls-Royce.

The concert began with a medley of Chopin, Rachmaninoff, Liszt, and Beethoven "with the dull parts taken out," accompanied by smoke and lighting effects. "I love to play that kind of music," Liberace remarked, dedicating it to his guru Paderewski. Another idol was Eddy Duchin, and he played the Duchin theme, the Chopin Second Nocturne.

Liberace did the dancing bit with a woman from the audience, then kidded his own image by asking her husband to dance. When he declined, Liberace sighed, "Well, some other time perhaps." After playing Strauss waltzes to the swaying, synchronized Dancing Waters, he commented, "I know what effect running water can have. Thank you for holding it in."

More piano, more costumes, a movie to show off his fingers and the massive rings ("I'm glad you want to see them because—let's

face it—you bought them"), a high-stepping dance with the Rockettes, the Chopin medley dedicated to Mom ("She is up there in the
best seat in the house, listening to it"), the Gershwin medley, and the
surefire crowd-pleaser: the request medley. He combined "New
York, New York," "Chopsticks," "Let Me Call You Sweetheart," and
other songs with startling virtuosity. Finally a stirring rendition of the
Chariots of Fire theme, and two and a half hours of relentless entertainment were over. "I'm having so much fun, I'm almost ashamed
to take the money," he announced. "But I will."

At the end he stood on the stage apron as people crowded to see
his rings and feel his red-sequined cape. "I feel like the Pope," he said.

The reviewers were surprisingly benign. Expectably, the *Village
Voice* attacked Liberace as "a celebrity whose only portfolio is sheer
excess" and attacked his "countless arpeggios and melodramatic
pauses; it all sounded like Jane Wyman was about to die." But the
Times recognized him for what he was: "Liberace has arrived at a
style that is not classical, jazz or pop but an ornamental genre unto
itself. . . . [He is] a one-of-a-kind musical monument." The *Post*
declared he "gave a fashion show, an all-singing and all-dancing revue
and endless, good-natured shtick in his well-paced Radio City Music
Hall show."

These were blue-skies days for Liberace: never had he seen things
going so right. New York was at his feet. Seventy thousand tickets
for the fourteen performances at the Music Hall were completely sold
out, smashing every record in its fifty-one-year-history. The audiences were not solely the blue-haired women who had followed him
throughout his career. They all came: yuppies and teenagers, blue
collars and white mink, secretaries and Broadway stars. Commented
the British actor Jeremy Irons: "If you want to see kitsch, there it
is. I couldn't live on it, but it is fun to see."

Every television talk show wanted Liberace as guest, and sophisticated magazines suddenly rediscovered him. Liberace luxuriated in the adulation. Shunning the limousine that was always parked outside the Hilton Hotel for his use, he strode the few blocks to the Music Hall waving a breezy hello to those who recognized him. Aides struggled to keep pace with him, watching nervously for muggers.

Backstage at the Music Hall he was king. Stagehands had seen a generation of entertainers come and go, many of them with good riddance. The backstage workers had grown hardened to bad manners and aloofness, hence they were unprepared for Liberace. Within a few days he knew all of their names. He said thank you whenever they did something for him. He invited them to his opening-night party.

When they had visitors backstage, he took them into his dressing room. "You like my rings?" he asked. "Here—try them on." When the engagement was over, he handed each stagehand an envelope on which was written: "To _____, Love, Liberace." Inside was $25.

After the night performance, Liberace often grabbed Denise Collier and one or two others and went for a stroll down Fifth Avenue. He loved to stare at the elegant goods in the windows and make comments: "Oooh, isn't that gorgeous? . . . I gotta have one of those. . . . Tacky, don't you think? I love it."

Following an afternoon of interviews, he often took Collier and others to an Italian restaurant for an indulgent meal before the evening performance. He preferred to sit in the window where he could be noticed, but he had one proscription for fans: he did not want to sign autographs or to be photographed while he was eating. If people asked, he took their hands and said, "Oh, darling, I'm eating right now, but just as soon as I'm finished, you come back over, and we'll do it. Thanks a lot."

Before and after dinner he smoked, and he averaged two or three packs of Carltons a day. When he was chided for the habit, he admitted, "Yes, I know, I know. I've tried to quit, several times. The best thing about quitting is hiding cigarettes so you can sneak them later.

I used to slip a carton under the seats of my cars in Palm Springs. Then I'd say I was going shopping, and I'd drive out in the desert and smoke to my heart's content."

Only once did Denise Collier see Liberace without his aura of equanimity. He had been invited to appear on a television show that both Seymour Heller and Roger Vorce considered important. "I won't do it," Liberace replied. He didn't explain why, but apparently something or someone on the show had offended him. The manager and agent asked Collier to persuade Liberace to change his mind.

"I'm sorry about this, Lee," she said, "but Seymour and Roger say you've got to do this show."

He gazed at her with a stony look she hadn't seen before. "Denise," he said coldly, "I don't gotta do nothin'. Ever."

End of argument.

Liberace went home to Milwaukee in early December 1984 for a thrilling honor: the christening of a theater bearing his name.

It had been the Ward Memorial Theater since its dedication in 1882 by General William Tecumseh Sherman, the Union general who marched through Georgia. First an assembly hall on the grounds of the Old Soldiers' Home, it became a theater in 1895 and had seen such performers as Will Rogers, Eddie Foy, Jr., Ed Wynn, Eddie Cantor, and Bob Hope. In 1984 local citizens formed a committee to restore the theater and rename it the Liberace Playhouse for Milwaukee's famous son.

Liberace arrived at the Veterans Administration grounds in a shiny red Duesenberg II, wearing a black suit and black-and-white striped tie, a full-length Canadian lynx coat, a large gold cross, and several rings. An army band played "On Wisconsin," and Liberace exuberantly grabbed a baton and conducted the musicians.

"Ya know," he told the crowd, "I grew up right across the street, over there at 4905 National Avenue. When I was a kid, I used to come over here and play for the old soldiers. I'll bet you there aren't many entertainers today who can say they played for Civil War veterans. Well, *I* did."

He gave a pitch for the fund-raising drive, signed his name to a donors' wall, and remarked, "A lot of people have theaters named for them after they're dead. I'm glad I'm still around."

Back to the Music Hall at Easter 1985, this time for twenty-one performances. "Just give us the same show," said the management. "No way," replied Mr. Showmanship. "Ya gotta give 'em something new and different." He had already planned his entrance, emerging from a giant Fabergé egg in a hundred-pound cape of pink-dyed turkey feathers.

Liberace was shopping for another apartment in New York, even though he would be there only a few weeks during the year. He had negotiated for a penthouse floor in a new building overlooking the East River, but the owners decided to convert it into a residential hotel, and Liberace didn't like the idea of living in a hotel. One day before the Music Hall opening, he took Denise Collier of the Solters, Roskin and Friedman office to his appointment at the Trump Tower. He liked the Fifth Avenue location and the glitz of the new shopping center–residential complex, and, ever starstruck, he was impressed that Steven Spielberg had bought an apartment there.

Liberace and Collier walked into the Trump Tower, and he asked the concierge to call the sales agent. The lobby elevator opened, and out stepped Donald Trump, the real estate magnate. Recognizing Liberace, he announced, "This sale is too important for me—I'm going to show you the apartments myself."

Trump escorted his visitors to the upper floors and showed where Spielberg had bought his place and then had a wall knocked down to provide a bedroom for his baby, Max. "This should be just right for you," Trump said, opening a spacious, two-bedroom apartment. As he recited the features, Liberace interrupted: "Yeah, but what about the kitchen? That's what I'm interested in."

Trump offered to let Liberace use the place during the Music Hall engagement, and Liberace readily accepted. Afterward, he and Collier sat on the carpet in the empty living room, and he gazed at the white and beige decor. "What this place needs is some color," he declared. "Let's go shopping!" He conducted her on a shopping spree, buying a huge abstract painting in Bloomingdale's, also a triangular, lipstick-red bar and other items in red, black, and gold.

The 1985 Music Hall engagement was an easy sale for his press agents. This time the media eagerly sought interviews with Liberace instead of having to be persuaded. Even *Interview* did a breathless article on Liberace, with Andy Warhol participating. He reveled in his newfound role as elder statesman of pop entertainers, and in interviews he offered commentary as well as advice to those who were undergoing the same white-hot fame that he had experienced in the mid-1950s.

"The audience wants fantasy plus," he expounded. "After all, living in the space age is a fantasy. Consider who are the top stars today: Michael Jackson, Boy George, and Prince. They realize the value of fantasy and showmanship.

"I was the first to create shock waves. I've been able to establish that kind of identification that, fortunately, works for me. It has become my trademark. For me to wear a simple tuxedo onstage would be like asking Marlene Dietrich to wear a housedress.

"There was a period when performers went through a sloppy, unkempt look. Thank goodness that's over. Glamour is such a part of show biz today. Look at Joan Collins and Liz Taylor. Liz will let herself get fat from time to time. But sooner or later she'll shed the pounds and return to her glamorous self. Then all of a sudden her career takes off again."

Reading that Boy George had cut his hair and was wearing conventional clothes, Liberace recalled the disaster when new managers tried to change his own image.

"I've never met Boy George," he remarked, "but I was tempted to call him and say, 'Hey, kid, you're twenty-three years old; you had a good thing going—don't kill it.'"

Liberace analyzed the troubles that led to Elvis Presley's early death: "A lot of it was self-inflicted. I knew him very well. He always felt somebody was after him. When you have that kind of fear, that kind of attitude, you attract people who want to do you harm. Have you ever noticed that?

"Years ago when I started doing TV and making appearances in big arenas, the place would put security guys up there, and I said, 'Please don't do that. It's very distracting to see ten cops in front of the stage. Everybody's looking at the officers instead of me. I don't want that.'

"I also found that people will *dare* to break a barricade. If there is a barricade, someone will try to jump over it. I've found the more open I am, the better."

During the 1985 engagement at Radio City Music Hall, the *Daily News* was insatiable in its coverage of Liberace. The paper suggested a photo spread on a Liberace shopping spree, and he responded enthusiastically. "Let's see now," he said to Denise Collier, "we'll go to Rolls-Royce and Tiffany's and Rita Ford's music box place and Fortunoff's and Balducci's and . . ."

Collier called the stores in advance and explained that it was a publicity stunt, strictly for photos, but Liberace ended up buying things at every stop. At the Rolls-Royce showroom he arranged for a car for opening night, a half-million-dollar automobile with mink carpeting. At Rita Ford he bought a music box in the likeness of Judy Garland that played "Over the Rainbow"—"I adore Judy Garland." In Tiffany's he was shopping for a silver-plated shovel, which he wanted gold-plated for the groundbreaking of his new, expanded museum. He looked up from the counter and his face turned white. "Oh, my God, it's Felicia Gallant!" he exclaimed.

Felicia Gallant was the glamorous romance novelist of the soap opera "Another World," and she was played by actress Linda Dano. Liberace was fiercely devoted to her and to the series; no one was allowed to disturb him between two and three in the afternoon while his eyes remained fixed to the television set.

"It's really Felicia Gallant—I can't believe it!" Liberace cried, taking her hand. He burst into tears, and she replied, "I can't believe it's Liberace!"

He invited her to attend his opening-night party in the Trump Tower, and he told a reporter, "At the top of my list were Donald Trump, Liz Smith, and Linda Dano. I love Linda Dano. She is the Joan Collins of daytime television." When she suggested that he make a guest appearance on "Another World," he readily agreed. The script called for him to meet Felicia Gallant at an autographing party and invite her to a party at his Trump Tower apartment, where the show was taped.

From soap opera to big-time wrestling—Liberace used every means to publicize the Music Hall show. He appeared on "Saturday Night Live" along with Mr. T and Hulk Hogan, then turned up on a closed-circuit television show from Madison Square Garden, "Wrestlemania," along with rock singer Cyndi Lauper, baseball hellion Billy Martin, Muhammed Ali, and such wrestlers as Rowdy Roddy Piper and Big John Studd. Liberace's contribution was a kicking act with the Rockettes.

The *New York Times* considered Liberace's return to the Music Hall newsworthy enough to begin a feature story on page one. The reporter interviewed the star backstage and described the show, with special attention to costumes and jewelry.

"To shake his hand is to flirt with laceration," wrote William E. Geist. "Let's see, left to right, we have the enormous topaz and gold ring, the grand piano of diamonds and gold with the top that opens, the simple hunk of amethyst ring, and then we move to the right hand, where we have the diamond candelabra ring, the gold record-player ring with moving turntable, and a large gold structure of a ring that looks as if it were designed by Buckminster Fuller, possibly for human habitation."

Also noted was a near-disaster when the comedian Billy Crystal encountered Liberace in the Rainbow Grill in Rockefeller Center. The pair embraced, and Crystal became entangled in Liberace's jewelry.

The hoopla hardly seemed necessary because the Music Hall had sold out for all seventeen days of the engagement, another record. The show offered new costumes and scenery but the same jokes ("Look me over . . .") and the usual smattering of Gershwin, Duchin, Chopin, Tchaikovsky, plus "Mack the Knife" as it might be done by Mozart, Debussy, and Strauss as well as the roaring "Beer Barrel Polka" accompanied by fireworks.

After forty years as an entertainer, Liberace's repertoire, his self-mocking jokes and his manipulation of the audience had scarcely changed. He had become a show-business commodity, *sui generis,* astounding new audiences with his brand of showmanship while retaining his loyal, longtime fans. He seemed always the same, exulting in his patented role of Liberace both onstage and off.

But a few observers discerned subtle changes. There seemed to be a remoteness behind the ever-present charm. For years whenever he appeared in Milwaukee, he had always entertained his fellow players from the high school band backstage. But in later years when the old musicians and their wives tried to visit him, they were turned away at the stage door. "Mr. Liberace is resting," they were told.

After all the 1984 hoopla over the naming of the Liberace Playhouse in his old neighborhood, the fund-raising drive to renovate the theater faltered. The Soldiers' Home Foundation asked Liberace for a donation to help its campaign for $1.6 million. The foundation received a letter withdrawing Liberace from the project and forbidding the use of his name on the theater.

The circle of advisers drew tightly around Liberace, insulating him against matters that might prove upsetting. In his daily life he had little contact with those who were not in his employ. More and more he savored the privacy he shared at The Cloisters and at Malibu with Cary James.

In his desperate fight against age, his face sometimes resembled a grotesque mask of Liberace of the 1950s. Plastic surgery had eliminated character along with the wrinkles, and makeup contributed to the air of unreality. So did the pompadoured toupees.

Duke Goldstone, director of the Guild Films show, visited Lee at the Beverly Boulevard penthouse in 1985. They hadn't seen each other in many years, and they laughed as they reminisced about the old days—taking the nun out of the audience for "Ave Maria," finding an alley cat for "Kitten on the Keys." Then Lee began talking about the triumphant return to the Music Hall, his immense salary in Las Vegas, his appearance at the Academy Awards. The conversation dwelt on Liberace until Goldstone departed. "My God, how he has changed!" the director said to himself. "He really believes his own publicity!"

Chapter 16

A FLYING RETURN TO THE MUSIC HALL
ACCOMPANIED BY A DISTURBING CIRCUMSTANCE

Milton Berle and Liberace had known each other since the early 1950s. During the first years of Liberace's fame he appeared on "Texaco Star Theater" and he later performed sketches with Berle on "Hollywood Palace." They had a common bond.

"I have great affection for you, Milton," Lee once said, "because of the way you treat your mother. You're so considerate of her, and you're not afraid to let people know you love her. The way I am with Mom." From Milton's earliest years, Sandra Berle was his greatest audience, leading the laughter at every performance.

In 1984, Berle and his wife, Ruth, paid a visit to Lee's dressing room after his performance at the Riviera in Las Vegas. The two performers had a joyful reunion, recalling when Lee showered Berle with seltzer water in the "stand-in" routine on "Hollywood Palace." Berle noticed that the room was crowded and stuffy, and he glanced over and saw George Liberace sitting in a corner. George's face had a yellowish pallor.

"Hiya, George, glad to see ya—don't get up," Berle said breezily, glancing down as he shook hands. He saw that George's nails had a bluish tinge. His hands were moist, and sweat dotted his forehead.

Berle excused himself and went to a telephone. "This is an emergency," he said. "Send paramedics to the backstage of the Riviera."

Just as the ambulance arrived, George fell over. It was a heart attack. His life was saved, but he was diagnosed as having leukemia as well as heart disease. He seemed to recover, and he spent his days greeting tourists at the Liberace Museum and signing autographs when they purchased books or albums. He became thinner and weaker and died on March 9, 1985, in his Las Vegas home. It was Lee's shattering duty to bury George alongside Mom in the family crypt at Forest Lawn. Now only Lee and Angie were left.

George's death sent Liberace into an uncharacteristic depression, exacerbated by the Scott Thorson affair. His morale was buoyed by the fan mail, which overwhelmingly supported him versus Thorson, but the best treatment for his depression came, as always, on the performing stage. There he could bask in the love and admiration of thousands, healing his battered soul.

Performing encompassed his life, to the exclusion of all else. His houses, the antiques, the dogs were important, but they served only as diversions until he could return to the stage. He had hundreds of acquaintances but few real friends, and nearly all of them were on his payroll; he boasted that twenty-six families depended on him for their livelihood.

Liberace was content in his relationship with Cary James, who had been given the title of private secretary. Cary adapted to the Liberace lifestyle with great ease. In fact, his lean frame had gained sixty-five pounds during his first year with Lee, and he subjected himself to a Lean Cuisine diet to make amends.

The two most important women in Liberace's life were his housekeepers, Gladys Luckie and Dorothy MacMahain.

Gladys had been with Liberace for thirty years and had weathered Mom's resentment of another cook in the house; the two women became close friends in Mom's later years. Gladys had been a caterer and could prepare any kind of food with extraordinary skill, but Lee's favorites were simple dishes like fried chicken and meat loaf. Gladys was more than a cook and housekeeper. Lee shared his secrets with her as with no other person, knowing they would remain confidential. Liberace admitted: "I would confide things in her that I didn't even think of telling my mother when she was alive." Gladys's responses could be blunt. "People who come here think I'm just a dumb old black woman," she once told a Liberace aide. "But I hear everything that's goin' on."

After Liberace had rebuilt The Cloisters, he had difficulty finding domestic help who could approximate Gladys's loving care. A succession of cooks, butlers and housekeepers came and went. Liberace believed he had solved his problem with an English couple. She prepared excellent meals, and he appeared the perfect picture of a British butler. Except for one thing. Whenever he prepared a drink for Liberace's guests, he poured one for himself.

One evening in Palm Springs, Liberace gave a dinner for a few guests, including Tido Minor, who had remained a close friend from the years when she was married to Don Fedderson. After the excellent meal, Tido excused herself for a visit to the powder room. "Would you like an after-dinner drink?" the butler asked. "Yes, please; I'll have a Drambuie," she replied. "We don't have Drambuie; I'll give you a brandy, dearie," the butler said, patting her on the behind.

The English couple departed, and Liberace resumed his quest for help at The Cloisters. Then he found Dorothy MacMahain.

One of fifteen children of a migrant farm worker, she had married at fifteen and had four sons by her early twenties. When Liberace hired her as housekeeper at The Cloisters, she traveled sixty miles from her home in Riverside each day. Lee admired her industry, resourcefulness, and discretion, and she remained with him for more than fifteen years, caring for both the Palm Springs and Malibu houses. Like Gladys in Las Vegas, Dorothy possessed the most important trait of all: she loved Lee's "children," the dogs.

Lee adored showering gifts on Gladys and Dorothy—furs, jewels, automobiles. He also flew them to his important engagements, such as Radio City Music Hall in New York, and installed them in hotel suites. In late 1965, Lee asked Dorothy, "How would you like to meet the President?" He had been invited to be among the celebrities attending a Variety Club television special honoring Ronald Reagan. When Dorothy worried that she might embarrass Lee, he paid to have her teeth capped and outfitted her with a stunning gown and sparkling jewels. The high point of her Cinderella evening was meeting President Reagan.

On the following day, Jamie James's publicity office received calls from the media asking, "Who was that attractive blonde with Liberace last night?"

Liberace decided to write his fourth book. After the autobiography and the cookbook had come *The Things I Love*, edited by Tony Palmer and published in 1976 by Grosset & Dunlap. It was a large-format book filled with photos of the Liberace treasures and accompanied by chatty text and a brief autobiography. Now Harper & Row wanted to update the Liberace saga, and a writer was assigned to help him. When Liberace read the manuscript, he was appalled. It included such matters as Rudy's alcoholism and Sam Liberace's adultery. Not at all in keeping with the Liberace image, even though he had sometimes touched on those matters in interviews. He wanted the book to be intimate though not confessional.

"I'll write it myself," he declared. But expressing his personal life, not merely recounting the time-worn anecdotes, proved more difficult than he expected. He found assistance in Shirley MacLaine after they met by chance at the Malibu market.

They had been good friends for fifteen years. Often they met while appearing in Nevada casinos, and Liberace found pleasure in entertaining Shirley and her troupe of dancers and musicians at his houses in Las Vegas and Lake Tahoe. She was always impressed by his air of total serenity, even amid the hoopla of Las Vegas. Only once had she seen that serenity shattered. They had met in the lobby of the Dorchester Hotel in London during the height of the Scott Thorson scandal. Liberace was in "a raw state of anger," she recalls, and he hotly denied an intimate relationship with Thorson. He was furious that someone would attempt to destroy the illusion that he, Liberace, had devoted his life to creating.

When they met at the Malibu market, Shirley discerned a change in her friend. He was thinner, which he attributed to dieting. He remained calm and balanced, but there was an added depth she hadn't recognized before.

Lee and Shirley went to his beach house, and he poured out his difficulties in writing his fourth book without assistance. She had recently completed *her* fourth book, *Dancing in the Light,* and she told him: "Lee, you have already written your life. You can write a book, too."

The Wonderful Private World of Liberace became a coffee-table book jammed with photographs depicting his life, past and present. The text was largely devoted to his houses, housekeepers, cooking (including the Liberace lasagna recipe), clothes, dogs, etc. Liberace's plan to include some revelations in the book were discouraged by the publisher. The sole autobiographical chapter, "I Lost My Virginity at Sixteen," described in polite terms his seduction by a roadhouse singer he whimsically called Miss Bea Haven.

"I've become a hot ticket," Liberace declared to the *Washington Post,* which seemed to confirm his boast with a page-and-a-half article during a 1985 engagement at the Kennedy Center.

"While it is entirely possible to suspect some rock sensations of profiteering in outlandishness," theorized *Post* writer David Richards, "Liberace's sincerity is beyond reproach. He genuinely revels in his fantasy world. Judgments of good taste or bad taste are irrelevant. It's *his* taste, and his joyful flamboyance is rooted in a child's wonderment. He's still the kid with his nose pressed up against the window. Only the window is Tiffany's.

"His image is not lost on the acquisitive 1980s."

Indeed, the Me Generation accepted Liberace as a minor icon because of his conspicuous affluence, and in an era of alternate lifestyles, nothing in his personal life provided any shock. His ability to earn money appeared unlimited. By working only fourteen weeks in 1985, he had gross receipts of $3.5 million. The Caesar's Palace contract paid him $400,000 a week. A furriers' trade show in Dallas offered him $600,000 for a two-night stand, and he said he'd think about it.

"It's funny," he commented, "the moment it gets out that you're not all that available, your price keeps going up and up. Sometimes I'm a little ashamed to take the money . . . but I will."

In February 1986, Liberace worked for union scale, playing piano for a very special wedding: Felicia Gallant to Zane Lindquist on "Another World." It was his second appearance on the soap opera, which starred his friend Linda Dano as Felicia, and he was effusive in praising her: "She fits into the pattern of legendary stars of the past;

she sets styles rather than follows them." He planned his selections carefully: "Let Me Call You Sweetheart" and "You Made Me Love You," followed by "My Funny Valentine." As sometimes happens in soap operas, the wedding was called off at the last moment.

In Las Vegas at Caesar's Palace in March, there were glimmers that the Liberace policy of excess was beginning to pale. He gave the opening-night audience two and a half hours of show, and many left after the first two hours. Dick Maurice of the *Las Vegas Sun* printed a scathing review, terming the performance tired and "old camp."

Maurice wrote: ". . . it hurts to see this unique man fall into the trap of allowing himself to be surrounded by so-called 'friends' who are not advising him correctly. They're quick for the paycheck but slow on creativity. . . . Those cars have had more mileage onstage than on the highway. . . . His latest outfit for Easter is more ridiculous than outrageous. Quite frankly, all that pink and feathers make him look like a female impersonator auditioning for 'An Evening at La Cage.' "

Members of the Liberace entourage were horrified by the *Sun* review. Liberace was characteristically unperturbed.

In April, he made another of his sentimental returns to Milwaukee, appearing for a week at the Riverside Theater. He had made his professional debut there in a Fanchon and Marco stage presentation. The theater had outfitted him with a proper costume then, but in 1986 he returned with his own wardrobe. It was enough to dazzle his fellow Milwaukeeans, and he set a house record for the Riverside: $454,830 in seven concerts.

Always on his return to his hometown, Liberace indulged himself at Usinger's, an old-time restaurant with typical Milwaukee food. One night after the show he was leaving for a dinner in a khaki two-piece suit, and a reporter overheard the conversation. "Lee, why don't you put a coat on?" called his dresser, Terry Clarkson. "I don't have anything that goes with this," Lee answered. "Silver fox goes with anything," Clarkson suggested. Lee replied firmly, "The only thing that would go with this would be my lynx, and I left that back in Las Vegas."

In August, Liberace returned to Caesar's Palace in Las Vegas for a two-week stand. Besides the usual publicity, he gave interviews to national media in preparation for another engagement at Radio City Music Hall in October. Among the interviewers was Ron Reagan, who was reporting for "Good Morning, America." Liberace reminisced about his friendship with Reagan's mother and father and also discussed knowledgeably the merits of certain rock groups.

After Ron questioned him about the onstage costumes, Liberace volunteered, "Did you know that I buy some of my leisure clothes at K-mart? You can get some wonderful bargains there."

During the two-hour break between shows, Liberace always enjoyed receiving visitors in his dressing room, especially other performers. One night he spent the entire time reminiscing with Robert Goulet and his wife, Vera. Goulet reminded Lee of the first time they met. Both appeared on a Toronto television station in 1957, and afterward Goulet had the nerve to play the only piano piece he knew, "Whispering." Lee smiled and commented, "Don't ever stop singing."

Jamie James came to Las Vegas for the annual ritual of selecting the Liberace Christmas card. James had prepared a silver design with a stand-up star and the message: "The star is the sign of Christmas—the light in darkness." Liberace gave his approval: "It's a bit more serious than what we usually have, but I like it."

During the Caesar's Palace engagement, backstage people thought they detected a change in Liberace. They noticed he lacked his customary high energy, and he rested in his dressing room more than usual. But that was not unusual for a sixty-seven-year-old star, they concluded. His performance onstage was unchangingly vital, ever responsive to the roars of laughter and applause.

Liberace was determined to make the Radio City Music Hall appearance more sensational than before. This time he would make his entrance—flying. He arrived in New York in mid-October, set up housekeeping in Trump Tower—with an extra apartment for his costumes—and began planning the entrance by wire, the stunt that had dazzled audiences at the Nevada casinos. The first-act finale would be a tribute to the Statue of Liberty centennial, with Miss Liberty holding a candelabra and Liberace arriving in a stars-and-stripes Rolls-Royce and wearing an ermine robe and red, white, and blue hot pants to lead the band while Rockettes kicked and skyrockets exploded.

Denise Collier arranged the usual round of interviews, though she was surprised that he was sometimes not available. Happily, he was no longer asked the palimony questions, and he could enthuse about his future plans: licensing of a new line of Liberace clothes, furs, and perfume; franchising the Tivoli Gardens as a nationwide restaurant chain; breaking ground for a greatly expanded Liberace Museum in the shape of a grand piano. *The Wonderful Private World of Liberace* was being published at the same time as the Music Hall appearance.

"I thought I'd better write my book before Kitty Kelly did," he said, smiling. He added about the Kelly book on Frank Sinatra: "If she had written about my mother the way she did about Frank's [alleging that Dolly Sinatra had been an abortionist], I'd kill." Both Kelly's books on Sinatra and Elizabeth Taylor were "trash," he maintained. Then why did he read them? Again, the smile: "I love it. I buy the rags in the market every week, even though I know there may not be a shred of truth in them."

As always, Liberace shrugged off any questions about retirement. His ambition, he said, was to end his career in the style of Yul Brynner: "He was just as brilliant in his last performance as he was in his first. If I thought for a moment that my performance gave the impression I was failing, I wouldn't do it. But I don't like to dwell on thoughts like that. They have a final sound to them."

Was he failing?

At times he seemed to have the same high spirits. He practiced the flying enthusiastically and laughed because he always landed facing toward the back of the stage. "Don't worry," he told the Music Hall flyman, Jimmy Anderson, "I've got three weeks to get it right." In fact, Liberace never did land facing the audience until the last of the twenty-one performances, and he always joked with the audience about his goof.

It was obvious that Liberace was not well. He was affable to the stage crew, but the camaraderie of the two previous engagements was lacking. There was no stream of visitors to the dressing room. Cary James was ever present, telling people that Liberace was resting. As soon as the performance ended, Liberace left the theater.

At his request there was no big opening-night party, only a gathering at Maxwell's Plum for those closest to him: Cary, Angie, her children, Gladys and Dorothy, Seymour, of course, and a few others. Phyllis Diller flew in from California.

Some reviewers noted that Liberace seemed thinner, but most of them praised his energy and showmanship. Only *Variety* suggested that some rethinking was needed to restore the pizazz: "The thrill is gone. Maybe not for some of his adoring fans, but certainly for the less-than-committed and apparently for the performer himself. . . . All the shticks which once were fresh, like his myriad fancy pianos and costume changes with valet, a car onstage, etc., no longer have much excitement."

Liberace's health was the subject of backstage conjecture. Obviously he was ill, but what could it be? There was talk of emphysema, and Liberace himself kidded about ending up in an iron lung: "Even with rhinestones I couldn't make it attractive." He continued smoking two or three packs of Carltons a day.

The final performance came on Monday, November 3. At the opening, two of the glittering costumes sailed through the air and then came Liberace himself soaring above the mammoth stage like Peter Pan, trailing a cape of silvery scales edged in purple feathers. He returned to earth—miraculously facing the audience for the first time. The 5,874 people in the Music Hall roared their welcome.

Two and a half hours later, he had given them everything he could: six costume changes, four cars, three-minute Gershwin, Chopin, and Strauss, a dance with the Rockettes, the maid-in-the-bathroom routine, a waltz with a woman from the audience, the offer to let fans feel the costumes, the "you-paid-for-it" and "now-I-own-the-bank" jokes, a Christmas medley.

Finally, "I'll Be Seeing You."

They stood in the wings crying. Angie, who had pushed her brother in a baby carriage. Seymour Heller, who had attended almost every Liberace performance for thirty-four years. Cary James, the companion and protector. Ray Arnett, who had toured with Liberace for thirty years and had produced the Music Hall shows. Eric Hamelin, the fourteen-year-old pianist whose career Liberace had fostered. Denise Collier, the press agent who had become devoted to Lee.

Then it was over.

Musicians, stagehands, Rockettes, all gathered on the vast stage to drink champagne and celebrate the record achievement—fifty-six Music Hall shows before more than 300,000 people. No other performer came close. A Liberace-style cake was wheeled out—six-tier, all-white, decorated with spun-sugar flowers, ribbons and bows, and a grand piano on top. The management presented Lee with the original artwork for the posters advertising the engagement, and he responded with a toast: "I love you all."

Because the opening-night party had been intimate, everyone was invited to the final celebration in the Michael Todd Room at the huge Palladium disco. Lee arrived with his entourage and graciously signed autographs and chatted with Rockettes and carpenters and violinists.

Mark Felton shouted over the rock-music din: "Lee, we want you back at the Hall next year, anytime you say. Can we talk about it?" Lee didn't respond. He seemed distracted, as if he hadn't heard the question. It seemed odd to Felton. Always before, Lee would grab at such a suggestion.

Lee departed from the Palladium after an hour. Underneath the cacophony of the Grace Jones and U-2 music was an air of foreboding among the Music Hall people. None of them had received a gift from Liberace this time, and that was totally unlike him. What was wrong?

Phyllis Diller knew. Two months before, Liberace and Bob Hope had appeared on a "Merv Griffin Show" saluting Phyllis's thirtieth anniversary in show business. When Lee walked onstage, beaming under heavy makeup, she felt an instant of breathtaking terror. His face was angular, not cherubic as before, and she recognized something in the eyes that she had seen in other friends she had lost in recent times. "Dear God," she gasped inwardly, "he has AIDS!"

Chapter 17

"I'LL BE LOOKING AT THE MOON, BUT I'LL BE SEEING YOU"

In late 1980, Michael Gottlieb, a thirty-two-year-old immunologist newly appointed assistant professor of medicine at UCLA Medical Center in Los Angeles, came upon a patient who puzzled him. A young man was suffering from an unusual kind of pneumonia, pneumocytis carinii. What surprised Dr. Gottlieb was that the patient, who until recently had been perfectly healthy, was almost totally devoid of the kind of immune cells that would have protected him from such an infection.

Soon afterward Dr. Gottlieb encountered another young man with the same disease and the same lack of immunity. And another. Within a few months the immunologist had encountered a total of five young males who had been previously healthy but now were afflicted with pneumocytis carinii and had no protective immunity. One of them developed Kaposi's sarcoma, a rare cancer normally found in elderly men. The five patients were all homosexuals.

Obviously something fairly recent had happened to the patients' immune system to make them susceptible to disease. On June 5, 1981, Dr. Gottlieb and a private physician who had referred some of the cases to UCLA, Dr. Joel Weisman, published a brief report for the Center for Disease Control's weekly bulletin citing "evidence for a new severe immune deficiency syndrome."

Within days, reports of similar cases were pouring in from San Francisco, New York, Miami, and other urban areas. The ailment was given a name: acquired immune deficiency syndrome—AIDS for headline writers. The evidence developed slowly. Not only were homosexuals susceptible because of sexual contact, but dirty needles could pass AIDS to drug addicts. Blood donors could also transmit the syndrome, and women, children, and heterosexual males could be infected. In 1983, the virus that causes AIDS was discovered by various researchers. AIDS was found to be rampant in parts of Africa and in Haiti. Health officials warned of an impending epidemic.

At first AIDS was treated as a medical curiosity. Some evangelists even preached that it was divine retribution for lifestyles that displeased God. By mid-1985 the epidemic warnings could not be ignored. The spread of AIDS was causing widespread alarm and even panic. Concern was galvanized in December 1985 with the death of Rock Hudson, the first international celebrity to fall victim to AIDS.

Vince Fronza and Ken Fosler, Lee's "personal" neighbors from Palm Springs, were among those who had come to New York for the Music Hall engagement. The pair had a vacation home in the Pocono Mountains, and Lee accepted their invitation to spend a few days there, along with Cary James, Dorothy MacMahain, and her sister. The party departed November 3 in a limousine, stopping at the Baldwin showroom on Seventh Avenue for Lee to put his signature on two pianos. During the two-hour journey, Lee was in a state of exhilaration.

"Oh, boy," he enthused, "I'm starting a year's vacation! Think of it—a whole year to do all the things I've been putting off all these years. I've told Seymour: don't schedule anything. I want to travel and relax. I want to rent one of those what-do-you-call-'em—recreational vehicles—and camp out in the wilderness with the dogs. I want to take a trip on the Orient Express. And oh yes, I want to rent a railroad car and make a circle tour of the United States, hitching rides on trains. I cut out an article in the paper that tells all about it, how much it costs, how you can park on sidings in the big cities and use the car as a hotel. That's something I really want to do."

But first he had the unfinished business of selling *The Wonderful Private World of Liberace.* He returned to New York for television talk shows and bookstore autographings and did more book promotion in Chicago, Dallas, and Los Angeles. In Chicago he was the sole guest on "The Oprah Winfrey Show" despite Seymour Heller's concern about Liberace's appearance. He seemed gaunt and sallow, and heavy makeup could not disguise his haggard appearance.

The show was taped in late November and broadcast on December 30. Liberace summoned his customary energy and talked bubblingly about his love of Christmas, the forthcoming party at Malibu, his love of houses and cars, the palimony suit ("I don't think the public much cares"), his loss of virginity with "Miss Bea Haven," shopping for bargains with Donald Trump.

Liberace also spoke of his rendezvous with death in Pittsburgh and concluded: "It taught me a great lesson, that the most important and valuable thing in one's life is your health, and if you have that, you're a rich person."

The book promotion ended with an autographing at a Los Angeles department store, and Liberace went home to The Cloisters for a quiet Thanksgiving with Cary James and a few others. Tido Minor came by for a lengthy visit, and she was shocked by Liberace's appearance. She hadn't seen him since June, when they had returned on a plane together after his appearance at the Expo in Vancouver. He had seemed in vigorous health then and had even stopped smoking. But now in Palm Springs he seemed painfully thin. And he was smoking as much as before.

"Lee, what's the matter?" Tido asked her old friend.

"Nothing, dear," he assured her. "I went a little overboard on the diet, that's all."

He made the same excuse to guests at the Malibu Christmas party, but his explanation didn't stop them from worrying.

Liberace planned to spend Christmas at The Cloisters, as was his custom. Before leaving, he visited the Beverly Boulevard penthouse to collect some belongings. In the hallway of the building he encountered Jamie James, who gave the common greeting when fans encountered Liberace: "Are you him?" Liberace responded as he often did: "Are you him?" The two men exchanged holiday wishes and embraced in parting. Strange, James thought afterward. Liberace always had that thick, peasant body, but now his back was thin and bent. James remembered embracing George Liberace in his last months and sensing how that once-powerful body was withering. But there was no chance of that happening to Lee, James convinced himself. Lee was too strong, too vital. He would live as long as his parents.

Liberace had a joyful reunion with his "children": the Chinese Shar-peis, Wrinkles, his special protector, and Prunella; the West Highland terrier, Lady Di, whom Lee called "the Highland Terrorist" ("She thinks she's a doberman"); and a Dutch keeshond, Gretel. Vince Fronza and Ken Fosler noticed that Lee seemed to have little energy and took frequent naps. But they couldn't imagine that he was really sick, not if he could endure twenty-one performances at the Music Hall and a book tour.

The face changed. With the loss of weight, the surgical nips and tucks tightened, and makeup couldn't hide the cruel caricature of Liberace. He saw few visitors besides Fronza and Fosler and his dear friend Tido Minor.

Liberace was visited by his California doctor, Ronald Daniels of Whittier. Alarmed by his patient's condition, Daniels ordered him admitted to the Eisenhower Medical Center in Rancho Mirage for tests. Liberace exhibited his customary optimism by buying six pairs of bedroom slippers.

The guests at the Malibu Christmas party had wondered why Liberace had not given his usual Palm Springs celebration, which often extended from Christmas Eve through New Year's Day. In January they received a curious letter. In essence it said: "Please don't inquire about my health. . . . I am on the road to recovery . . . when I feel better, I will call you." The signature read "Liberace."

His associates puzzled over this. They hadn't even known he was ill. How serious was it? Did he have leukemia, like George? Why would he issue seemingly a form letter to his intimates? Was it really his signature?

"What's wrong with him?" Jamie James asked.

"I don't know," Seymour Heller admitted.

Tido Minor telephoned Gladys Luckie in tears. "So you got the letter, too?" Gladys asked. "Yes," said Tido, "and I don't understand what's going on. It's so unlike him so send such a cold letter. What is happening?" Gladys admitted, "I don't know any more than you do."

On January 22, Liberace signed a document that began: "I, Liberace, also sometimes known as Walter Valentino Liberace, Lee Liberace, and Wladziu Valentino Liberace, domiciled in Las Vegas, Nevada, being of sound and disposing mind and memory, do hereby make, publish, and declare this to be my Last Will and Testament. . . ."

The will bequeathed the entire estate to his attorney, Joel R. Strote, as trustee for the Liberace Revocable Trust. The bulk of the estate, Strote declared later after the will was filed in Las Vegas, was to go to the Liberace Foundation for the Performing and Creative Arts. No individual bequests were listed. Witnesses to the will were Ken Fosler, Vince Fronza, and Dr. Daniels. The familiar Liberace signature with the scroll-like *L* was affixed, though the last three letters of the name appeared wobbly.

The day after the signing, Liberace entered the Eisenhower Medical Center. The hospital announced that he was suffering from anemia and would remain for tests and evaluation of his condition. The event attracted little notice until the following day, when the *Las Vegas Sun* printed the headline: "Liberace Victim of Deadly AIDS." The copyrighted story by Jeffrey M. German declared that Liberace had been told he had between two months and a year to live. Citing "knowledgeable sources," German said that in the past few months Liberace had displayed symptoms of AIDS: decline of appetite and energy; loss of twenty to thirty pounds.

Not so, insisted Seymour Heller, declaring, "I never heard the word AIDS mentioned by anyone." Liberace had lost the pounds on a watermelon diet, Seymour maintained, and had gotten out of the habit of eating. Dr. Elias Ghanem, Liberace's physician in Las Vegas, would not comment on the *Sun* report. Other newspapers and news services were wary of printing the AIDS report without confirmation.

Fosler and Fronza visited Lee in the hospital and found him cheerful but impatient with the hospital routine. When they called for him on Monday after his weekend stay, his feet were tapping in the wheelchair. "Let's get moving," he muttered. "I want to get home to my children."

By Tuesday it had become apparent that the severity of Liberace's condition could no longer be veiled by optimistic pronouncements and watermelon diets. To relieve some of the media pressure at The Cloisters, Denise Collier of the Solters, Roskin and Friedman office in New York would make the announcements. Collier issued the statement that Liberace was gravely ill with pernicious anemia, emphysema, and heart disease. Asked whether his condition was complicated by AIDS, she replied: "All I know is this statement. He's only being treated for emphysema and heart disease. It seems to me that all this is heavy enough."

Angie Farrell arrived from Las Vegas to help care for her brother. Gladys Luckie came, too, filled with foreboding. She knew Lee as intimately as anyone. And she had noted something ominous when he left Las Vegas in September after his last Caesar's Palace engagement. He had shipped his favorite Rolls-Royce to Palm Springs, and she suspected he believed he would never return to Las Vegas. Gladys gave no hint of her apprehension after her arrival at The Cloisters. She cheerfully cooked Lee his favorite dishes—her meat loaf and patented fried chicken with dumplings.

Lee remained in the Napoleon bedroom, surrounded by the dogs, his energy ebbing. He watched entertainment shows on television, but newscasts were purposely kept from him so he would not be alarmed by the attention being paid to his illness. A few close friends and associates were allowed to see him, with cautions to keep their visits short. Dr. Daniels made regular visits, and a nurse was in attendance around the clock. She was English, and Lee called her Florence Nightingale II.

By Friday Lee seemed to be more alert. He was eating solid food, and he was able to sit up by himself instead of being helped. But the improvement was temporary. The decline resumed, and the bulletins from Denise Collier in New York grew more somber. Liberace was dying.

The death watch had begun.

Reporters and photographers converged on Palm Springs, scenting more than the death of a world-famous entertainer. If the *Las Vegas*

Sun's report proved true, Liberace's death would produce headlines akin to those for Rock Hudson's illness and death. News services, television networks, and newspapers sent staff members. The *National Enquirer* had eight people working on the story.

The Cloisters was a convenient location to cover such an event. In the heart of Palm Springs, it was faced by a city parking lot that was also used by parishioners of Our Lady of Inspiration Catholic Church, directly to the south. Television crews parked their vans facing the house. Reporters and photographers lounged in their cars as they awaited developments across the street. Whenever an announcement was made, the media converged on the front of the house. Police were able to confine fans and curious onlookers behind the three-foot wall surrounding the parking lot.

Most photographers remained in the parking lot, where they could peer into the courtyard from atop their cars. Others became more bold and parked next to The Cloisters' eight-foot stucco wall, allowing them to focus their cameras in the windows. That was the signal for the security staff, headed by Dorothy MacMahain's twenty-two-year-old-son, Tommy, to turn on the sprinklers. After a few soakings, photographers abandoned the ploy.

A photographer for the *National Enquirer* vaulted the wall and was discovered wandering among The Cloisters' buildings. He was arrested and taken away in handcuffs by police.

The number of journalists would swell to fifty when an announcement was imminent, diminish to a handful at dinnertime, then grow again. By midnight only two or three remained for the all-night vigil. The crowd of spectators, one hundred and fifty at its peak, also fluctuated according to the time of day and the expected events. They included local residents who expressed pride in having Liberace in Palm Springs, visitors who saw the spectacle as one of the tourist attractions, and longtime Liberace fans who came with their scrapbooks of faded clippings.

One Palm Springs resident told reporters she had driven by Liberace's house every Christmas since 1962 and had enjoyed the decorations and the carols on the loudspeaker. Another said he brought his children there for Halloween, when Liberace always appeared in costume. Self-proclaimed faith healers appeared in the crowd and tried vainly to gain entrance to The Cloisters. A woman taped a message to the door: "My dear friend, my prayers are with you. I hope you are taking at least 3,000 mg of Vita C. God bless."

Bonnie Ward, reporter for the *Desert Sun,* was preparing for a long, dull nightwatch at 1 A.M. when two carloads of teenagers drove up before The Cloisters. They were freshmen at San Diego State University who had heard on the 11 o'clock news that Liberace was dying. They had made the two-hour drive to pay their tribute.

"He's not of our era, but we respect him as one of the greatest," said one of the youths. Said another: "Liberace has style. Other entertainers like Elton John tried to copy him, but he was the original." The leader of the pilgrimage said that, after hearing the news, he had invited others to make the trip to Palm Springs for a vigil. One of the students had responded: "So what? He's a fag. Why drive two hours to watch a fag die?" The leader commented, "That comes from someone who is insensitive. Liberace was the best. He lived the way he wanted to. He wanted rings, he bought them. He could wear those crazy costumes and get away with it. He was classy."

After a few more comments, the students turned away from the reporter, saying they hadn't come there for publicity. They huddled in blankets against the parking lot wall until dawn, when they had to return to their classes.

The long days and nights of the deathwatch wore on as Liberace clung to life. Fans stopped in the driveway and left lighted candles, which cast an eerie glow on the white walls of The Cloisters. All day and into the evening, automobiles in a steady stream drifted by the house. Reporters heard a repeated refrain from the passersby: "Is he dead yet?"

Liberace's condition worsened over the weekend. He seemed to be in no pain and he took no medicine, but his pulse grew weaker and his breathing more labored. He was moved from the bedroom to the lighter, sunnier sitting room, which had been his favorite place in The Cloisters. On Sunday morning, Vince Fronza came from next door and said, "Angie and I are going to Mass. Wanna come along?"

Lee smiled wanly. "I wish I could," he said. "I'll just stay here and watch my shows." He was playing tapes of one of his favorite television programs, "Golden Girls," which starred Betty White, his friend from KLAC-TV days.

By Monday morning he could only respond yes or no to questions. The room was filled with flowers from Elton John, Tom Jones, Tony Orlando, and others. Also four red roses from a bush outside that Dorothy had nursed back from near-extinction. When asked which flowers he enjoyed the most, he pointed a wavering finger toward the four roses.

That evening he was unable to speak at all. Denise Collier told the media: "I don't think there's much time. I don't know if it's going to be a day or two days, but I don't think it's going to be much more than that."

Jamie James arrived from Los Angeles on Monday. He was shocked to see the man he had always known to be pulsing with vitality. Now the skin was colorless, the arms unmoving. And the eyes. Always they were a piercing brown, with a small blood fleck from a boyhood accident; James had it retouched out of the official portraits. The color was all gone now, replaced by a pale yellow.

Liberace seemed to notice nothing, not even the sunbursts of photographers' lights whenever someone arrived at or left the house. The outside hubbub was not audible in the room, only the soft sounds

269

of music. Among the tapes was Barbra Streisand's new album of Broadway tunes, which Liberace had enjoyed.

"You can go ahead and talk to him," the nurse suggested. "I think he might be able to understand you."

James sat beside the bed and held Lee's hand, which was wrapped with a rosary, his only jewelry. James spoke of past triumphs and future hopes, rubbing Lee's arm and remarking to himself how young the skin felt. When James finished talking, Lee gave no indication he had heard anything.

Tuesday, another day of vigil. Dr. Daniels came to the house and noted no change in the patient's condition. Lee seemed to give a flicker of recognition when the dogs appeared, but the steady stare returned.

On Wednesday morning, February 4, the nurse telephoned Dr. Daniels that Liberace was in critical condition. They gathered in the room: Angelina, who had been there when Lee was born; Dora Liberace, George's widow; Seymour Heller, who had guided the Liberace career, with one brief interval, through its glory days; Jamie James, who had promoted the Liberace image; Gladys Luckie and Dorothy MacMahain, who had managed his houses; Cary James, his last intimate companion; his "personal" neighbors, Vince Fronza and Ken Fosler; Tido Minor, who had remained at the bedside from morning to midnight for five days; Angie's daughter Diane and her husband.

They talked quietly among themselves, their eyes focused on the still figure on the bed. At 10 A.M. the Shar-pei Wrinkles entered the room and approached Liberace, licking him once on the face. Wrinkles walked to a bedroom and lay down, and the dog remained there for hours afterward, unwilling to move.

Only Angie, Tido and the nurse were in the room shortly before 11 when Tido noticed Liberace's breath growing slower. The nurse took his pulse and detected no change. But the breaths became fainter. Then at 11:02, with a long sigh, Liberace died.

The reporters outside had spent the morning in an atmosphere of nervous anticipation. But the handful of people going in and out of the house that morning gave no indication that Liberace had died. Angie and Fronza walked to the church and lighted candles and attended the final Mass. They declined any comment to reporters, saying Strote would make all the statements. A priest was asked if Liberace had been given last rites of the church. That had been done the previous Thursday, the priest said.

Strote emerged from the house at 11 A.M. and departed without speaking to the media. Another long wait, and the crowd thinned out. At 2:05 the newspeople became alert when a large, dark blue station wagon with tinted black windows arrived. It came from Forest Lawn Memorial Park in Glendale, which had been requested to send a vehicle that did not resemble a hearse. Three men in black suits emerged and entered The Cloisters. They left twenty minutes later, then returned at 2:50. At 3:05 several men appeared in front of the house, including Angie's son-in-law, Don McLaughlin. He read a statement:

"Liberace passed on this afternoon. Any formal statement will come from Denise Collier. The family is very aware of all the love and support, and we are very grateful for it. A memorial service is planned later this week at Our Lady of Solitude and next week in Las Vegas."

A few minutes later, the mortuary attendants wheeled the covered body out of the house on a gurney and loaded it into the station wagon. Angie, Seymour, Cary, Jamie, Gladys, Dorothy, and the others who had seen Liberace in glorious life and in his last moments stood in the doorway and wept and hugged each other and waved as the dark blue station wagon inched its way through the crowd and turned to begin the journey to the Liberace crypt at Forest Lawn.

In New York, Denise Collier released the news that Liberace had died of congestive heart failure brought on by subacute encephalopathy, a general term for degenerative brain disease.

The tributes soon came from Liberace's fellow performers. Bob Hope: "He was my friend for forty years. He will be sorely missed." Frank Sinatra: "That he was a consummate artist is not really as important as my telling you that he was one of the finest human beings I've ever known." Phyllis Diller: "He was the greatest positive thinker I've ever, ever known. He loved life, he loved to laugh, he loved people." Mickey Rooney: "He was one of the greatest entertainers the world has ever known. I loved him, as did the world." Phyllis McGuire: "Not only was Lee a dear friend, he was a great artist." Debbie Reynolds: "Lee was one of a kind, like all the beautiful treasures he collected." Shirley MacLaine: "Lee was the nicest person in show business."

Red Skelton termed Liberace "the P.T. Barnum of the symphony halls" and added warily: "I hope the cynics don't make a circus of his death. God wouldn't like that."

The death of Liberace was front-page news across the country, and the network news programs featured pictorial biographies. ABC included an excerpt from the previous December's "The Oprah Winfrey Show," Liberace's last television interview. "The most important and valuable thing in one's life," he said, "is your health, and if you have that, you're a rich person."

CBS showed a clip of Liberace in a 1950s "Person to Person" interview with Edward R. Murrow declaring, "I remember being very poor once and making a promise to myself if I could do anything about it, with God's help, I'd never be poor again."

The CBS account closed with Liberace at the piano singing, "I'll be looking at the moon, but I'll be seeing you."

Sabas Rosas, a supervisor in the Riverside County coroner's office, was in his office in Indio, forty miles south of Palm Springs, on Friday when a telephone call came from the Health Department in Riverside. "The L.A. County Department of Health Services says Forest Lawn applied for a permit to bury Liberace," said the official. "Has the coroner's office been contacted?"

"No," said Rosas.

"Do you know if a contagious disease is involved?"

"No. Was a physician in attendance at the time of death?"

"No."

"Then we'd better look into it. Especially with all that publicity about Liberace and AIDS."

Rosas notified the Riverside County coroner, Raymond Carrillo, who demanded to know the underlying cause of the encephalopathy. The disease itself did not cause heart failure; many things could cause encephalopathy, including alcoholism, syphilis, old age, toxins, viruses, and—AIDS.

The coroner ordered the body returned from Forest Lawn for tests. Even though it had already been embalmed, tissue samples could reveal the cause of death. At 10 A.M. Liberace's body was loaded into a van at Glendale for the journey to Riverside.

At the same hour, Our Lady of Solitude Church was filling with fans and friends of Liberace. The first to arrive were two women from British Columbia who had been devoted to him. The 350 seats of the church were filled an hour before the 11 A.M. service and folding chairs were brought in to accommodate the overflow. The celebrities included Kirk and Anne Douglas, Dolores Hope, Isabel Sanford, Charlene Tilton of "Dallas" and her husband, Dominic Allen, who had appeared with Liberace.

Father William Erstad recited the liturgy and read the message from President and Nancy Reagan: "He built a bridge of friendship across the generation gap. Lee was a gifted musician who truly earned the title 'Superstar' and a caring individual who time and again responded generously when called upon to benefit those in need. . . ." Vince Fronza delivered the eulogy, concluding, "I'm sure Lee is looking down and saying, 'Thanks to all of you, and I'll be seeing you.' "

That afternoon, Raymond Carrillo, who had been chosen Riverside County coroner a few months earlier, announced at a news conference in Indio that Liberace had been exposed to the AIDS virus. The coroner said he had subpoenaed records of blood tests that had been taken at Eisenhower Medical Center three weeks before.

"The records did indicate that he was tested for HTLV III [antibodies to the AIDS virus] and the test came back positive," declared Carrillo. But did Liberace have AIDS or was he merely carrying the virus? That could not be determined until tissue samples had been tested. They had been sent to a laboratory at Colton, in San Bernardino County, because Riverside County did not have facilities for the tests.

The body of Liberace was at last released to begin the final journey to Forest Lawn. On Saturday, friends and family gathered for the entombment. Lee joined Mom and George in the six-foot-tall white marble sarcophagus, a major feature of the cemetery's Court of Remembrance. Imbedded in the marble was a reproduction in shiny brass of the Liberace signature, a music staff, and a piano.

"Somebody along the line tried to pull a fast one on us," muttered the coroner in an outburst of civic indignation.

Raymond Carrillo stood on the steps of the Riverside County administrative building in Indio on an overcast Monday afternoon. Beside him was Sabas Rosas, the investigator who had been the first to blow the whistle over the Liberace death certificate. They faced forty reporters, photographers, and television crews, including one that was transmitting the news conference live to a Los Angeles station.

"Mr. Liberace did not die as the result of cardiac arrest due to cardiac failure brought on by subacute encephalopathy," declared Carrillo. "He died of cytomegalovirus pneumonia due to or as a consequence of human immodeficiency virus disease. . . . In layman's terms, Mr. Liberace died of an opportunistic disease caused by acquired immune deficiency syndrome."

How long Liberace had been infected with AIDS could not be determined, said Carrillo. He added his belief that the doctors caring for Liberace had attempted a cover-up, and he criticized Forest Lawn for removing the body without notifying the coroner.

"It's too bad it went to this extent," said Rosas. "If protocol had been followed the way it should have been, it probably wouldn't have ended up where we're at. We're doing our duty to the public."

The newspeople scurried to file their stories, and other reporters sought reactions from the mortuary and Dr. Daniels, who had signed the death certificate. Forest Lawn said it had assumed the death certificate and the notifying requirements were in order. Daniels's attorney, William Ginsburg, commented: "We categorically deny there was an attempt to cover up, flimflam, or pull a fast one." He declared that Liberace's symptoms did not fit the normal patterns of AIDS and that Daniels "had tried to get Mr. Liberace into several programs to diagnose, identify, and treat AIDS and was unable to do so because his symptoms didn't fall into those sets neatly."

The controversy was kept alive for another day or two, and on Thursday the final memorial service was held for Liberace's fellow workers in Las Vegas. Stars and showgirls and stagehands crowded into St. Anne's Roman Catholic Church, where the organ softly played "I'll Be Seeing You." Three priests conducted a Mass, and Robert Goulet delivered the eulogy.

Debbie Reynolds came with Donald O'Connor, and it was the first funeral she had attended in forty years. She didn't believe in funerals, and her last one had been her grandfather's when she was fifteen. She had reasoned that in view of the AIDS controversy, Liberace's "straight" friends needed to demonstrate their devotion to him. At the service she told reporters: "Liberace was a wonderful man and should be remembered as a loving, dear person and not for any other reason."

He was remembered as the supreme showman—who died because of AIDS. Certain questions, most of them unanswerable, remained. How did Liberace acquire the disease and from whom? How long did he have the virus? Did he know he had AIDS? If so, why didn't he admit it and thus add to the public's consciousness and concern about the scourge? Did he know he was dying?

Certainly he knew his life was ending; the signing of the will thirteen days before his death attested to that. Undoubtedly he knew the nature of his illness; every homosexual who becomes sick must face the terror of AIDS. He was probably told the results of the Las Vegas hospital tests in September. Yet he chose to keep his closest associates—except Cary James—in the dark and to go forward with the Music Hall engagement and the book tour as if nothing was wrong.

Why?

Because he didn't want to grieve those who loved him. Because he didn't want news of his affliction to leak to the press, eroding his image as the faultless Mr. Showmanship. Because he would never admit publicly, either by statement or by the inference of AIDS, that he was a homosexual. That would sadden and confuse all the women who had loved him as a son for so many years.

He had devoted a lifetime—all his waking hours—to the Magic of Believing. First he had fashioned the masterful illusion that became known as Liberace, and then he had made the admiring millions believe in it. It was a brilliant invention, unsurpassed in the history of American show business. And Liberace, the former Wladziu Valentino Liberace, the onetime Walter Buster Keys, wanted nothing to tarnish what he had so lovingly created. Not even death.

INDEX